─SUBURBAN─
S·T·Y·LE

SUBURBAN STYLE

THE BRITISH HOME, 1840-1960

HELENA BARRETT AND JOHN PHILLIPS

Little, Brown and Company

BOSTON   TORONTO   LONDON

LITTLE, BROWN AND COMPANY
BOSTON · TORONTO · LONDON

A LITTLE, BROWN BOOK

Copyright © Little, Brown and Company 1993
Copyright © Macdonald and Company Publishers 1987
Text copyright © Helena Barrett and John Phillips 1987

First published in 1987 by Macdonald and Company Publishers
This edition first published in 1993

ISBN 0-316-90644-1
A CIP catalogue record for this book
is available from the British Library

Editor: Sarah Chapman
Designer: Ruth Prentice
Picture Researcher: Philippa Thomson
Indexer: Monica Kendall

Printed and bound in Great Britain by
BPCC Hazells Ltd., Paulton, Bristol

Little, Brown and Company
165 Great Dover Street
London SE1 4YA

Title page picture: detail from a London
Transport poster of 1908 extolling the virtues of
Golders Green. Behind the Arts and Crafts house in
its semi-rural idyll can be glimpsed an idealized
version of what is now the Northern Line.

C·O·N·T·E·N·T·S

◁ *Home* by F. C. Whitney, the frontispiece for *The Art and Craft of Homemaking* (1913) by E. W. Gregory.

F·O·R·E·W·O·R·D

The phrase 'surburban style' may sound incongruous, but it is the architecture and design of the average suburban street – its style, in fact – as it evolved from Victorian times until after the Second World War, that are explored in this book. The idea that any aspect of suburbia is worthy of closer inspection, least of all its architecture or design, has always been considered unlikely: the suburbs have traditionally been a target for vilification, their architecture an object of derision. They have proved, however, to be a disarmingly resilient and popular form of housing, highly satisfactory to millions of Pooters in their Victorian villas and Browns and Smiths commuting to and from Metroland.

Recent years have seen a general upsurge of interest in preserving and restoring the modest homes of 1840–1960, in much the same way as stately homes and bijoux cottages have always been prized. This concern for ordinary domestic architecture has slowly spread from the Georgian terrace to the Victorian and Edwardian villa, and can now be seen to be gradually extending to houses built more recently. Even the semi-detached houses of the thirties are now being valued, perhaps because they are under threat, if only from the advances of double-glazing and stone-cladding vendors.

To appreciate fully the suburban home, the wealth of features and decorative detail to be found in even the most modest semi-detached or terraced dwelling must first be recognized and their origins understood. The fact that suburbia has an enduring style has already been appreciated by some, if not overtly. The new housing developments that are today winning awards owe much of their popularity and distinction to their adoption of the varying 'styles' that have already been tried and tested in Victorian and Edwardian suburbia. The fact that estate agents' literature is now peppered with references to 'original features' rather than to 'complete modernization' is another indication of this trend. Increasingly, householders are being encouraged to recognize that the stylistic integrity of their home is a substantial part of its value.

But suburban style is not simply a matter of particular arrangements of bricks and mortar: it reflects an outlook and a way of life as well, a lifestyle which has itself greatly influenced the appearance of both individual houses and the suburban environment in general. For this reason it is important to consider the social and economic factors that helped to shape suburbia. Understanding the context in which these houses were built – the people who first lived there, their occupations, the services that were, or were not available, and the fashions that dominated particular periods – gives an insight into why they look as they do.

We hope that by writing this book, we will encourage those (the majority of us) who live in suburbia to appreciate and value the myriad details and distinguishing features of its 'style', and hopefully to preserve it.

Helena Barrett
John Phillips

▷A major factor in the development of the suburbs was the need to escape from the squalor and overcrowding of inner-city slums (right), but almost more important was the demand for new houses created by a rapidly expanding middle class. The Industrial Revolution had created unprecedented employment opportunities, not only in factories and small businesses but in the huge financial system which grew up round it, and which required vast numbers of clerks, such as these in a Sheffield office (far right), to keep it going. This new generation of white-collar workers had a clear idea of their enhanced status in society, and required this to be reflected in their homes.

1. THE DEVELOPMENT OF THE SUBURBS

Introduction

By the beginning of the reign of Queen Victoria in 1837, Britain's cities had scarcely doubled in geographical size since Roman times. The next hundred years, however, saw urban expansion accelerate at an unprecedented rate, eating into the countryside in an unplanned sprawl and creating a nation of suburban rather than urban dwellers. The reasons for this rapid suburban growth, and why it took on the character and appearance it did, are complex. Despite popular prejudice, no two suburbs are exactly alike, yet they all share common features. In general they can be defined as largely residential areas that owe their existence, initially at least, to nearby centres of industry or commerce. Efficient transport systems, although necessary in the more far-flung developments built since the 1920s, were, like suburbia itself, essentially the result of the rapid expansion of the middle classes.

The traditional English middle class, between the landowning aristocracy and the labouring masses on the social scale, had always been active and entrepreneurial, but comparatively small. The Industrial Revolution, however, brought with it unparalleled opportunity for upward social mobility, as new jobs and professions in the engineering and manufacturing industries were created. Even more important was the system of finance which underpinned the new industrialism, and which spawned a host of bankers, insurers and financiers. They established major businesses and of necessity employed an army of accountants and clerks.

THE DEVELOPMENT OF THE SUBURBS/2

The expanding civil service also demanded a new class of administrators, and the needs of this group as a whole created more jobs for teachers, doctors, shopkeepers, builders and many other trades and professions. This new social group, while often earning little more than many of the artisan class, nonetheless had a different set of aspirations, and a quite different view of their social position. While the physical manifestation of this might change from one generation to the next, as fashions changed, its basis remained the same: that of making one's status visible and apparent. The house was a perfect vehicle for achieving this.

The First Suburbanites

Throughout the nineteenth century millions of people joined the various 'middle classes' – a term which encompassed anything from rich city merchants in the Soames Forsyte mould to the Pooterish clerk earning £150 a year. Although this class probably comprised only a sixth of the population in 1841, even then it established a very particular culture and a set of values quite different from those of other social classes. Most significant was the emphasis on the importance of family life, within rigid social dimensions. To speak of the 'family' however, is somewhat misleading, for Victorian homes often housed many more individuals than just the immediate family. While middle-class households varied considerably in size – for example, eighteen per cent of marriages in the 1870s produced ten or more live births, while eight per cent were childless – they were on the whole large, and live-in

▷ **Salvation Army leaders were among the many philanthropists offering a solution to the degradation of inner-city life, as shown in this chart of their scheme (1890).**

servants were essential, for practical as well as social reasons. Lodgers were common in less well-off families. The absence of state care for the elderly often meant that they lived with their children; and with women outnumbering men in Victorian times, space might also have to be found for maiden aunts or sisters. The role of the male as head of the family and provider was unquestioned; the role of his wife was to run the home (i.e. give orders to the servants), attend church, and above all to have children.

This type of household was seen as a microcosm of an ordered, dutiful, Christian society; its social rigidity perhaps reflected the insecurity of people from often humble origins seeking to establish a higher position in society. Professor John Burnett, in *A Social History of Housing* (1980), explains how important the house itself was to this aspiration:

The home then had to fulfil these many functions: to comfort and purify, to give relief and privacy from the cares of the world, to rear its members in an appropriate set of Christian values, and above all, to proclaim by its ordered arrangements, polite behaviour, cleanliness, tidiness, and distinctive taste that its members belonged to a class of substance, culture and respectability. The house itself was to be a visible expression of these values.

The impetus behind the rapid development of the early suburbs was the need to provide housing that fulfilled these requirements.

Early Styles and the Rejection of Flats

The suburban houses built by speculators after 1840 pandered to the middle classes' desire to emulate their social superiors, and to reflect their aspirations. Increasingly ornamental exterior details, based either on the Italianate style, which drew its inspiration from the grand palaces of the Italian Renaissance, or the Gothic Revival which took as its source the great cathedrals of northern Europe, seem to have proved particularly attractive to the average clerk and his family. The basic design of the houses remained, however, that of the Georgian terrace – closely packed together with dark basements and difficult garden access – and was essentially an urban style. Mid-Victorian suburban life was not in any way seen as an escape to the countryside, and the pioneers of the new territories still regarded themselves as town dwellers.

There was, however, a deep repugnance for living in flats. To the suburban mind, one of the great advantages of houses over flats was that a housing estate lent itself more readily to social exclusivity. A great deal of thought was usually given to how the 'tone' of an area might be maintained; the European system of large apartment blocks housing all ranks of society – the wealthy on the first floor and the other occupants falling in social status the higher one ascended the stairs – was anathema to the British middle-class desire to be quite separate from the lower orders. To make matters worse, flat dwelling was associated in the mid-nineteenth century with the tenements erected by benefactors such as the Guin-

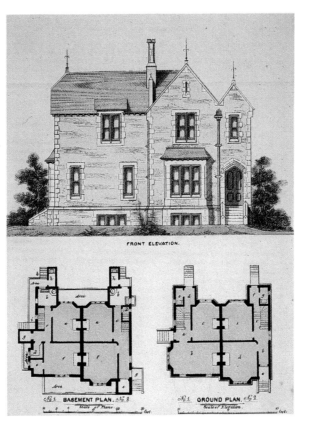

FRONT ELEVATION.

Nº 1. BASEMENT PLAN. Nº 2.   Nº 1. GROUND PLAN. Nº 2.

◁Many historical styles provided inspiration for Victorian suburban architecture, but the most popular were the Italianate and Gothic, providing as they did both a degree of ostentation and the potential for a variety of detail that appealed to the new suburbanites. This design for a pair of semi-detached villas in the 'Domestic Gothic Style', and suitable for a plot at the junction of two streets, appeared in E. L. Blackburne's *Suburban and Rural Architecture* (1869), in which he states that 'The object of the designer has been to obtain as much picturesqueness of outline and play of light and shade as is possible in houses of so small a class.'

THE DEVELOPMENT OF THE SUBURBS/3

▽ THE DEVELOPMENT OF A SUBURB.
The map of 1745 (left) shows the small village of Crouch End with its attendant hamlets of Muscle (Muswell) Hill and Stroud Green. Hedges and fields are clearly shown, and the road pattern – converging on what has now become 'The Broadway' – is clearly established. The New River, built in the early seventeenth century to carry water from springs in Hertfordshire to Sadler's Wells in North London, is the only other major feature. The map of 1864 (centre) shows a great change from this rural scene; three railways cut through the fields, and its proximity to the city has littered the area with large mansions set in private parks (shown darker than the surrounding fields). But the presence of several brickfields and one or two rows of terraced and semi-detached housing is an indication of greater changes to come. The map of 1896 (right) shows the grounds of the grand mansion covered by streets of byelaw terraces. Extra stations have been built to cope with the commuters.

ness and Peabody Trusts, and 'five-per-cent philanthropy' land companies which attempted to provide decent homes for the working classes away from the slums.

Putting a distance between themselves and the working classes was not entirely a question of status and social position for the suburbanites, because it also had a practical basis. Flight from the inner cities was an attempt to escape serious health problems. Overcrowding and poor sanitation in the cities' slums increased the risk of disease: cholera and typhoid epidemics were common, and child mortality was very high. Slum conditions were also linked in respectable Victorian minds with lax moral attitudes and questionable behaviour – something with which they particularly did not want to be associated.

Social superiority, as reflected in the house itself, was undoubtedly a major attraction of the suburbs, however, with privacy an important additional factor.

Ideally, houses were well hidden behind high walls or shrubberies, and entire estates were often enclosed and gated in an effort to keep out the hoi-polloi and maintain an air of exclusivity. Other, smaller details also lent the new suburbs a superior and individual quality, as one writer pointed out in *The Builder* magazine (1848) when considering the rash of new building, which he notes is directed only at 'the gentry':

You may get a new house, of almost every conceivable pattern and at any conceivable price down to £60 per annum. You may take your choice, according to the length of your purse, of 'noble reception rooms' and 'neat parlours'. But your purse must have some length to accomplish even the latter. *There is a leaven of aristocracy in the parlour with folding doors.*

The same writer also points out the importance of the names given to houses

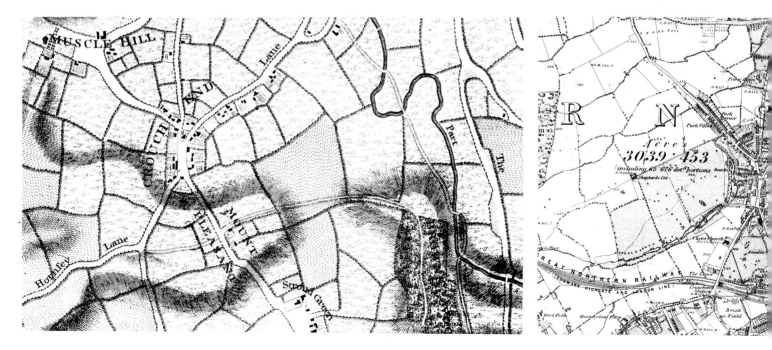

and streets as a further indication of the social pretensions of the first suburban occupants (and a feature of suburbia that has remained ever since). If the estate on which the houses were built had originally been held by a well-known family, its name might be borrowed to add tone to the neighbourhood; the de Crespigny estate at Camberwell in south-east London is a good example. Otherwise family names of the great aristocratic dynasties were freely used to adorn many a Victorian home – Grosvenor Villa, for example, did not necessarily mean connections with the Duke of Westminster. The ancient term 'street' was also thought to have plebian associations, and suburbia has always preferred the word road. Towards the end of the nineteenth century, and particularly in the twentieth, 'groves', 'ways' 'parks' and 'avenues' became popular as the focus of suburban dreams and aspirations began to change, and attractive street names became important.

ARTISTIC AND RURAL INFLUENCES

Several developments, broadly beginning in the 1870s, exerted considerable influence on suburban homes and aspirations. The 'aesthetic' fashion, a reaction against the opulence and extravagance in design that had characterized the High Victorian period, took hold, and aesthetic values now had a place beside those of status and social position. The Arts and Crafts Movement (see pages 99–100) also had a profound effect on British domestic design, and provided the middle classes with welcome instruction in 'artistic' taste. A further factor, which assumed importance towards the end of the century, was a major change in attitudes towards rural Britain, and this was to be a prime influence on housing style and the development of suburbia until the Second World War. To the average town dweller up to this point the country had been simply the domain of those directly or indirectly involved in the agricultural industry, with the town offering most in the way of opportunities and entertainment. By the end of the century, however, this highly urban population began to look on the country in a new light, and the 'countryside', as it became known, was seen as a place for recreation and leisure. The railways and, later, 'metalled' roads which gave the newly popular cycling clubs easier access were instrumental in developing this new diversion. Those who could afford it bought and restored derelict agricultural workers' cottages (the result of the agricultural depressions of the period), and country cottages became fashionable as second homes.

Concurrent with the beginnings of this trend, new architectural ideas were emerging, notably the Queen Anne style

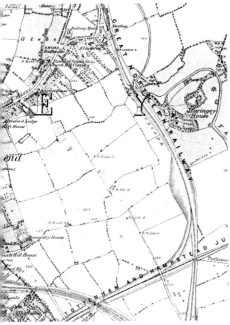

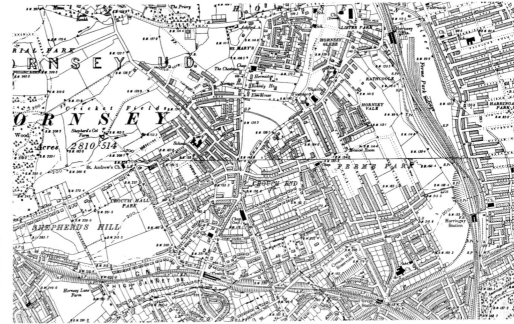

THE DEVELOPMENT OF THE SUBURBS/4

which made its first appearance in a suburban setting in Bedford Park in London. The 1870s also saw the first stirrings of the science of town planning and a move away from the city or at least from the predominantly urban view of housing. The Garden City Movement and some pioneering model housing estates such as Port Sunlight, Bournville and Hampstead Garden Suburb, as well as a remarkable series of country houses by Arts and Crafts architects, all played a part in drastically changing housing design in the 1890s. It was part of a new, romantic view of home, in which a rural cottage retreat was the ideal, and in trying to achieve this the new suburbs adopted vernacular styles based upon traditional and country-town building types, styles that were to remain popular well into the 1930s.

▷**Bedford Park, a London suburb built in the 1870s, was to influence both the style and setting of future housing, even as much as sixty years later.**

PRIVATE HOUSING IN THE 1920s AND 1930s

The middle-class suburbanite of the inter-war period had different requirements from his pre-war counterpart. The house was still an essential status symbol, and had to fulfil many romantic and symbolic images of the ideal home, but it now had also to meet many more practical requirements. The changing pattern of employment brought about by the growing service industries had increased the number of managers, administrators, teachers and clerks in relation to manual workers, so that the middle class grew disproportionately.

Individual households were smaller than previously: the average number of children per family fell from 5.8 in 1871 to 2.2 in the 1930s. This social group was

also poorer in relation to the working classes than its Victorian and Edwardian counterparts, and servants were no longer a standard feature of the suburban home. Social upheavals caused by the war, and better paid, higher-status jobs becoming available for women, had resulted in a shortage of people willing to be employed as domestic servants for the low wages most people could afford. The effect of these factors was a need for smaller, more convenient houses that could be easily maintained by few staff, or by the housewife alone. Owning rather than renting one's house became a source of status as the building of homes for mortgage rather than rent became the norm. Fierce competition

△**The galleon in full sail was a familiar motif of suburbia between the wars.**

between building firms and falling costs reduced the price of housing considerably in the 1930s, and low interest rates further encouraged buyers.

The style chosen by the builders – mock Tudor or 'Jacobethan' – satisfied a curious ambivalence towards the home among the middle classes of the day. The typical mock-Tudor semi with its rose-filled front garden was highly functional and modern in some respects, particularly in the kitchen and bathroom, but at the same time cosy and cottage-like, much more rural in atmosphere than any previous speculative housing. Half-timbering, perhaps with herringbone brick infill, leaded lights, inglenooks, tile-hung bays, porches, red brick or pebble-dash walls and gabled roofs all combined to give a picturesque if not positively romantic image of a country cottage. As Professor Burnett points out, the reasons why this style was so pervasively popular may have much to do with 'the assumption that every English gentleman was, or felt he was, a disinherited country gentleman', yet many of the motifs seem to be even more fanciful than those required to emulate the country life. The escapist imagery may have had more deep-seated and immediate origins. Many home buyers had first-hand experience of trench warfare, and the world economic depression and political chicanery in Europe made many fear another conflict. Against this background, modern architecture was firmly rejected as too uncompromising, and a 'beamed' cottage with rose-covered porch represented a return to a cosier and more secure age. The galleon in full sail, one of the most popular images of the time which found its way on to everything from windows to lampshades and ashtrays, perhaps best represents this past era, when England was prosperous, happy and, above all, militarily secure.

SUBURBIA SINCE THE SECOND WORLD WAR

The astonishing expansion of suburbia, which the outbreak of war had brought to an abrupt halt in 1939, did not resume at the end of the conflict. Although the housing shortage of 1945 was comparable to that of 1918, the development of housing in Britain took a new direction with the advent of effective planning legislation introduced in the late 1940s. Aerial bombardment had destroyed many dwellings, and demographic trends aggravated the shortage because, although the population as a whole was growing relatively slowly, the number of individual households was increasing, particularly in the post-war marriage boom. Improved life expectancy also caused the proportion of people over retirement age to rise relative to the rest of the population, and they tended to maintain their own homes independently. A large number of the households in Britain thus consisted of only one or two people, and the standard three-bedroom house of the inter-war period no longer matched the needs of a large part of the population.

The death knell for the inter-war suburban style was, however, sounded most effectively by the political attitude of the nation, which was quite different in 1945 from that of 1918. The new Britain was to be a planned Britain, one in which the effort and government co-ordination used to win the war would be directed to domestic problems; no longer would the nation's economy and environment be left to look after themselves. Part of this new mood was a fundamental change of view towards the provision of housing. In the years following 1945 Britain saw the revival of urbanism rather than suburbanism, a form of planned suburbia in which towns and cities themselves, if well thought out, were now perceived for the first time in many generations as good and proper places to live. The prevailing view that country was preferable to town, and that suburbia with its 'country cottage' styling was a reasonable compromise, was completely overturned, and it was the classically severe and unadorned Georgian inner-city terrace that became a source of inspiration. The plainness of Modernism was now seen as the latest manifestation of this tradition of 'good taste' and three-storey town houses again became fashionable.

Another characteristic of the new urbanism was the provision of mixed developments, in which different types of dwelling were built together to cater for different types of occupier, partly in an attempt to mix social classes; but this idea was not a success. In the absence of a distinctive decorative architectural style for the house itself, new status symbols were sought, and cars, white goods and European holidays took on this role.

△ **Stevenage New Town, an example of the new approach to planning after 1945.**

THE BUILDERS/1

The building of suburbia, which began in earnest in the 1840s, was, until effective planning Acts of a hundred years later, for the most part the result of private enterprise. With the exception of a few philanthropists and, in the twentieth century, local councils who turned their attention to providing homes for the working classes, most of the building was concerned with the provision of houses for a growing social group – the middle class.

The scale of the enterprise was vast and often risky for the builders and developers involved. Those drawn to hopes of a quick profit from house building in the 1840s boom came from many walks of life. Not only bricklayers, masons and carpenters took up the challenge, embarking on small developments on which they did much of the work themselves and subcontracted the rest, but shopkeepers, small businessmen and even clergymen with small sums to invest were also tempted to try their luck. The scale of operations was equally varied: one speculative builder might be responsible for just three or four houses in a street (which explains to some extent the many variations to be found in one apparently uniform row of houses) while others, including Thomas Cubitt (the most successful nineteenth-century builder), undertook whole estates.

The land on which the new houses were built usually came from large country estates, as landowners breaking up their property found that leasing to builders was more lucrative than collecting rents from market gardeners or farmers. Having first secured an Act of Parliament to abolish manorial rights on their land, landowners then offered portions of their estate on building leases to individual builders who built houses for rent. As all the property would eventually revert to the landowner under this system, he had a vested interest in maintaining, as far as was practicable, high rental values, and attempted to ensure this by laying down certain stipulations concerning the size of houses and the type of occupant that would be acceptable. The builders also needed to attract the best tenants possible since their rents were needed to finance their next enterprise and to provide their income. As a consequence a disproportionate number of estates were aimed at the 'top end' of the market.

Builders would often take on only a few of the available plots, as their resources allowed, and this resulted in a piecemeal development which was unsatisfactory for a number of reasons. On a practical level, since the development had not usually been planned in

◁◁**This group of builders is posed outside the house on which they were working in London's East End in 1882. (The boss is presumably the man in the frock coat with a peg leg.) Speculative builders might build a whole estate or just a few houses in a row.**

◁**From its earliest beginnings, the expansion of suburbia was looked upon with misgivings, as this engraving of 1829 by George Cruikshank, showing the departure of trees and hayricks under the onslaught of troops of bricks and mortar, graphically demonstrates. Both the speed of suburban development and its blight of the countryside were major sources of concern.**

LONDON going out of Town. — or — The March of Bricks & Mortar! —

THE BUILDERS/2

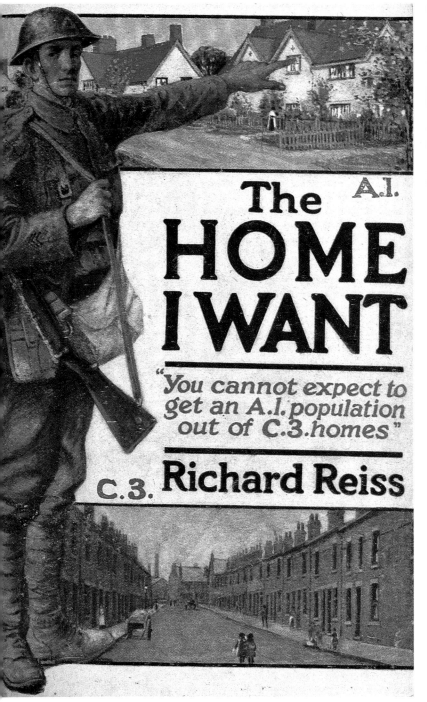

△Falling interest rates and generous grants put the dream of home ownership – the ideal behind this romanticized poster for a private firm – within many people's grasp.

◁The urgent need for a large number of acceptable homes after the First World War meant that for the first time the State became involved, both by building houses and by creating conditions to encourage the private sector.

any way, the provision of such services as were available was haphazard; even more important from the landowner's point of view was the fact that gaps left between the houses might be filled later by more smaller houses, thus increasing the density to an unacceptable level, or even by something like a fever hospital which would drastically lower the value of the whole development. Efforts were made to maintain the tone and therefore the value of an estate, and ranged from enclosing it by means of gates, with gatekeepers preventing the lower orders or tradespeople (unless on genuine business) from getting in, to simply not letting houses to people in 'unsuitable' occupations, even if they could afford it. Despite these measures, however, mishaps were inevitable, whether troublesome sewers or undesirable individuals, or simply the proximity of those (such as laundresses and shopkeepers) who actually serviced the grander houses, and the estates were gradually abandoned by their carefully courted occupants, often only ten years after being built. Landlords would then turn the houses over to multiple occupancy by working-class families, in order to make some return on their money.

Legislation and Control

There was little centralized control over house building until about the 1870s, either in terms of the planning of estates or the specification of individual houses, and complaints about 'jerrybuilders' were numerous. Such legislation as did exist before the 1875 Public Health Act varied from district to district, and in many cases was only concerned with restricting the building of 'back to backs' rather than with any more general guidelines. For the most part building was confidently undertaken by builders armed with nothing more substantial than their pattern books.

The 1875 Act gave local authorities the power to lay down regulations concerning the sanitary conditions of their houses, as well as byelaws concerning the layout, width and construction of new streets, and the space around houses, which were to form the basis of the so-called byelaw street. Further Acts included legislation on the internal spaces of houses and their structure. The controls were not as effective as they might have been, however: the adoption of byelaws was voluntary, not mandatory; and work was supposed to be inspected by already stretched Local Board surveyors, while in practice the schemes were open to corruption – not least because many builders found their way on to the Local Boards. This system continued in much the same way until the First World War. Nevertheless, the vast majority of the houses, as their current condition testifies, were soundly built.

THE PUBLIC SECTOR

After the First World War, the shape of suburbia was greatly influenced by a major new factor – the State as a provider of housing. The influence of the State was quite direct, as local authorities actually built much of suburbia and set very high minimum standards which private developers were forced to copy. There was also an indirect influence on private housing in that many owner-occupiers sought new ways to ensure that their houses looked privately owned. Two strongly opposed philosophies can thus be seen in the contrasting styles of each type of suburbia: the style of the private estate emphasizes the desire to express individuality, whereas the style of local-authority architects veers towards notions of social egalitarianism. (Tenants who now buy their former council homes often quickly demonstrate an affinity with the bourgeois style and attitude of the classic owner-occupier.)

Local-authority housing had theoretically been possible since the Housing Act of 1890, but only a few councils had used their powers to build, and then only in a very modest and piecemeal way. It was the acute housing shortage aggravated by the Great War that provoked the State into building in earnest. Until then the received wisdom had been that market forces and private builders would continue to provide the nation's housing. Several factors brought about this change of heart. Soaring rents caused by the housing shortage led to the passing of an Act in 1915 to hold rents and mortgage interest down to pre-war levels. After the war it became apparent that to repeal this measure would lead to extortionate and politically unacceptable rent levels. Rents were thus kept artificially low, and in such a climate builders would not build new housing for rent. The return on capital was simply too low, at least for the more modest, low-rental homes which the nation so badly needed. Builders therefore tended to prefer to build larger houses whose rent was not controlled, or increasingly, as it became clear that rent control was to be a permanent fact of life, houses for sale. Thus the twentieth-century trend towards owner-occupation rather than rental was established, and as decent homes for a reasonable rent were no longer economically viable, it was clear that the poor who could not afford to buy would suffer most from the shortage.

This situation was hardly new, but the other factor in favour of State intervention was the belated recognition that private enterprise and market forces had never provided a decent standard of housing for the poor, and that the situation should be tolerated no longer. The King himself stated that decent, sanitary homes were necessary to social progress and to the rearing of a healthy race, as well as the conversion of unrest into contentment. Provoked either by social conscience or fear of revolution, Parliament at last turned its attention to the nation's chronic housing problem. The practical outcome was the Tudor Walters Report of 1918, named after the MP who chaired the committee which produced it, but written largely by Raymond Unwin of garden city fame (see also page 126).

The report set out minimum standards which it hoped would profoundly affect the general standard of housing 'for at least sixty years', and created a form of suburbia not seen before. It adopted many of the ideas of the garden city movement, and was also influenced by planned suburbs such as Letchworth

THE BUILDERS/3

and Hampstead Garden Suburb with their model working-class houses. It recommended a maximum density of twelve houses to the acre, arranged in cul-de-sacs and around open spaces, avoiding the byelaw monotony. Wider cottage frontages (they did not call them houses) with no 'tunnel back' rear projections ensured that sunlight shone directly into as many rooms as possible. Three bedrooms and two living rooms were regarded as the minimum, all with stated minimum sizes. Fixed baths were essential, although they were often placed beneath a 'work-top lid' in the scullery. Rear access to gardens of good size and adequate privacy with no shared facilities were to be the new norms. For aesthetic reasons the semi-detached form was rejected in favour of terraces of four to six houses, with tunnels to provide access to the rear, even though semis would have been cheaper to build. Generally speaking the report was realistic in terms of costs, although it stressed the need to take aesthetic as well as practical considerations into account when designing estates. The grouping of houses and layout of roads to preserve existing trees and shrubs and create pleasant vistas were regarded as essentials of good design and were in fact seen more often on council than on private developments.

The Housing Manual turned the report into instructions for local councils, but it was not until the Housing Act of 1919 that councils were actually required to build houses for the first time, with a government subsidy. The councils often did so to a standard higher than the Housing Manual suggested. The attitude that private enterprise could not provide housing adequate for the nation's needs and that the State should shoulder some of the burden prevailed throughout the inter-war period, though with some inevitable

fluctuations in response to cuts in public spending. By 1934, nearly a third of the 2.5 million houses built since 1919 were council owned, but by the late 1920s the high standards of Tudor Walters had had to be modified as cost yardsticks were reduced, and minima tended to become maxima in matters such as room sizes. Nevertheless, these standards represented a significant attempt to deal with the housing problem, and provided 'ideal homes' for many people.

HOUSES FOR SALE

The factors affecting the entry of local authorities into house building also had an effect on the private sector. The rent freeze which had been introduced during the war and continued afterwards also forced those who had money to invest, and who had up to this point put it into houses for rent, to seek other outlets; an obvious answer was building societies. Building societies had been slowly developing since the eighteenth century, beginning as small groups of people getting together to acquire and build houses, and were organized along the lines of friendly societies. They grew very rapidly in the period immediately after the First World War. The measures of 1919 which had involved local authorities in building houses had also been extended on a limited basis to speculative builders, and in 1923 the grants on offer to them were made more generous. This encouragement, together with the money that was flowing into building societies and favourable interest rates, were the important factors that paved the way for the inter-war building boom that created privately owned, semi-detached suburbia.

Until the First World War the majority of builders involved in speculative development had continued to work in small units along the lines established in

the nineteenth century, but after the war new and much larger firms quickly emerged, and those that had been working before the war expanded considerably. Alan Jackson, in his detailed account of the growth of suburban London, *Semi-Detached London* (1973), notes that names still associated with house building today – Laing, New Ideal Homesteads, Costain, Wates and Wimpey – were all at work during this period, particularly in the years of the most building activity at the end of the 1920s and beginning of the 1930s. As in the nineteenth century, individuals not usually associated with the domestic building industry were tempted to get involved, and their lack of experience in many cases led to financial ruin. For example, Jackson cites a bankruptcy report of 1937 which 'records the former occupations of two Edgware building partners as "maker of silk ties" and "gown manufacturer", whilst another in similar straits had been a Liverpool iron and steel merchant and haulage contractor.' The large and successful companies, however, were now in a position to undertake every aspect of estate development, from the initial purchase and layout of the land, to marketing the houses and encouraging the maximum number of potential buyers.

The most significant point about the new houses from their future occupants' point of view was that they would be bought rather than rented. Until the

▷▷Competition between the building companies was intense as the market became saturated in the 1930s. Inducements to potential buyers ranged from free electrical appliances to assistance with the deposit, as offered by New Ideal Homesteads in their 1935 advertisement. Morrell's, however, were content to let the 'sun and tonic air' of their estates and their proximity to railway stations do the selling for them.

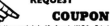

THE BUILDERS/4

war, with few exceptions, it had been the custom to rent accommodation, but just as it became more attractive to invest in building societies at this period, the possibility of investing in a home also assumed a new attraction. Initially the houses built were too expensive for most people, but as the housing boom gathered pace the building societies and builders found ways to ease the situation. The early 1930s saw a reduction in the mortgage interest rate, together with an increase in the repayment period; in addition, some local authorities offered loans of up to ninety per cent with a maximum repayment period of thirty years. The problem of the cash deposit remained until the 'Builders' Pool' was established: this was a fund which lent the deposit to the prospective purchaser's building society, thus reducing the amount required or even removing the impediment from the buyer altogether. Jackson suggests that this move was the result of the fierce competition for buyers which had increased towards the middle and end of the 1930s. Already ambitious advertising campaigns were intensified and more obvious techniques were employed, such as offering free electrical appliances or even motor cars.

The rush to put houses up and to sell them was not always the best way to ensure good quality, and complaints were often heard about damp, leaking roofs and other structural defects, a situation which even led some proud new home-owners to default on their mortgages. Legislation affecting house building in the inter-war years was still comparatively limited, and patchily enforced. In theory, builders had to take account of local byelaws concerned with basic standards of health and safety, sanitation, foundations and so on, and any restrictions stipulating price and maximum density, as well as town planning schemes. Building standards relat-

RICHARD COSTAIN & SONS, LTD.

CROHAM HEIGHTS

UPPER SELSDON ROAD, SANDERSTEAD.

Estate Office. Norfolk Avenue.   Tel:- Sanderstead 2429

The "Teakwood" Home. (Four Bedrooms & Garage)

£1,180 Freehold:-

Includes:-
> Roads paved for adoption, and legal expenses.
> Choice of modern fireplaces and decorations.
> Electrical installation, all services.
> Paths, Drives and Fencing.

The Sanderstead Woods form a fine background to this portion of the Estate, and fine views of the Croham Hurst and Golf Links are obtained. Limited to six houses to the acre, it yields large gardens with a well drained chalk subsoil.

South Croydon Station and the shopping centre are reached in less than ten minutes by the frequent No. 54 'bus service, in addition to the Chelsham and Edenbridge Green Line service passing the Estate. There is a good local shopping centre, within a few minutes walk.

◁◁**These advertisements for houses built by Wates and Costain illustrate the cottage styling and an air of exclusivity that were the most important features of 1930s' suburbia. The 'Teakwood' home is at the upper end of the market, well placed near shops, transport facilities, and with a large garden, fine views and a golf club nearby.**

first, in the rush to provide houses after the war, developers were allowed to go ahead without waiting for planning schemes or with 'interim' approval; later, as the legislation was developed, it was found that individual planning authorities were too small to function effectively and were unwilling or unable to work together. Criticism of the increasing suburban sprawl gained ground consistently up to the Second World War, and much of it was directed specifically at so-called ribbon development, which was effectively defeating the object of the new bypass roads. The Ribbon Development Act of 1935, which gave councils the power to restrict frontage development along main roads, was the first of many measures which were to curtail the kind of suburban development that had been established during the 1920s and 1930s.

After the Second World War, the new emphasis on centralized planning was reflected in the Planning Act of 1948, which gave unprecedented powers to local authorities to control development in their areas. It required them to draw up overall structural plans to ensure the proper segregation of, as well as adequate provision for, housing, industry, shops, offices, transport, amenities and open spaces. A separate Act established the green belt around London, which halted the suburban sprawl around the capital to the limit it had reached in 1939. Later Acts did the same for other large conurbations. To alleviate the inevitable pressure on the space available in cities, the New Towns Act of 1946 envisaged a new type of development – self-sufficient towns within commuting distance of major cities – to replace the unplanned sprawl. Urban renewal was also to be the new focus for building attention and thus suburbia in its traditional form was finished.

ing to materials used and building practices were barely covered until 1937, when the National Federation of House-builders (under the Chairmanship of Sir Raymond Unwin) instituted a voluntary scheme which recommended specifications and kept a register of builders whose houses were in line with them.

Although some form of planning legislation had been in existence since 1909 in most authorities (initially enabling them to plan the use of their land), and was further extended in the 1920s and 1930s, little of it was successful. At

THE SERVANTS

The employment of servants played a major role in shaping the character of suburbia. Servants were necessary for two reasons. Firstly, they did the vast amount of work that the Victorian household generated: the design of houses as well as their contents required constant labour to maintain the standards of cleanliness demanded by the middle classes. The second reason for employing servants was one of status: the Victorian lady of the house was not expected to work, and there was no shortage of advice in contemporary household guides as to exactly how many servants one was expected to engage according to income. (Despite the almost total disappearance of servants in suburbia today, the snob value of employing a 'daily' has not diminished.) In the last quarter of the nineteenth century, when servant employment was at its highest, four or even five servants would not have been unusual in a well-to-do middle-class household.

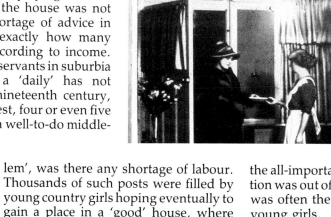

As might be expected, servants had a strict hierarchy of their own. The linchpin of the system was the cook, assisted by a scullery maid. Other maids did general housework, although one of them might double as a lady's maid, helping with the mistress's toilette. A specialist nursemaid looked after the children. Male servants were more expensive and consequently status-enhancing, but rare in suburbia except in wealthy areas, where the 'carriage folk' would of course employ grooms; and when butlers were employed it was not uncommon for the hierarchy to be extended so that the higher servants had servants of their own.

For most suburbanites before the First World War, however, such an extended household was an ideal they were unable to emulate. The usual compromise was a 'cook-general' who did everything, and possibly a nursemaid to look after the children. Wages were about £25 per annum, with 'all found', that is, food and lodging provided. Even this paltry sum was too much for a clerk on £200 a year, and a 'maid of all work' on less than £20 a year had to be the answer. Nor, despite the 'servant prob-

lem', was there any shortage of labour. Thousands of such posts were filled by young country girls hoping eventually to gain a place in a 'good' house, where servant-keeping was not such a financial strain and better facilities could be provided. They were sent into service in the city for the first time by their caring but impoverished families when often as young as fourteen.

What the majority of them saw, of course, was suburbia, and it undoubtedly held terrors for these children, many of which were well founded. The upper-class home in which the servants' duties, if onerous, were at least strictly defined, and in which their territory was held sacrosanct, was not always replicated in suburbia. A maid of all work was expected to labour for extremely long hours and, with no cook or butler to protect her, was completely at the mercy of the mistress of the house. It is hardly surprising that many unhappy and lonely girls mistook the attentions of the elder sons or head of the family for simple kindness, and illegitimacy and even infanticide were the not uncommon results. A pregnancy was unlikely to endear one to the mistress, and without

the all-important reference another position was out of the question. Prostitution was often the only alternative for these young girls.

Many servants were, however, happily employed, but as other, more highly rewarded jobs became available to women there did begin to be a shortage of servants. In fact, the proportion of women in the workforce remained remarkably static, being thirty-one per cent in 1871 and thirty per cent in 1931. But whereas before 1900 nearly half of them were in domestic service, by 1931 inventions such as the telephone and the typewriter had created a large additional demand for female labour. The wartime munitions factories, too, had given many women a taste of independence and the better wages that now made domestic service seem demeaning. Between 1911 and 1921 the number of resident servants in the London suburbs was halved from twenty-four to twelve per hundred families.

The loss of servants naturally had a major effect on housing design. Large Victorian houses had been planned with two communities in mind. Servants usually shared cold attic bedrooms, but the

warm kitchen was theirs, and the family of the house did not penetrate beyond the green baize door which traditionally separated their living quarters from the domestic offices. Later Victorian domestic commentators such as J. J. Stevenson, author of *House Architecture* (1880), deplored the poorer living conditions of servants and demanded a more humane attitude towards them, while advocating the retention of their own territory. By the end of the century new houses were being built with maid's sitting rooms, previously an unheard-of luxury, in order to tempt staff by making the job – which was still rather poorly paid – more attractive.

In America, where the 'servant problem' had been felt earlier, Catherine E. Beecher (sister of Harriet, the author of *Uncle Tom's Cabin*) had already pioneered labour-saving housing design incorporating continuous work surfaces like those in ships' galleys, in the nineteenth century. Although her idea of the fully fitted kitchen was not generally adopted in Britain until well after the Second World War, the trend towards more easily maintained houses is the major feature of housing design in the twentieth century. In *Semi-Detached London*, Alan Jackson says that as early as 1911 houses in Harrow were being advertised as 'specially designed to meet the requirements of a small family not wishing to incur the worry and expense of keeping a servant'.

After the First World War, live-in servants became a rarity in suburbia, and housing, almost without exception, was designed to accommodate only the family that occupied it. This did not prevent the more pretentious from attempting to recreate the splendours of the past. Alan Jackson describes Golders Green in the 1920s thus:

Few of the houses were large enough to accommodate servants, but many families hired a maid, making sure that she was in attendance at least for the evening meal, which would be taken at the front of the house, with curtains drawn well back and lights blazing.

The trend away from servant keeping has continued; virtually no houses built today make special provision for live-in staff. Despite this, estate agents, who know well the preferences of their market, are still apt to refer to an odd room above the normal complement as a 'maid's sitting room'. Snob value dies hard in suburbia.

△△Servants were an essential status symbol in suburbia for most of the period – until they were ousted by a battery of modern domestic appliances – even though many households had only one 'maid of all work'. As always in suburbia, appearances were very important, for polishing the silver as much as for greeting visitors at the front door.

◁The Army and Navy Co-operative Society was a supplier of maids' uniform, which might include a trimmed or mob cap, a morning dress and afternoon dress, and a 'tea apron'.

G.P. 207.—Frilled Cap, finished Black Velvet, 2/9

G.P. 207a.—Afternoon Apron, good wearing, finished tucks and embroidery insertion, 3/6

G.P. 208.—Cap, of dainty Muslin, trimmed embroidery and beading, 2/1

G.P. 208a.—Tea Apron, of fine Muslin, finished wide hems and beading, 2/9

G.P. 209.—Muslin Cap, trimmed insertion, 2/1

G.P. 209a.—Strong Cambric Apron, finished fine embroidery, 3/6

G.P. 210.—Organdi Muslin Cap, 2/9

G.P. 210a.—Muslin Tea Apron, daintily trimmed fine lace, 3/3

G.P. 211.—Mob Cap, of Spot Muslin, 2/9

G.P. 211a.—Tea Apron, of fancy Spot Muslin, 2/11

G.P. 212.—Maids' Alpaca Afternoon Dress, of reliable quality, well cut and finished. Can be supplied with 1 in. collar band if desired. Colours: Black, Navy, Brown, or Grey, 27/6

G.P. 213.—Frilled Cap, of soft Muslin, 1/11

G.P. 213a.—Smart Tea Apron, of fancy Spot and Plain Muslin, 1/11½

G.P. 214.—Simple Muslin Cap, 1/6

G.P. 214a.—Afternoon Apron, of good quality Lawn, finished fine embroidery beading, 3/11

G.P. 215.—Alpaca Coat Frocks, loose at waist. Price 25/6

G.P. 216.—Maids' Morning Dresses of strong Washing Gingham, with Peter Pan collar or 1 in. collar band, in Blue, Grey, Butcher, or Steel. Price 12/11

Waist.	Skirt Length.	Waist.	Skirt Length.
Sizes ..	26 in.	32 in.	Sizes ..	28 in.	36 in.
„ ..	26 „	34 „	„ ..	30 „	34 „

PUBLIC TRANSPORT/1

The cliché of the bowler-hatted suburban man catching the 8.05 to town reinforces the belief that the suburban way of life is somehow dependent upon the ebb and flow of commuting menfolk, and it is therefore often assumed that suburbs owe their existence to good public transport. This is not strictly true. Until mass car ownership, a suburb and its transport system were indeed often inextricably interdependent, but the existence of both was the result of the increased wealth that a large city could generate and which could support a middle class with enough surplus income to be able to live remote from its place of work. The early and mid-Victorian suburbs in fact housed a vast army of clerks who walked two or three miles twice daily in all weathers, and were not dependent on transport at all. Landowners were able to make considerable sums by charging penny or half-penny tolls to commuters taking short-cuts across their property. The wealthier commuters – the so-called 'carriage folk' – had their own independent transport, and were thus able to live much further from city centres.

As the nineteenth century progressed, the rapidly increasing size of many towns and cities made mass public transport more and more desirable. While many suburbs suffered for years from inadequate communications with their cities, others were built because the presence of a railway, driven through open country, turned the surrounding fields into valuable development land. Many Victorian railway companies were not interested in commuter traffic, and those who did see its rich potential were often prevented by law from developing the land they had made valuable. Again, in other areas they might negotiate with local building speculators, who could often be persuaded to bear the cost of building a station, to their mutual benefit. By the turn of the century, however, many transport companies were adopting a much more aggressive, pioneering approach to their territories, realizing that, to survive in a business notorious for low profit margins, they had to create their own new markets. The most famous of these was the Metropolitan Railway which used a unique legal

▷**Although horse-drawn buses were more expensive than trams, this painting by G. W. Joy,** *The Bayswater Omnibus* **(1895), is an idealized view: disturbances were common among the rush-hour crowds struggling to use the unregulated transport system.**

loophole to set up subsidiary companies to develop and market its own housing estates in north-west London. This swathe of suburbia became known as 'Metroland' after the magazine published by the company to advertise its attractions.

The story of public transport is one of the rapid growth of private companies which operated unplanned and haphazard networks of trains, trams and buses which could be infuriatingly uncoordinated. Gradually, the companies merged to form larger corpora-

tions which were eventually, in the twentieth century, taken into public ownership in order to make some sense of the systems. London, in Victorian times the largest city in the world, faced the need for mass transport earlier than most other places, and developed many of the systems that other cities were later to adopt.

The Nineteenth Century

Throughout the nineteenth century, the horse-drawn omnibus, and not the train,

△Ludgate Hill Station (built in 1846 on the site of Fleet Prison whose ruined walls remained) was among those offering cheap day-trips to the coast and elsewhere.

▽The interior of Cannon Street station in 1874 shows that commuters were seen as captive targets for advertisers, then as now; W. H. Smith already ran the bookstall.

was the major carrier of passengers. In 1829 a Mr Shillibeer introduced the first horse-drawn 'bus service (from a Parisian idea) which ran from Paddington to the Bank and, although his company failed, the subsequent bus mania quickly established routes all over London and the larger cities. Cut-throat competition led to races between buses from rival companies, but the ancient system of tolls and turnpike roads slowed the traffic and kept costs high. (Bus travel was beyond the reach of the working classes, still in any case living in

PUBLIC TRANSPORT/2

the inner-city areas.) Eventually, the rival outfits combined to form larger, more organized companies, though boundary disputes persisted well into the twentieth century, and pirate buses would poach passengers on busy, profitable routes. Buses were excluded from some areas on grounds of social exclusivity, or to protect existing services such as the hackney carriage system in the City of London. Similar vested interests often also prevented railways from penetrating city centres – London's mainline stations ringed the city – and trains thus presented no threat to the bus services; in fact, they complemented the bus services by supplying huge numbers of passengers as well as the vast amounts of hay and oats needed in the city centres.

Railway companies were slower to value commuter traffic. The first railway building boom of the 1840s ignored the suburbs: stations were only added to main lines passing through suburbs as an afterthought during the second boom of the 1860s. The unplanned building of the railways did, however, have some unexpected effects on Britain's cities. The increased flow of people and business activity helped to make cities important places in a flourishing industrial society – places able to support larger middle classes and larger suburbs. More horse buses were needed in the city centres to cope with the extra traffic, and congestion quickly became intolerable. New roads built to relieve the chaos were prevented from penetrating well-to-do areas, and, like the railways, were

often deliberately driven through slum districts for 'sanitary' reasons, the assumption being that the displaced inhabitants would move to new homes in the suburbs. Travelling costs inevitably prevented this, however, and so one consequence of the Victorian road and rail boom was homelessness for thousands of the poorest city dwellers.

After the 1870s, two new developments provided some relief for the overcrowded working classes. Trams, larger and more comfortable than buses, but slow and cheap, were introduced at this time and were regarded as an essentially working-class means of transport (they were excluded from wealthy areas such as the West End of London). The cheaper commuting now possible for the working classes prompted the building

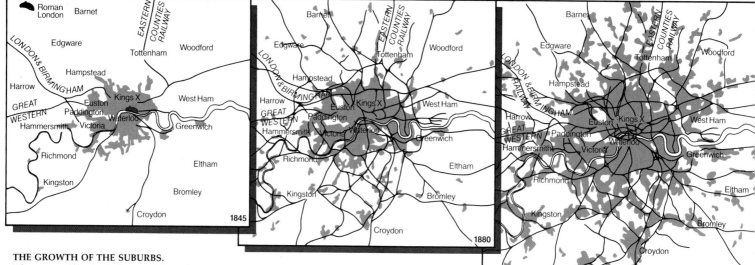

THE GROWTH OF THE SUBURBS.
The maps illustrated are of London, though similar expansion could be traced for any of the major conurbations in Britain.
1. London in 1845 was still concentrated around the Roman City of London, with small fingers of development reaching to outlying villages such as Hampstead and Clapham.

2. By 1880 the outline of the city had extended perceptibly, and the villages along the rapidly proliferating railway lines, such as Bromley, Croydon, Edgware and Barnet, were also expanding, although as yet there was little commuter traffic from these relatively farflung areas.

3. By 1914 the potential value of commuter traffic had been recognized, and stations were built along the railway lines, followed by a new burst of suburban building which filled the gaps between existing urban areas.

of suburbs specifically for them rather than for the middle class. In addition, Parliament, in response to the misery that had been caused by the cutting of railways through slum districts, required some companies (notably the Great Eastern) to provide, as a condition in the Private Acts which they needed to operate, cheap workmen's tickets to enable the poor to commute. Eventually the Cheap Trains Act of 1883 required all companies to do this, and they usually ran special early morning trains. Many hundreds of thousands took advantage

▷ Railway companies ran cheap workmen's trains in the early morning and evening to enable the poor to commute from the working-class suburbs. Gustave Doré's rather grim engraving shows Baker Street Station.

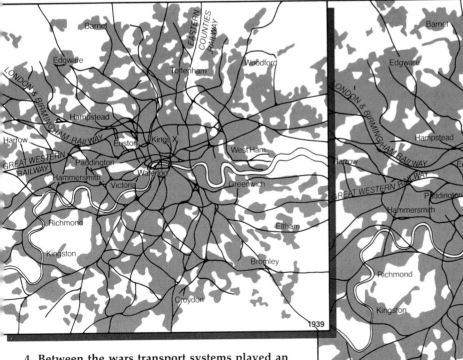

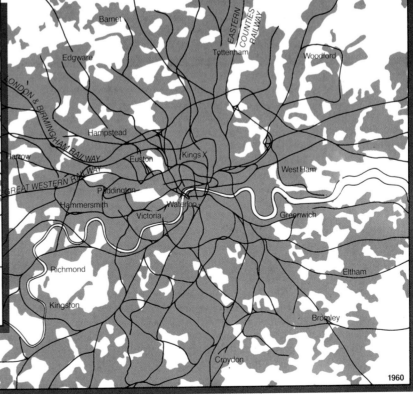

4. Between the wars transport systems played an even bigger part in suburban growth and by 1939 an outer ring of suburbs had grown up.

5. By 1960 this outer ring was almost solid.

PUBLIC TRANSPORT/3

of this scheme. Some companies were more generous than others, and this may be why parts of north-east London's suburbia are predominantly upper working class in character, while those of north-west London, where the companies operated a markedly stingier scheme, retained their exclusivity.

The Twentieth Century

By 1900 Britain's major towns and cities had transport systems which were largely privately owned, although some local authorities had bought out companies to try to impose some planning. The haphazard growth had, however, already led to some appalling conditions. Fights to get on workmen's trains and overcrowded buses were common, as were unnecessary breaks in journeys where different companies or local authorities reached their boundaries. The unrestricted competition also kept company profits very low. London, as hub of the Empire, had particular problems: it was under enormous pressure to expand, and its sheer size gave it special transport problems. The way it solved these, both technically – by converting to electric rather than horse power – and politically – by nationalization – was ultimately to influence cities not only in Britain but throughout the world.

Perhaps the greatest innovation in transport was the tube system. The world's first underground passenger railway had been built in 1863 and ran from Paddington to Farringdon. Its steam engines ran on tracks just below street level, and although it was extended to form what is now the Circle Line, it was prevented, in common with the other railways, from entering the City and the West End. It was not until 1890, when the first deep-level 'tube' was burrowed, and the coincidental invention of electric engines (initially it had been intended to haul the trains on cables), that the new tube trains gained a real advantage, for they could penetrate the very heart of cities without legal restriction or the need to demolish buildings. The age of fast, simple commuting was at hand; and by 1910 central London was criss-crossed by tube lines.

This speed of building was largely due to the efforts of the American financier Charles Tyson Yerkes, who persuaded his compatriots that there was money to be made out of the English commuter. He masterminded the core of the system we know today, including all those Edwardian stations clad in distinctive oxblood tiles. Yerkes typified the hard-headed pursuit of profit which brought the transport systems into being. In the case of the tube trains, this profit motive meant a disastrous lack of planning which left whole areas without trains (for example the poorer parts of north-east London, until the Victoria Line was built in the 1960s), while in other places the tracks of rival companies ran side by side. Also, as with overground railways, the development itself instigated major new suburban building programmes. Yerkes extended the Hampstead Railway (now the Northern Line) into the meadows of Golders Green which, helped by the simultaneous building of nearby Hampstead Garden Suburb, rapidly became a built-up area. The same thing was to happen twenty years later when the line was extended to the village of Edgware. The railway companies, actively generating new markets, helped to shape suburbia.

The other major change in the transport system was the imposition of centralized control and planning. The London County Council since its creation in 1888 had been buying tram and bus companies in an attempt to impose some order on the system. In 1933 the Council established the Passenger Transport Board to run the tube, tram and bus services. (The shareholders of the private companies had long realized that public transport would never be profitable.) Two men from the largest of the former private companies – the Underground Group – dominated the new Board. They were Albert Stanley (later Lord Ashfield) and Frank Pick, and between them they did much to create the public style of London's transport services in the inter-war years, and set new standards which were unfortunately not copied in other towns.

Stanley used Government funds, provided under schemes to relieve unemployment, to extend the tube lines into the countryside, areas that are now deepest suburbia. Frank Pick, the commercial manager, realized that the system itself must be attractive if it were to bring in the required level of custom, and it was he who was responsible for giving London Transport its reputation for good design. He commissioned famous artists to create posters (many of which are now collector's items) to persuade people to use the system outside peak hours for shopping and recreational purposes; but of more lasting impact was Pick's choice of architects for the stations themselves. Charles Holden's stations, the most famous, epitomize the best inter-war style.

The expansionist policies begun by Yerkes in London were continued by both public and private companies as they attempted to generate demand for their services in Britain's other conurbations by advertising the attractions of 'their' suburbs. After the Second World War, the nature of suburban development was drastically altered, not only by new planning legislation but by mass car ownership which reduced middle-class dependence on public transport. Today, its strategic importance in the life of a city is again being questioned.

TRAVEL UNDERGROUND

INTO THE HEART OF THE SHOPPING CENTRES

△Staff from the British Aeroplane Company's works at Filton, Bristol, fill the rush-hour trams in 1939 (top). Trams and trolley buses disappeared from London in the 1950s – replaced by motor buses and trains – but were retained for much longer in many provincial cities. Piccadilly Circus underground station (above) was devoid of advertising in 1908, although the tiling is familiar today. The trains were very different from today's streamlined stock: access was by doors at each end of the carriage, which must have caused delays at busy times.
▷This London Transport poster of 1908, depicting the interior of the same type of tube train as that shown above, is an attempt to encourage suburban housewives to use the system outside the rush hours.

SHOPS IN SUBURBIA/1

The development of shops in Britain is closely bound up with the growth of suburbia; the massively increased population which caused the housing boom also had to be fed, clothed and shod. In the early nineteenth century, shops as we now think of them catered for only the aristocracy and upper middle classes. Retailers usually had close links with the producers of their wares, and were highly specialized, selling only a narrow range of goods, be it hats, shoes or cheese. The great majority of people relied for their everyday purchases upon street markets, which were supplemented by an army of street traders hawking what were then considered luxury goods such as ribbons or fruit, and whose cries have become part of the mythology of Victorian town life.

Such a state of affairs was satisfactory when towns were small, and many councils built special covered markets which are still in use today. As towns grew, however, central facilities became increasingly out of reach, and a corner shop selling every requirement became essential for most suburbs, while those with pretensions might boast an entire parade. Such shops were essentially a new phenomenon. Factory production meant that specialist knowledge of a product was no longer necessary, and anyone with a little capital and a mind to work extremely long hours could set up a general retail business. Even so, street traders remained a common suburban sight well into the twentieth century, the 'onion johnnies' and itinerant knife grinders disappearing only in the 1960s, and the milkman still an element of British life today.

▷This photograph, taken around 1905, shows Manor Park Dairy in a lower middle-class but eminently respectable suburb of East London. The business seems to have been long established and running a little to seed, judging from the faded paintwork and window displays, a poor imitation of the mountains of produce that could be seen in the multiple stores of the period. The sign behind the man in plus-fours advertises a dairy show at the Agricultural Hall in Islington, North London, a reminder that cattle and sheep were still a common sight in inner-city and suburban streets. Some trade names are familiar today.

Independent suburban shops were rarely the 'little goldmines' some held them to be, but they did offer the convenience of being local. They thrived in the last decades of the nineteenth century because real wages rose and commodity prices fell, leading to greater affluence for a large proportion of the population, particularly the new suburban middle classes. After 1870 Britain imported huge amounts of grain from the newly sown American prairies, causing a fall in grain prices. Similarly, new refrigerated ships could import cheap meat from the Argentine, and trains could whisk fish inland from the ports. The falling commodity prices and cheap mass production which made the retail trade feasible also led to very low profit margins which made the independent retailers vulnerable to competition, especially from the larger 'multiple' or chain stores.

Chain Stores

The first of these multiple stores was the Co-op. The co-operative retail movement, based on the philosophies of the Owenite Rochdale Pioneers who founded the first successful consumers' co-operative in 1844, expanded rapidly, from half a million members in 1881 to three million by 1919. The members, who were both customers and the contributors of the capital, all received a dividend – a share of the company's profits – which varied according to how much they had patronized the stores. As the co-ops diversified from foods into drapery and other goods, they became the subject of vitriolic attacks by the independent shopkeepers, who feared that the intrusion of such shops into their suburban domains would undermine their position.

A much greater threat to the independent shops, however, was the development of private chain stores. Among these were W. H. Smith and Menzies, which had established themselves as booksellers in railway stations as early as the 1850s, to cater to the reading habits of suburban commuters. After 1870 names such as Home and Colonial, Maypole and Lipton's began to appear in many suburban shopping parades. (Lipton's, which had begun in Glasgow in 1870, had 242 branches by 1898.) Their retailing formula was simple: they bought in great quantities the cheap foodstuffs then being imported, and sold them at very low profit margins, relying on rapid turnover. High turnover was ensured by the chains' exploitation of another new phenomenon: advertising. Men such as Lipton were great self-publicists, and used many gimmicks. For example, his gift of a five-ton cheese to Queen Victoria was politely refused, but achieved the desired result nevertheless. The independent shopkeepers could not compete on this scale, but their increased consciousness of the need to advertise resulted in the tightly packed and elaborate window displays that seem so characteristic of the period, and feature in so many old postcards.

Many of the chains established at this time have become well-known names in

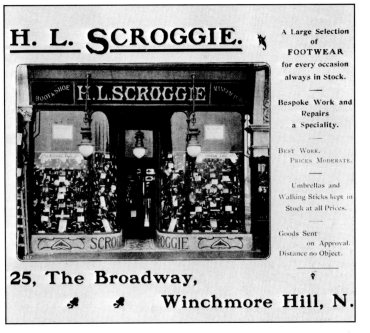

H. L. SCROGGIE.

BOOT & SHOE H. L. SCROGGIE FAMILY BOOT

A Large Selection
of
FOOTWEAR
for every occasion
always in Stock.

———

Bespoke Work and
Repairs
a Speciality.

Best Work.
Prices Moderate.

———

Umbrellas and
Walking Sticks kept in
Stock at all Prices.

Goods Sent
on Approval.
Distance no Object.

———

25, The Broadway,
Winchmore Hill, N.

◁ Scroggie's boot and shoe shop bears lettering in a style common in Edwardian times, but the gas lamps and huge stock displayed behind curved plate glass windows were ahead of their time. The mosaic work below the windows was often destroyed when a business changed hands.
▽ The suburban shopping centre, dominated by its mock-Tudor parade, is like hundreds of others that sprang up all over the country in the 1930s.

the larger suburban shopping centres. Clothiers such as Hepworth's, Hope Brothers and Dunn's, and footwear retailers such as Freeman Hardy Willis, were household names by the early twentieth century. Possibly the most successful of all was Jesse Boot, who applied the techniques of bulk purchase, low profit margins and high turnover to drugs with astonishing success. By also selling gifts, stationery and cosmetics, he demolished the prevailing view that medicine should be sold from premises reminiscent of a medieval alchemist's and that the higher its price the more efficacious the product must be. Such a policy put a Boots store in every major town by 1907, and in almost every suburb by the 1930s.

Semi-detached suburbia between the wars was usually served by a parade, a self-contained row of essential shops such as baker, butcher, grocer, greengrocer, newsagent and confectioner. The parade itself was often built in mock-Tudor splendour by the builders responsible for the estate as a whole. A row of shops and the increased income that they could provide (along with the flats above for the shopkeepers) were a more attractive proposition to the builders than other amenities such as churches, schools, libraries and social centres; and it was particularly desirable to be able to persuade one of the multiples to take premises, in order to secure a good return on the investment.

Stores such as Marks and Spencer, which was established as a series of 'penny bazaars', and Woolworth, an American firm which arrived in Britain in the 1900s, were originally set up to cater for a working-class market, all goods being sold at a fixed low price, usually no more than sixpence ($2\frac{1}{2}$p.). When these stores established branches in predominantly middle-class suburbs during the 1920s and 1930s their price

limits were scarcely increased, since it was realized that even though the more affluent could spend more they were just as eager to have value for money.

Some of the small independent suburban shopkeepers were themselves so successful that they were able to buy out their neighbours and expand into department stores. These were often just glorified draper's shops, but some actually sold a great many kinds of goods from their own purpose-built premises, and were modelled on the great department stores of the West End of London which had been established in the 1870s. These catered for an upper middle-class clientele and were places of fashionable resort where women could meet and purchase almost anything. For example, Whiteley's, the famous store in Westbourne Grove, was known as the 'universal provider', although it lacked the chic of Harrods. New standards were set by the American Gordon Selfridge, who opened his Oxford Street store in 1909. He was the first to use window displays which, electrically lit until midnight, attracted large crowds. He also insisted that cosmetics, previously hidden away to preserve their air of mystery, be fully displayed. Thus the first sensations to greet the customer were the opulence and headiness of the perfumery counter – a practice continued in almost every suburban department store to this day.

Shops and the Suburban Taste

While the development of shops and stores was important in suburbia simply to provide the basic needs of life, it also played an important part in the development of style and taste in the suburban home. In the mid-nineteenth century home furnishing was still very much in the hands of professional craftsmen such as upholsterers and decorators who,

with the help of pattern books from suppliers, gave advice on the selection of furniture and furnishings. At this period the rising middle classes were more concerned with creating an air of nobility and obtaining value for money than with more subtle considerations of taste.

By the 1870s a number of factors had arisen to change this situation. The income of the middle classes began to increase, and books appeared to advise them on the importance of 'artistic' interiors and 'aesthetic' colours. At the same time the rapid development of retail outlets and department stores sup-

◁Retailers played an important part in the formation of suburban taste, not least by means of their presentation. Creating an inviting image to entice the prospective buyer was always a prime concern, and this design for a shop front from E. L. Blackburne's *The Mason's Bricklayer's, Plasterer's and Decorator's Practical Guide* (1859) would have been the choice of the fashionable, featuring as it does polychrome brickwork and Gothic detailing.
▷Later methods of attracting customers were pioneered in London's Tottenham Court Road by Heal's, who recognized the importance of both presentation and education: they opened the Mansard Gallery in 1917 for the regular exhibition of the latest in art and design.

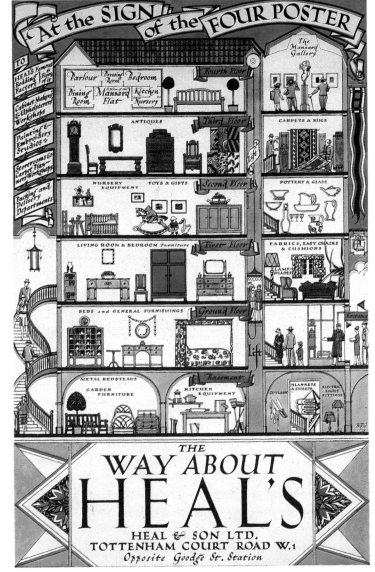

plying home furnishings meant that the newly affluent and newly style-conscious suburbanites were now in a position to make decisions about furniture and furnishings for themselves. Shops such as Morris & Co. (see page 99), whose Oxford Street premises, opened in 1877, became particularly influential,

were quick to take advantage of the new interest in domestic design and decoration.

By the early years of the twentieth century, manufacturers and retailers were taking an active role in the creation of a fashionable suburban home. Glossy catalogues illustrating their wares were

produced, and department and furniture stores displayed their products in room settings to inspire their customers. Harrods even marketed furniture in house 'sets' so that all the requirements of a new home could be met in one step, each item preselected for the buyer. (Another enticement to the home decorator was the introduction of hire-purchase arrangements.) Fashionable retailers also attempted to influence the public taste in more far-reaching ways. Heal's, based in London's Tottenham Court Road (a major shopping street for home furnishings even in the nineteenth century), opened their Mansard Gallery in 1917 for the regular exhibition of avant-garde art and design, and all their customers received invitations.

After the First World War many new magazines concerned with the home and its decoration appeared on the market. In addition to providing a whole new field for advertising, these magazines promoted particular stores and manufacturers in their feature articles, primarily by illustrating their ideas on the latest fashions by room settings or individual items of furniture which were credited to particular stores.

By now the suburbs had become the most important focus of attention for the retailer, whether he ran a grocery or a furniture store, and their importance increased with the massive growth of housing developments between the wars. The suburbanites' particular emphasis on the importance of family life and therefore of the home meant that a large proportion of disposable income would be spent on the maintenance and decoration of the house and garden, and retailers responded to this need as much as to all others, and it was at this time that suburban shopping centres as we think of them today were truly established.

RECREATION IN SUBURBIA/1

Throughout the period 1840–1960 the pioneering settlers in newly built suburbia found few recreational opportunities. This was caused partly by a simple lack of facilities, as housing usually preceded other amenities by several years, but the problem often lay deeper than that. New suburbs either swamped existing village communities, or were built on a metaphorical 'no-man's land' that could engender no immediate community spirit. The situation was aggravated by the administrative complexities of local government and the often unseemly squabbles between local boards and councils about who should provide amenities such as schools for the new settlers. In short, new suburbanites often had to make their own communities rather than fit into long-established ones.

The very nature of the typically suburban lifestyle did not help this process. Husbands commuted to the inner city and spent very little of their conscious lives in the home neighbourhood, and local allegiance was therefore not automatic. Women, too, found opportunities for social encounter very limited, especially if they had no children. Even though most migrant families moved outwards from the inner cities along existing lines of transport and new settlers often came from the same areas, the move outwards often indicated a rise in social status which prohibited mention of one's lowlier origins, and an opportunity to make friends through shared experience was thus studiously avoided. Even the most thriving and sought-after estates today were once the setting for what would now be called 'New Town Blues'.

Aged parents were occasionally persuaded to leave the inner cities and join sons and daughters in the new suburbs but, generally speaking, new estates attracted young families. As owner-occupation became the norm in the twentieth century, the building societies favoured those with safe, steady, unexciting jobs, prepared to make the necessary long-term financial commitment. Thus suburban life became synonymous with routine, regularity and dullness, a life dictated by train timetables and monthly repayments. So often lacking in community spirit, the suburbanites took little interest in politics (everyone was assumed to be Tory) or national—let alone international—affairs, except when directly affected by them. They established a highly introspective home-centred way of life which has been the norm in Britain ever since. For the suburban wife at home all day, the lack of social life and worries about money and home often led to neurosis. (By the 1930s, this condition, compounded by the artificial and unattainable values of the Hollywood dream factory, began to be taken seriously by the medical profession, and bored suburban housewives found themselves used as research fodder for psychologists.)

Not all was gloom, however: the ever-inventive Victorians quickly organized churches, clubs and societies to cater for a wide variety of sporting and cultural activity, and to provide the necessary social contact. Many of these thrive today. In the twentieth century, spectator sports, radio and cinema have also helped to fill the longer leisure hours. The general trend seems to have been away from participatory activities towards spectatorship, both inside and outside the home, and the coming of television obviously reinforced this. Even mass car ownership, which made escape from the home and suburbia easier than ever, often meant that the family was taken to see rather than to do something.

VICTORIAN FAMILY LIFE

The new suburban settlers clearly had to act themselves to prevent their estates from becoming bleak, soulless dormitories. The Victorians were, we are so often reminded, good at making their own entertainment. Parlour games (and 'ladylike' pastimes such as needlework) were popular, and after 1850 even the most hard pressed would contrive to buy a piano on hire-purchase, as music in the home was a virtue established by the Queen herself, although on Sundays it might be restricted to hymn singing. No doubt households were better able to entertain themselves, but with six or eight children and various other inhabitants under one roof, this was not such a difficult task. The week revolved around Sunday when Father did not go to the office, and the activities on this day were highly ritualized. Father would take the family to morning service, while cook (or mother and the maid) prepared the Sunday roast. After lunch, the whole family would go for a walk dressed in their 'Sunday best', perhaps to the local park to hear a brass band, or, commonly enough, to the cemetery where the children would put flowers on the grave of a half-remembered brother or sister. After tea, the whole family went to church again. For more leisured suburban matrons, it was the day to see and be seen, and the high point of a week that consisted of equally ritualized social calls, 'at homes' and a little charity work.

▷Middle-class distaste for pubs, like this one photographed in 1896, caused many to champion working men's clubs as an alternative. The snooker hall of 1912 (far right) hardly resembles the idealized view of such clubs (below).

The Church

The Church was the key to social contact; almost the first building to appear after the houses in any Victorian suburb was a 'tin chapel', usually soon replaced by a neo-Gothic edifice, paid for by generous public subscription. Towards the end of the century, many fine Arts and Crafts churches were built, particularly by Nonconformist congregations. In the eighteenth and early nineteenth centuries the Church of England had lost ground in the towns to the radical zeal of Nonconformism which better suited the values of independence and self-help of the merchant class of that time. The Census of 1851 showed that seven million out of a population of eighteen million regularly attended Church, and while this may seem a high proportion today, it was then thought low and caused much consternation. The Anglican revival of the mid-century coincided with the growth of suburbia, when the new aspiring middle class generally rejected dissent and Catholicism in favour of the Church of England, with its Tory and Establishment connotations. The working classes were not, it seems, touched with the same sense of piety, and church-going remained an essen-tially suburban rather than urban activity. For the middle classes, the Church not only fulfilled the spiritual needs of the community but also had a major role as a provider of concerts, outings, talks and lectures, clubs and Sunday school, as well as of general companionship.

The Public House

Public houses have always been viewed with ambivalence in suburbia. The Victorian middle classes, while using them to a limited extent, felt they could not officially condone their presence, a view which stemmed from their popularity with the Victorian working classes. With beer and gin cheap enough to provide an anaesthetic to the harshness of life, the corner pub with its warmth, light and conviviality was a clear attraction in working-class areas, and in the mid-nineteenth century no respectable middle-class man would enter one. However, the old villages swallowed up by suburbia usually had at least one inn to which a suburban gentleman could stroll for refreshment without qualms. When new suburban pubs were built they were often called hotels whether they took in guests or not, to preserve an air of respectability. They also tended to

RECREATION IN SUBURBIA/2

▷Only the well off would have had 'radio-telephony apparatus' in 1922. The original caption to W. R. S. Stott's painting reads: 'The Christmas Party Up To Date: Fairy Tales By "Broadcast". Christmas parties this year will possess a new and fascinating attraction both for young and old in the shape of the latest wonder of wireless telephony.'

△The bandstand in the background suggests that the tennis players in Eric Ravilious' triptych of c.1932 (top) are taking advantage of municipal facilities, not the more exclusive private clubs.

△This Jacobethan roadhouse (above) was intended to recreate the atmosphere of a village inn, with beams, bargeboards, stone-mullioned, leaded windows and herringbone brickwork.

be very grand in both size and style, using a more ornate form of the local housing style.

Theoretically at least, the middle classes favoured temperance, especially for the working classes to whom they had to set an example. Beer consumption per capita reached its all-time peak in 1870, at the very time when both the Temperance Movement and the 'Sweetness and Light' generation were calling for the provision of 'rational recreation' to provide an alternative to pubs. The Club at Bedford Park, for example, was envisaged as a sort of 'temperance pub' serving tea and coffee and providing a library and recreation and meeting rooms for the local community. Similar institutions were established elsewhere, but with limited success. Many local authorities began to establish recreational amenities such as libraries, museums, parks and gardens, gymnasia and swimming pools towards the end of the century, but although middle-class suburbia

△Walking in Surrey in the 1930s. The inter-war craze for hiking caused many legal battles with farmers and landowners, and the technique of 'mass trespass' led to the confirmation of the legal right to the countryside that walkers enjoy today. (The houses are typical of the English Vernacular that was an inspiration for much of suburbia.)

benefited greatly from such schemes, they did little to affect the popularity of alcohol elsewhere.

It was not until the arrival, in the twentieth century, of mass entertainment, in the form of football matches and the cinema, that the working classes were provided with what the Temperance Movement had failed to offer – a real alternative to pubs. This helped to give pubs a rather more respectable image, especially after the restriction of opening hours introduced during the First World War. Between the wars a large number of suburban pubs were built. They were sometimes massive in size (especially the 'roadhouses' built along the new bypasses), but tended still to favour mock-Tudor styling, not only for its cosy image and instant sense of tradition, but also because it reflected the image of a quiet and respectable village inn rather than a rough and boisterous Victorian corner pub.

Sporting Activities

For the non-drinking atheist, suburbia offered other ways of making social contact. After the 1880s tennis clubs were very commonly established on odd pockets of land left by the developers, and provided the more athletic with the opportunity for pleasant flirtation. Croquet and archery facilities were often provided, too, as both these sports were regarded as genteel and therefore appropriate for ladies. Suburban tennis clubs were notoriously snobbish but probably less so than the many golf clubs established after the 1890s in areas with pretensions. These institutions prided themselves on social exclusivity, and the status that membership brought held more attractions than the game itself. Golf and tennis clubs were also the usual venues for the dances that were such an important part of the suburban social ritual.

The invention of the pneumatic tyre in 1890 gave bicycling a fresh appeal, one that could be enjoyed by women as well as men. Coinciding with the new desire to visit and use the countryside for recreation (a desire that has never waned), bicycling clubs were quickly established, and provided a major means of rural exploration which was only superseded by the car after the Second World War.

After 1900, leisure in suburbia tended to rely less heavily on organized social activities, as further technical inventions – the gramophone, wireless and, in particular, the cinema – were introduced.

RECREATION IN SUBURBIA/3

THE TWENTIETH CENTURY

Music halls were the closest things the Victorians had to mass entertainment apart from pubs, but relatively few were built in suburbia – with notable exceptions, such as the Golders Green Hippodrome in London – even after their transformation into respectable variety theatre. In 1908, a brief roller-skating craze hit Britain from America, and several rinks were built, but it was almost immediately overshadowed by another American import – moving pictures – which were to become probably the main form of suburban recreation for the next forty years.

The Cinema

At first, makeshift cinemas were made out of converted church halls or now redundant skating rinks, but the danger posed by the highly combustible film in ramshackle buildings led to the passing of the Cinematography Act of 1909, which required local councils to license cinemas. The first purpose-built cinema was probably the Phoenix (c. 1910) at East Finchley, North London (still operating), and henceforth no suburb was complete without one. With names such as the Electric, the Corinth, or the Imperial, they emphasized exotic luxury, with plush fittings, bevelled glass and mahogany doors that enticed one to a world of hitherto undreamed-of pleasures.

While some of these pleasures were supplied by the products of a rapidly growing film industry, the chance of a kiss and cuddle in the darkness was also quickly appreciated. Even though the 'double fauteuils' advertised by some cinemas seemed to condone if not encourage such activity, suburbia did not take kindly to lax moral habits. Films were heavily censored, and some local authorities took it upon themselves to intervene further by appointing 'decency supervisors', and it was not unknown for house lights to be switched on suddenly from time to time to ensure rectitude.

The silent films were, of course, accompanied by pianists who played music appropriate to the scene, and by the 1920s some cinemas had quite large orchestras. In 1929 these suddenly found themselves redundant: the talkies had arrived. Their arrival heralded the golden age of cinema, and another suburban building boom. Oscar Deutsch ringed London with Odeons in the 1930s, and most suburbs could boast two or three more by the end of the decade. Huge 'super cinemas' were built, with 1500 to 2000 seats, a ballroom, a café and a mighty organ. By 1939 the county of Middlesex had one cinema seat for every ten inhabitants. Although there were fears of over-provision, the cinema building boom continued as demand reached new, ever higher levels. Entire families would often attend, but it was mainly the sixteen-to-thirty age group who would regularly go to the 'pictures' at least twice or more a week. Cinemas, often occupying prominent sites, thus became an essential part of suburbia and its way of life, and their chosen names – such as Majestic, Regal, Ritz, Dominion and Embassy – continued the themes of wealth and grandeur.

The architecture chosen also reinforced the escapist nature of cinema-going. With few exceptions, the mock-Tudor nostalgia then favoured for houses, shops and pubs was out. Since the cinema was about entering a different world, the building could be

◁ The Woolwich Odeon, built in 1937, is typical of the Moderne style adopted by many cinema chains. Its uncompromising outline proclaims anything but suburban dullness and promises a few hours' escape from reality. The starkness of the cream-coloured faience-ware façade completes this image, and the whole thing sits – as is so often the case – rather uncomfortably next to a mock-Tudor pub.

unashamedly modern or 'modernistic'. Large, plain façades were covered in cream or beige faience-ware, often floodlit at night. Art Deco styling seemed suitably up-to-date and American, and other, more exotic themes such as Egyptian were also used. Odeons usually had flat-topped towers to attract attention and act as floodlit beacons at night. Interiors were, if anything, even more exotic, and the architectural theme might be reinforced by murals depicting romantic scenes such as distant hills and waterfalls, or castellated walls. These rather clumsy attempts to create 'atmosphere' were invariably aided by concealed lighting that could be changed from one lurid hue to another.

Tawdry as many of them later became, new cinemas were nearly always welcomed by the residents of suburbia, although in wealthy areas it was sometimes thought that they would provide entertainment for only the servants. The image, if not the fact, of opulence, with extravagant foyers, exotic ballrooms, and luxurious powder rooms, provided a glimpse of the lifestyle of the Hollywood stars, and a touch of glamour that suburbia evidently sorely needed.

Entertainment at Home

For those who did not want to go out, the home itself provided many new forms of leisure after the First World War. Reading had always been popular, but books were generally quite expensive. Where public lending libraries were inadequate, the twopenny lending libraries – Boots the chemist ran a major one – provided ample reading material. Cheap paperbacks also appeared, notably Penguins in 1935, bringing ownership of many good works within reach, and the bookcase became a standard item of furniture. (Amateur dramatic or operatic groups were also popular.)

Gardening had also always been a popular activity, but the provision of larger gardens, the hallmark of twentieth-century suburbia, gave it an additional fillip, especially among men for whom it broke the sedentary job routine or for whom the shed was a welcome refuge. The chat in suburban commuter trains often concerned the new additions to the seed catalogues or the merits of the latest 'Atco' mower. Office gardening clubs were also established in the 1920s to take advantage of bulk purchasing of seeds. (See also Chapter Five, 'Gardens in Suburbia'.)

New gadgets such as the gramophone also profoundly affected home entertainment, none more so perhaps than the wireless. The BBC began broadcasting in 1922, and quickly became a major source not only of entertainment but also, in Reithian tradition, of information. Sundays were filled with religious and serious programmes but private stations such as Luxembourg and Radio Normandy were popular alternatives, providing 'light' programmes on Sundays, and entire families would gather round the sets to listen to particular favourites. Sets were not cheap but prices fell quickly, from about £15 in 1931, to £8 in 1934.

A few London suburbs also enjoyed TV reception, which began in 1937. By the outbreak of war in 1939, there were 20,000 sets in the capital but it was another eleven years before people could watch anything. Even useless TV sets were, however, important status symbols (as were so many of the new gadgets that appeared between the wars). Cinema attendance peaked in 1947, but the rise of television in the 1950s resulted directly in a decline in cinema-going, and many suburban cinemas were closed down after 1960, given over briefly to bingo or tenpin bowling before demolition.

△In the late 1920s the BBC was fast becoming a national institution, but receivers were expensive. Prices fell in the 1930s, and the separate horn-shaped speakers, as shown in this advertisement of 1928, disappeared. The wooden or bakelite wireless sets of the 1930s had built-in speakers which could be concealed behind a choice of fretwork screens.

ATTITUDES TO SUBURBIA

The phenomenon of the suburbs has always been the object of considerable criticism: the very word 'suburban', like 'provincial', implies a wealth of uncomplimentary meaning. The appearance of the houses, the spread of suburban developments, the suburban milieu, even suburban 'values' – however questionably defined – not to mention the suburb dwellers themselves, have all been roundly condemned by architectural critics and social commentators alike.

Criticism of the houses, and particularly their sprawling intrusion into the countryside, started early. In 1848 a writer in *The Builder* magazine described the 'building mania' that was rapidly covering the country around the major cities with a rash of 'Victoria' or 'Albert' villas, and showed that it already had unpleasant connotations: 'A suburb in these days is one congeries of crude brick and mortar. It is the most melancholy thing in existence.'

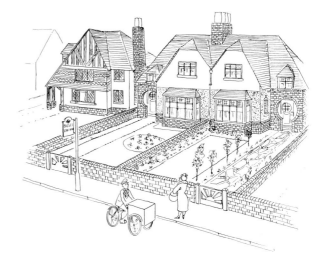

△ **'By-pass Variegated' suburbia, as seen by Osbert Lancaster in his satirical** *Cartoon History of Architecture*.

John Ruskin (see page 98), whose writings were to have such an influence on the appearance of much Victorian suburbia, took up the theme in 1878, this time emphasizing the loss of an imagined rural idyll where idealized cottages were 'neatly kept, and vivid with a sense of the quiet energies of their contented tenants'. He describes this now as 'of rotten brick, with various iron devices to hold it together', as a result of the energies of the speculative builder, and the occupants themselves as 'lodgers in those damp shells of brick, which one cannot say they inhabit, nor call their "houses" . . . but packing cases in which they are temporarily stored, for bad use'. What Ruskin shows is a lack of knowledge of the housing needs of people then employed in the cities, needs which the new suburbs were successfully meeting, as well as a lack of interest in, or conception of, the suburbanites' pleasure in these houses.

Of the few who attempted to redress the balance in favour of suburbia during this period, perhaps the best known are George and Weedon Grossmith, who in the *Diary of a Nobody* (1892) introduced Mr Pooter to the world. While the authors undoubtedly poke fun at the pretensions and absurdities of Mr Pooter in his Holloway 'villa', particularly in his often unfortunate dealings with servants and tradespeople, it is always with a clear and affectionate view of Pooter and his obvious satisfaction with his suburban home.

It was not until the 1920s, however, when the spate of house-building that resulted in semi-detached suburbia began, that the vitriol was brought out in earnest. The housing developments of this period were largely ignored by the building and architectural journals, which were more likely to feature the neo-Georgian or international-style 'Moderne' of Government housing schemes and *avant-garde* architects; the standard Jacobethan semi, when considered at all, was censured.

The reasons for this attitude are considered in *Dunroamin* (1981), a book subtitled 'The Suburban Semi and its Enemies', which examines the paradox of suburbia's bad public image and its success with those actually living there. The authors, Paul Oliver, Ian Davis and Ian Bentley, suggest that the architectural profession's almost total lack of involvement in the building of suburbia is one of the main reasons for its determination to disapprove, and the lack of coherent argument from the critics gives weight to their view.

The cartoonist and essayist Osbert Lancaster, in the introduction to his *Cartoon History of Architecture*, from *Pillar to Post*, written in 1938, makes a plea for everyone to develop an informed and critical eye for architecture, to learn to consider every building as 'architecture', whether it be a public convenience or a town hall, and yet his description of suburbia receives no such sympathetic consideration. In the essays he wittily gives his view of the architectural styles of the speculative builder, from 'the infernal almalgam' of past styles in 'By-pass Variegated' to the 'plentiful use of pebbledash, giddy treatment of gables and general air of self-conscious cosiness' that delineates Wimbledon Transitional, to the 'accurate reproductions of Anne Hathaway's cottage, each complete with central heating and garage' that characterize Stockbrokers' Tudor, and is convinced that they will not last:

It is sad to reflect that so much ingenuity should have been wasted on streets and estates which will inevitably become the slums of the future. That is if a fearful and more sudden fate does not obliterate them prematurely; an eventuality that does much to reconcile one to the prospect of aerial bombardment.

John Betjeman in the 1930s also hoped for the destruction of suburbia, expressing this wish in the poem 'Slough' (1937):

Come friendly bombs, and fall
    on Slough;
It isn't fit for humans now –

In the conclusion to his own 'history of architecture' entitled *Ghastly Good Taste, or, a Depressing Story of the Rise and Fall of English Architecture* (1933), he lays the blame for the decline of 'good' architecture at the feet of the Victorians – 'the Middle Class that represents industrialism' – and is particularly scathing of suburbia, both Victorian and modern. Like Lancaster, Betjeman writes with the aim of encouraging the 'average' man to have an informed opinion of architecture, although he feels this is a forlorn hope: 'Although he lives in a hideous suburb, surrounded by it, walking through it to his office . . . still he does not notice architecture . . . he is blind to the blatant ugliness.' The dead 'period' decoration of every villa in 'lovely Mill Hill, Hendon Heights or . . . Moderate Morden' all receive criticism. By the 1950s, however, Betjeman had moderated his views: his 'Metroland' television series expressed affectionate nostalgia for semi-detached suburbia.

Less vehement but no less effective

▷ **The architects' view of architecture, contrasted with the client's, by Hellman.**

than the architects and critics were the gently patronizing popular writers on the home such as Dorothy Peel. Advising in *The New Home* (1898) on the best situation for a domestic establishment, she writes: 'I must confess honestly that the suburbs of any large town appear to me detestable, but to be strictly just, suburban life has perhaps some decided advantages over town life.' Suburbia can only be an unsatisfactory compromise for her, however. In *The Art of the Home* (1897), Rosamund Watson points to another problem of the suburbs – they are always doomed to be several steps behind the latest fashion. Speaking of the 'artistic' and 'aesthetic' fashions in home furnishings which now, being *passé*, seem to her odious, she notes that 'to be sure they have mainly ebbed out to the suburbs, but that is only so much worse for the suburbs'.

In general, suburbia fares little better in literature, but in one novel, *The Semi-Detached House* (1859) by Emily Eden, it is placed in a more favourable light. The heroine, complaining of her imminent move to a semi in the suburbs, expects the worst of her neighbour with whom she will share a 'state of semi-detachedness', but in the event everything works out to the mutual happiness and contentment of both halves of the semi-detached arrangement, a situation which reflects that of the vast proportion of real-life suburban dwellers.

It is perhaps this very contentment and satisfaction with the compromise that is suburbia – a state that has been achieved without the help of architects or the diversions of town life – that has itself led to the criticism. Suburbia's persistent refusal to fall down or decay has always been a source of irritation.

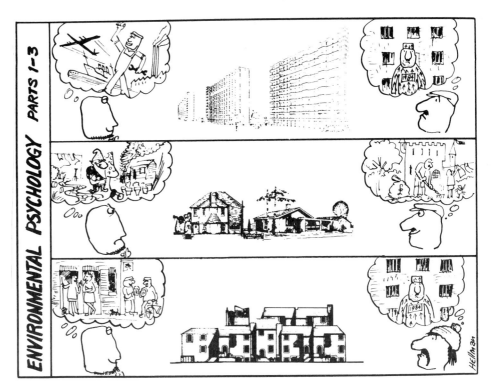

△This sitting room, photographed in about 1880, is heavily draped, patterned and ornamented in a manner typical of the High Victorian period, at a time when householders were just beginning to be concerned with questions of taste and 'art' furnishings such as oriental chinaware.

▷William Frith's painting *Many Happy Returns of the Day* (1856) is an idealized portrait of family life, and gives a good indication of the size of household that a middle-class Victorian gentleman might have been required to maintain.

2. THE HIGH VICTORIAN SUBURB (1840-1880)

Introduction

The phenomenal growth of suburbia in the nineteenth century was due to the equally large increase in the size of the middle classes relative to other social groups. The first generation of middle classes to move out of the cities into the new suburbs – taking with them a vivid memory of poor housing conditions there – created a new and enduringly powerful concept of 'home' as the central institution of civilized life, a sanctuary for the family and refuge from the workplace. The house, through its appearance and decoration, was the visible indication of the piety, position and social pretensions of its occupants.

'HE STRAIGHTWAY BUILDETH A VILLA'

The new suburbanites were uncertain about the ways and means of establishing themselves in society, and anxious to seek guidance on the correct ways of doing things. Accordingly, a growing trade in 'manuals of domestic economy' began. The earliest of these set rigid guidelines for the scale of household trappings appropriate to different levels of income. (The word 'household' is particularly important here: a Victorian middle-class marriage meant the creation of an elaborate establishment which would include at least one servant – the most obvious indication of status – as well as the possibility of resident in-laws or ageing spinster aunts, and perhaps a lodger as well as the family itself, often with a large number of

THE HIGH VICTORIAN SUBURB/2

children. One of these early guides suggests that a minimum annual income for 'families of superior condition in life' was £150, for which a servant for occasional housework could be afforded; at £250 a resident maidservant was part of the household and the 'wife' now referred to as a 'lady', a sure indication that the family had achieved a certain social standing. The guide also describes in great detail the appropriate allocation of proportions of income to various items of expenditure, including food, drink, education, servants' wages and rent.

A Position in Society

Once the basic outline of the establishment itself had been laid down, attention could be given to the social niceties and to questions of etiquette. Since the home was also to be the centre of virtually all the social life to which a family might aspire, it was essential that it was seen effectively to fulfil this role. In his book *A Social History of Housing, 1815–1970* (1980), John Burnett says that a well-understood code of etiquette ensured that only acceptable guests were received, and then only at certain times, and that this code was the main way newcomers could be placed in the 'social landscape'. He states that

. . . these rules were primarily arbitrated and enforced by women. Since active housekeeping and gainful employment were unacceptable for a 'lady', a life of conspicuous leisure was almost all that was open to her . . . The minimum requirements for participation were not too onerous – at least one respectable-looking maid to open the door and answer bells, and a house of a size and character of which one need not feel ashamed.

In this context it was important that the house should have a certain number of rooms, each with a purpose rigidly delineated. Social callers would be 'held' in the hall, prior to being received by the lady of the house, after which they would be shown into one of the principal rooms for the duration of the call. The role of the lady of the house was particularly important, and, according to the opinion of various social commentators, accounted for the taste, good or bad, displayed in the furnishings, fittings and conduct of the household.

One of the most famous ladies of the time was Mrs Isabella Beeton (1836–65), whose *Book of Household Management* (1859) became the social bible for all those who were uncertain of any aspect of running a household, such as the right number of servants, their duties and the correct organization of a dinner party. While most of the book is concerned with the provision and preparation of food, it also includes sections on the role of the lady of the house, with regard to both social intercourse and her management of servants. The first chapter is devoted to 'The Mistress', whose qualities are described thus:

As with the Commander of an Army, or the leader of any enterprise, so is it with the mistress of a house. Her spirit will be seen through the whole establishment; and just in proportion as she performs her duties intelligently and thoroughly, so will her domestic duties follow in her path.

Along with early rising, cleanliness, frugality and economy, the mistress of the house was also instructed to practise caution in her choice of acquaintances: 'society should be formed on such a kind as will tend to the mutual interchange of general and interesting information'; gossips were to be avoided, as was any inclination to profligate hospitality.

Every item of domestic life had an appropriate behaviour. Even spending an evening at home had its etiquette:

Where there are young people forming a part of the evening circle, interesting and agreeable pastime should especially be promoted. It is of incalculable benefit to them that their homes should possess all the attractions of healthful amusement, comfort and happiness; for if they do not find pleasure there, they will seek it elsewhere . . . Light or fancy needlework often forms a portion of the evening's recreation for the ladies of the household . . . [or] the reading aloud of some good standard work or amusing publication. A knowledge of polite literature may thus be obtained by the whole family, especially if the reader is able and willing to explain the more difficult passages of the book, and expatiate on the wisdom and beauties it may contain.

STYLE AND TASTE IN THE VICTORIAN HOME

Mrs Beeton's volume irrefutably set the pious and disciplined tone of Victorian domesticity, but yet more guidance was required on the exact style of the fixtures and fittings, and this was offered in numerous other popular publications.

One of the most popular or, more accurately, populist guides to domestic tastes was *Cassell's Household Guide*, first published in 1869. It gives a particularly good idea of what the Victorians felt they needed to know about their homes, once the basic necessities of the establishment had been achieved. The volume's subtitle is 'A Guide to every Department of Practical Life', and it begins with 'Abscess, Treatment of', and continues through 'Curtains, Construction of', to the identification and care of various types of wood, giving advice on the selection of furniture and the preparation of fish soups on the way. Its

◁ **A Victorian parlour in Leeds. The carpet and wallpaper are richly coloured and patterned, the furniture is substantial and almost every available surface is covered with the decorative bits and pieces favoured by the Victorians, including pairs of china dogs, brightly coloured embroidery and framed pictures.**

assumption is that the basic requirements for the maintenance of a position in society have been met, and so it is more concerned with questions of style and taste – particularly the quantity, fashion and quality of the furnishings and fittings. Accordingly, it lists the items required for each room, giving helpful hints on the best suppliers, average prices, and cheaper substitutions for certain articles if the household budget cannot stretch to the more expensive items. Like other guides of the period, *Cassell's* gives a table of recommended expenditure in proportion to income, but notes that the need to maintain a certain appearance might lead to the householder overreaching himself:

The style of a house in a degree determines the respectability, class, credit, or means of its occupier, even though he be without a fixed income, and living to the extent of, or beyond his means.

Cassell's also attempted to have a disciplining effect on the high-Victorian taste for novelty and exuberant decoration. Echoing the critics who made their opinions felt immediately after the Great Exhibition of 1851, it includes a section entitled 'Principles of Good Taste in Household Furniture and Decoration', in which the writer describes some of the styles and patterns available in furniture and furnishings, pointing out which are the most popular and which, by contrast, exhibit the 'right principles'. The writer advocated flat pattern and paler, subdued colours than were then the fashion, or at the very least, adherence to one 'leading principle', but given that the author favours restraint, the amount of decorative licence seems considerable:

[for the wallpaper] a pattern of some simple diaper, consisting of a geometric basis filled in with leaves . . . the carpet also flowers and foliage arranged on a geometric basis . . . the higher forms – groups of flowers, fruits, animals and the human figure – being reserved for the more important features [such as] a table with animals crouching underneath.

One of the most fascinating sections in the *Guide* is 'Household Decorative Art', which offers a fund of decorating ideas in embroidery, leatherwork and other media. The lengths to which Victorian ladies would go in order to produce the latest fashion in *objets d'art* is amply illustrated by instructions for the creation of a fire-screen embellished with a stuffed and mounted bird: they are instructed first to 'take a bird' and then carefully to dismember, stuff and mount it in such a way as to cause least damage to the feathers and to create a beautiful display. The arrangements of dried flowers and stuffed birds and animals under glass domes that were so much a feature of the Victorian domestic scene are perhaps also examples of Victorian 'home taxidermy'.

Significantly, some of the decorative suggestions are designed specifically to be applied to furniture or other items in order to 'elevate them to the rank of "art furniture"', a term that was to become increasingly important towards the end of the century. It appeared in more and more household guides, becoming better defined as the Arts and Crafts and Aesthetic Movements began in the 1880s to give a new direction to the decoration and construction of houses for the second, and more self-consciously stylish, generation of suburbanites.

ARCHITECTURAL STYLES/1

Most of the inner suburbs of Britain's cities saw a period of great decline in the first half of the twentieth century. The middle classes for whom they were built tended, often very quickly, to move as soon as they could to newer and more fashionable suburbs further out of the city, leaving many fine Georgian and early Victorian houses to the devastating effects of multiple tenancies and landlords too concerned by falling rental values to spend much on repairs. Second World War bombing took its toll, but did little damage compared with the destruction caused by Central Government policies which paid generous grants towards inner city redevelopment schemes, thus encouraging wholesale demolition rather than rehabilitation. Local housing authorities took advantage of the Government's generosity and in the 1950s and 1960s demolished whole tracts of potentially fine housing with very little resistance from the general public, simply because the style of the buildings had gone out of fashion. Even the owners of the Nash terraces in Regent's Park, now considered to be among London's finest domestic buildings, thought seriously about demolition in the 1940s because of their poor condition.

△**Strawberry Hill set an eighteenth-century fashion for a Gothic castellated style deplored by later Gothic Revivalists.**

Inner Suburbia – a Renaissance

Since the late 1960s there has been a reversal of the trend towards demolition, and many areas once in a very poor state have now been 'gentrified' beyond recognition. One of the reasons for this phenomenon was that building societies began to relax their lending restrictions on older properties, and local-authority mortgage schemes began to be effective. This meant that old houses could be bought rather than rented. In some areas which building societies had 'red-lined' (a policy, denied by the societies, of not lending money on properties situated in certain defined districts), the estate owners themselves acted as mortgagees in order to dispose of their rundown properties which could otherwise only be let at artificially low rents. Other reasons for gentrification are harder to define. Defying convention had a certain cachet in the 1960s, and buying a house in a run-down area in order to refurbish

it was, and still is, fashionable among certain middle-class couples. The financial benefits of an improvement grant were small compared with the attraction of the soaring property prices to be enjoyed as these vanguard purchasers were followed by their equally middle-class friends. Indeed, spotting the next area to become gentrified is now a major preoccupation of some potential inner suburbanites. Good public transport and an attractive architectural style are indicators of a possible up-and-coming area, but it is fashion that dictates property values in the inner suburbs, and fashion is fickle, although it has recently saved many fine early nineteenth-century houses for a few more years.

The majority of houses in the inner suburbs were built in the first half of the nineteenth century, and although an individual house may display a bewildering variety of styles, it can usually be classified into one of three distinct types: Georgian, Italianate or Gothic.

Strictly speaking, 'Georgian' refers to houses built before 1837 when Victoria ascended the throne. The rising middle classes of the 1840s quickly demanded rather more of their houses in terms of comfort and individual prestige than the preceding generation; they rejected the severe and undecorated Georgian forms which had dominated domestic architecture in favour of the more ornate Italianate and Gothic styles. It is thus usually possible roughly to date an inner suburban house by its architecture.

FROM GEORGIAN TO ITALIANATE

The inspiration behind most Georgian suburban architecture was the Neoclassicism of the great mansions and public buildings of the eighteenth century. The Classical style, which was based on Greek and Roman architecture and repopularized by the Italian architect Palladio in the seventeenth century, is noted for its simplicity. Its beauty is dependent on symmetry, form and proportion, and it is characterized by the restrained use of applied ornament, save perhaps for friezes and pediments. It was the overall effect that was valued: for example, the size and positioning of windows in a wall were considered to be more important than highly decorated window-cases. The speculative builders of the late Georgian period recognized this and built many rows of houses lacking decoration, and whose beauty lies in the uniformity and dignity of the group as a whole.

Today Georgian domestic architecture is again in fashion; it is valued for its very severity and plainness. But to the aspiring middle classes of the mid-nineteenth century the subjugation of individual houses in favour of the unity of the row was anathema to their desire for individual expression. Newly pros-

perous manufacturers and merchants thought that Georgian simplicity was merely poverty of dress, unbecoming in the house of a man of substance and newly made fortune. The growing supply of machine-made mouldings, castings and pressings meant that for the first time the lower middle classes could emulate the ostentation of their social superiors.

The time was ripe for drastic change, and the inspiration came once again from Italy, this time in the form of the Renaissance villa – as idealized in the seventeenth-century landscape paintings of Claude Lorrain and Poussin and espoused by a number of leading architects, not least Charles Barry who designed the Reform Club of 1837. For example, Florence's Medici Palace has many of the features adopted by the

△The inspiration for the Italianate style was the palaces of Renaissance Italy, such as the Palazzo Medici in Florence. The monumentality of the building, together with the impressive detailing of walls and windows, denote the wealth and position of its owners – an impression desired by suburban builders as well as the Medicis.
◁Osborne House, Queen Victoria's favourite home, was built in 1849 in the fashionable Italianate style, complete with formal terraces.

ARCHITECTURAL STYLES/2

Victorians for the Italianate style: the shallow pitched roof with overhanging eaves supported on brackets, the horizontal string courses delineating each storey, the use of the rounded or Romanesque arch, often containing double arcaded windows. Similarly, the Palazzo Farnese in Rome clearly displays the quoins (corner-stones) and window-cases capped by arched pediments that are to be found on many early Victorian homes. This architecture, originally designed to demonstrate the authority and power of great Renaissance families such as the Medicis, influenced not only the villas of the merchants and professional classes, but also the dwellings of the army of clerks who emulated them.

The House and its Furniture, written in 1859, states that the great merit of the Italianate style is its very irregularity:

well suited to every class of English domestic building from cottage to spacious mansion. It gives scope to as much or as little decoration according to the taste of the owner, and is capable of such treatment and modification in every respect as may render it suitable alike to the slender purse of the City Clerk or the well-filled money bags of the merchant prince.

1. PART OF A LATE GEORGIAN TERRACE.
No single house in the terrace stands out save the one in the centre which projects slightly to give a focal point and sense of symmetry to the group. The roofs are hidden behind a parapet to give the effect simply of a wall pierced at regular intervals by window openings. The windows are always the sliding sash type, never the small-paned opening casements sold as 'Georgian style' today. The ground floor has been stuccoed (rendered in lime mortar) and grooved to resemble stone-work. Such a terrace always has basements.

2. EARLY VICTORIAN TERRACED HOUSE, c. 1850. Based on the earlier Georgian terraced house, it displays Italianate features introduced at this time: window lights grouped in threes with decorative window cases, scrolled brackets supporting the porch and a cornice of stucco.

The space-saving qualities of the basic ground plan of the terraced house were, however, far too attractive to the speculative builder to be radically altered. Instead, the severe Georgian terraces were given an Italianate look. Initially this simply involved the addition of a moulded cornice to the parapet, but by 1850 roofs had developed overhanging eaves which were supported on scrolled brackets, and windows had elaborate moulded cases and string courses delineating the different storeys. Individual houses were distinguished from their neighbours by the addition of a porch over the door – often carried on columns – or by breaking up the frontage so that some houses stood forward from others, sometimes with stuccoed quoins to accentuate the divide. The multiplicity of builders each constructing only two or three houses also contributed to the lack of uniformity in many terraces built at this time. Grander houses might even display a tower or campanile, no doubt in emulation of the most famous contemporary Italianate domestic building, Osborne House on the Isle of Wight, built by the Queen and Prince Consort in the 1840s. But the demand for even more elaborate decoration seemed insatiable, and the Italianate style soon had an even more ornate rival – the Gothic.

3. ITALIANATE FAÇADE, c. 1860. **The broken frontage of this façade emphasizes the individuality of the houses, unlike Georgian terraces which stress the unity of the group. Further breaks with Georgian simplicity include the visible roof with gable end and overhanging eaves.**

4, 5. SMALL VILLAS, c. 1860. **The highly decorated Italianate house on the right makes the early Gothic-style house next door to it look quite plain. (In the 1930s modern International Style and mock-Tudor semis were juxtaposed with equal incongruity.)**

6. SUBSTANTIAL VICTORIAN VILLA **showing a typical Italianate shallow-pitched roof and string courses to delineate each floor. The tower was based on the 'campanile' of medieval Italian villas. The Queen gave the style royal approval when she built Osborne House.**

ARCHITECTURAL STYLES/3

THE GOTHIC STYLE

The Gothic style of architecture grew in popularity alongside the existing taste for the Italianate ornamentation of what were otherwise classical Georgian houses. However, by 1860, this 'Battle of the Styles' was over, the Italianate style was on the wane and Gothic forms were to reign supreme in one form or another for much of the rest of the century – at least for most suburban housing.

The term Gothic as applied to Victorian architecture is almost indefinable, since it was used by the Victorians to cover any style that was not classical. Like the Italianate style, the form was not new, and it, too, had grandiose origins, in the great church architecture of medieval England and Europe, based upon the pointed arch. After the 1840s Gothic forms began to become popular in the domestic architecture of suburbia. There were three major reasons for this. Firstly, the rapidly expanding middle classes were seeking more decorative styles to show off their new-found wealth; secondly, the religious revival of the mid-nineteenth century favoured the Gothic with its long ecclesiastical associations (not only could the newly arrived suburban family show its wealth to visitors but also its piety); and thirdly, one of the most famous public buildings in Britain, the Houses of Parliament, was built at this time in the Gothic style, and the interior was designed by the high priest of the Gothic Revival A. N. W. Pugin (see page 60).

Another eminent Victorian to give impetus to the Gothic Revival was John Ruskin, whose motivation was aesthetic rather than (as it was for Pugin) religious. In his book *The Seven Lamps of Architecture* (1849), he argued for the general acceptance of one style to replace the chaos of the many architectural

THE NEW HOUSES OF PARLIAMENT.—ST. STEPHEN'S PORCH.

◁The first major public building in the Gothic style was the Houses of Parliament, built to replace the Palace of Westminster destroyed by fire in 1834. This engraving shows building work still in progress. Sir Charles Barry's design was of a symmetrical Classical form, but because of its detailing, for which Pugin was responsible, the overriding impression is of a Gothic building. Pugin directed the masons and carvers, and through this building he established a style that was to influence architecture for the rest of the century.

fashions prevalent at the time, some indication of which can be gained from Richard Brown's *Domestic Architecture* (1841), which lists and illustrates many styles, including the following: Cottage Orné, Swiss Cottage, Norman, Lancastrian, Tudor, Stuart, Anglo-Grecian, Pompeiian, Florentine, Venetian, French, Persian, Moorish Spanish and Chinese. It excludes Gothic, however, because in Brown's opinion 'it exclusively belongs to sacred architecture and not to domestic'. Few of these styles in their pure form influenced the rapidly growing suburbs of the time, and it is

typically Victorian that no original styles are contemplated, only copies of older ones. Ruskin himself felt that 'the forms of architecture already known to us are good enough for us', and argued for various Gothic styles to be adopted universally, as being 'Augustan' in authority.

Standard pattern books were much used by the speculative builders of suburbia to provide ideas for decorative features which could be easily copied, and the aesthetic result of such random culling of inspiration is often limited. Most famous of these books was *The*

Encyclopaedia of Cottage, Farm and Villa Architecture and Furniture by John Loudon, published in 1833 and the standard reference work for many builders for fifty years. In it, Loudon, by profession an architect and landscape gardener, shows houses in a great many styles, and depicts roofs, chimneys, gables, towers, windows, door-cases and many other details which can still be seen in all Victorian suburbs today, often in quite bizarre combinations. Gothic became the basic style, but Swiss barge boards, Tudor chimneys and rustic porches might be added with cheerful obliviousness of any incongruity.

Ruskin's *The Stones of Venice* (1851) popularized, in particular, the carving of foliage in stone. The Museum of Science in Oxford, built to his design, incorporated elaborately carved capitols that provided the inspiration for thousands of suburban porches and bay windows decorated with capitols, mass-produced in artificial stone and sometimes incorporating angelic faces.

Pointed arches, carved stonework, and a faintly ecclesiastical feel are therefore the essence of the Gothic ornamentation of suburban houses, but the rejection of Classical form also allowed for more fundamental benefits in housing design. For example, roofs in Classical architecture were not considered respectable; after all, the Greek and Roman climate rendered them almost redundant. Georgian and early Victorian housing tended to hide them behind parapet walls, rainwater being disposed of via elaborately designed centre-valley gutters usually lined with lead. These are a source of worry, if not disaster, to twentieth-century owners. Gothic architecture, however, is based on a north European tradition, where the wetter climate meant more steeply pitched, conspicuous roofs, which are among the glories of many Continental cathedrals.

The early Victorian Italianate style popularized overhanging eaves, often supported on decorative plaster brackets, and these were undoubtedly much more efficient water-repellers; but the roofs themselves tended to have the shallow pitch of Mediterranean Europe. In the modest Gothic-style suburban house, the roof itself is conspicuous and generally of a much steeper pitch which is more practical for the climate. The Victorians' favourite roofing material was grey slate, which was cheap because of the development of the Welsh slate industry, and readily available because of the new railways. To offset its drabness, ornamental ridge-tiles of red clay or even cast iron were commonly employed, and on better-quality housing some rows of slates would be laid in 'diamond' or 'fish-scale' patterns to break the monotony. Even greater effect was gained from the design of the pitches themselves. The French-looking mansard roof (each pitch having two slopes) was sometimes used, as were turrets and domes, sometimes clad in lead or copper, which were especially common on corner sites, shops, pubs, and larger houses. Various byelaws often required party walls to project higher than the roof, to prevent the spread of fire. Otherwise most suburban houses contented themselves with a simple gable or semi-turret over what was one of the major features of the mid-Victorian house – the bay window.

The abolition of Window Tax in 1851, together with technological developments which made glass both cheaper and obtainable in larger panes, enabled the mid-Victorians to construct projecting bay windows, perfect devices for emphasizing the individuality of the houses themselves, and a complete reversal of the Georgian ideal. Many commentators deplored the blank effect produced by such large panes of glass,

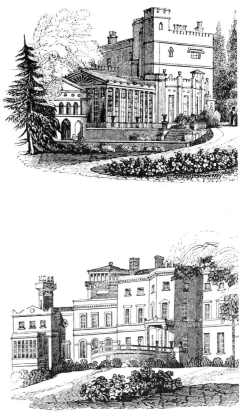

△ **Two large country houses from Loudon's influential *Encyclopaedia of Cottage, Farm and Villa Architecture and Furniture* (1833), which was a standard reference work for builders for at least fifty years.**

but in fact the classic Georgian window – a double sliding sash with six panes to each sash – had already been subtly altered in preceding decades. The glazing bars had become thinner to let in more light, and after 1820 a completely new pattern emerged: a large pane of glass surrounded by narrow border panes. The small corner panes were often of vividly coloured blue or red glass with star designs cut into them, a

ARCHITECTURAL STYLES/4

pattern that remained in vogue throughout the century, although, curiously, frequently confined to French doors and landing windows at the back of the house. By the end of the century a bay window had become standard for many working-class front parlours, while the middle classes demanded that the bay be carried up to include the front bedroom and provide the excuse for a gable and decorative finial on the roof. Window design also seems to have been signifi-

cantly influenced by the Venetian forms of the Gothic espoused by Ruskin. Pure Venetian windows – three lights grouped together and capped by Romanesque (fully rounded) arches supported on capitols of carved foliage – can be seen on many modest Victorian houses, often ornamented by polychrome (multi-coloured) brickwork which was another great favourite, but more often the style was adapted. Sashes were grouped in threes, two small side lights and a central

larger one, and more popular was the segmented (gently curved) arch, which, although used in the seventeenth century, is one of the few features that seems to be genuinely Victorian and not a copy of a past style.

The rise of the bay seems to have coincided with the demise of that notorious Georgian feature, the basement. An entire floor of many Georgian and early Victorian houses was below street level, and the main entrance of the

1. GABLED HOUSE WITH RECESSED ENTRANCE, 1860s. Stucco, popular for the ground floor in Georgian times, has here been continued right to the top of the house; the false quoins (cornerstones) and top pair of windows are Italianate.

2. ITALIANATE VILLA, c. 1865. This highly ornamented villa reflects the popular taste for showy polychrome brickwork, possible because the new railways made builders less dependent on local brickfields.

3. TERRACED HOUSE WITH BALCONY, 1860s. This house, like its neighbours, incorporates many decorative features – including ecclesiastical Gothic – to make it as imposing as possible. The entrance has been designed to impress visitors.

house usually approached by a few steps or a short bridge over the 'area' (the small yard below street level). Lit and ventilated at the front of the house only by a single window facing the area, basement rooms were acceptable as kitchens and sculleries when the house was occupied by single families. However, the social decline and multiple tenancies to which many inner-suburban dwellings gradually succumbed often led to basements being occupied by entire families, even though their lack of light and ventilation made them quite unsuitable for such a purpose.

Numerous byelaws and Public Health Acts began to regulate such things as minimum distances between buildings and ratios of window sizes to room sizes in order to improve living conditions for the poor, but these were slow to take effect. It was the realization, among those who could afford to choose where they lived, that damp basements were not conducive to good health, and the market's response to this, that led to changes. By 1860 semi-basements, only about a metre (3 feet) below ground level, were common but necessitated long flights of steps up to the front door. In new housing of the 1870s basements had risen out of the ground so much that they had largely disappeared, and the Classical Georgian terrace of forty years earlier had been completely transformed.

4. TERRACED HOUSE WITH DOUBLE BAY, 1870s. When this house was built, even semi-basements were becoming unusual. Two-storey bay windows began to be seen, and roof gable ends and porches displayed elaborate bargeboards.

5. GOTHIC-STYLE TERRACED HOUSE, 1870s. The Gothic elements – carved foliage and ecclesiastical pointed arches – are a travesty of Pugin's and Ruskin's principles, but satisfied the need for both ostentation and piety.

6, 7. ITALIANATE AND GOTHIC VILLAS, c. 1875–80. The house on the left has Italianate eaves, stuccoed quoins and classically inspired pilasters, while the right-hand house shows vestiges of Venetian Gothic in the carved capitols.

HOUSE LAYOUT AND APPLIED DECORATION/1

The internal layout of Victorian suburban houses, despite one or two regional variations, remained both remarkably uniform and distinctly English. The basic layout pattern was established in Georgian times, when the absence of Building Acts to regulate design (save in London) meant that economy in land use was probably the prime factor for the speculator, while the inhabitants wanted privacy and respectability. Living in a house rather than an apartment was the first essential. The second was separate access to every room – after all, that is what differentiates a house from a mere cottage. The nineteenth-century terraced house was tall and narrow-fronted (to save land) and generally consisted of two rooms on each of three floors, all connected by convoluted passages and staircases. The basement, usually entirely below street level, housed the kitchen and servants, and above that, at street level, were a dining room and parlour. The first floor, with no street entrance, could accommodate a room the full width of the house, and its more elegant proportions, often combined with the back room via folding doors, made it suitable as a drawing room for receiving guests. The floors above were for bedrooms, and often included cramped attics for the use of servants. As early as 1817 this design was considered odd enough by foreign visitors to cause one of them, Louis Simond from France, to remark:

These narrow houses, three or four storeys high – one for eating one for sleeping a third for company, a fourth perhaps at the top for servants – and the agility the ease the quickness with which the individuals of the family run up and down, and perch on the different storeys, gives the idea of a cage with its sticks and birds.

This basic layout seems to have been used across the social spectrum, from the spacious town houses of the gentry to the cramped working-class terraces of the industrial towns. Unfortunately, the lack of building regulations in the first half of the nineteenth century meant that many of these now very fashionable houses were built to standards unacceptable today.

The plethora of Acts of Parliament in the second half of the nineteenth century sought to control health problems by regulating building design, and from then on the decisions of local government also greatly affected the internal design of suburban housing. As regulations regarding such factors as ventilation, window sizes, ceiling heights, street and house widths, size of rear gardens and sanitation began to take effect, a new type of house evolved: the byelaw house. Byelaw housing has become synonymous with drab monotony, but it is important to recognize the huge improvement over their predecessors that such dwellings provided. Basements disappeared, and kitchens and sculleries became housed in a rear annexe projecting into the garden. An outside privy with flush pan was sometimes incorporated into the annexe, although access to it was still via the garden as the trapping systems of the water closets did not always successfully exclude sewer gas. Before long the rear annexe also had a first floor with one or two bedrooms and even a bathroom, and the hitherto standard plan of two rooms on three floors had become the three rooms on two floors format. With fewer stairs and more light, these were the dream homes of the second generation of suburbanites, adding increased standards of comfort to the requirement for privacy, segregation, order and ostentation.

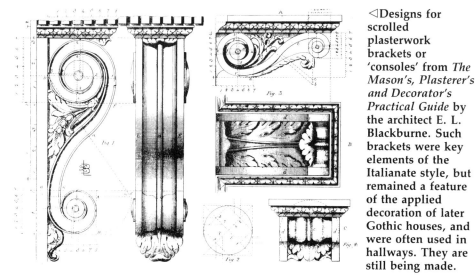

◁Designs for scrolled plasterwork brackets or 'consoles' from *The Mason's, Plasterer's and Decorator's Practical Guide* by the architect E. L. Blackburne. Such brackets were key elements of the Italianate style, but remained a feature of the applied decoration of later Gothic houses, and were often used in hallways. They are still being made.

That byelaw housing was built to high standards possibly accounts for its increasing popularity today, but whereas the twentieth-century occupier tears down walls to create large, multi-functional rooms, the essence of Victorian layout was the desire to segregate functions. This reflected the middle-class need to emulate the gentry, whose large houses afforded individual rooms for different activities, such as studies, smoking rooms or billiards rooms. Thus, in comparatively small suburban dwellings, much floor space was devoted to corridors connecting a succession of small rooms which were often given over to only occasional use – a waste of space few would find acceptable or affordable today.

Some sense of their priorities can be gained by taking a visitor's-eye view of the reception areas of a typical six- or eight-roomed middle-class house of the late nineteenth century. (The very words reception room mean 'fit to receive guests', as opposed to the more private quarters which only the family ever saw. The concept of dividing a home in this way is almost gone, and the word is anachronistic save in the jargon of estate agents trying to evoke the imaginary graces of a bygone era.) The front door is recessed into a porch and the whole entrance is ornamented to be as imposing as possible. A maid would open the door to the hall which, ideally, had to be wide enough to contain a seat so that guests could be 'held' while being announced, and well hung with pictures to entertain them during these potentially embarrassing few moments. In most houses, of course, the hall is merely a narrow corridor but its holding function is not forgotten: the ceiling and floor are often highly ornamented and designed to impress, and the first flight of stairs, seen by guests, is much wider than upper flights seen only by the family. Ornamental plaster brackets at ceiling height, and sometimes also a curtain or fretwork screen, separated the front hall from the rest of the house although the whole area might only be a 2.5-metre (8-foot) passage. The hall was in effect a formal vestibule for the most sacred place, the drawing room, as it was called by the upper middle classes,

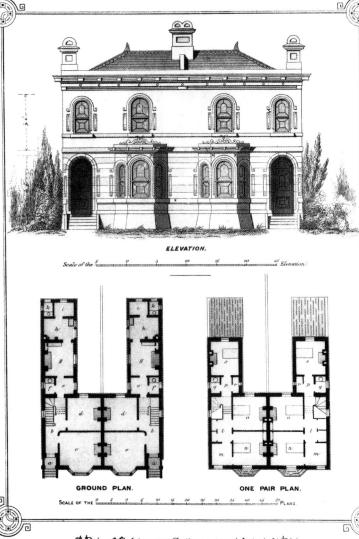

ELEVATION.

Scale of the   0   5   10   15   20   25 Elevation.

GROUND PLAN.   ONE PAIR PLAN.

SCALE OF THE   0   5   10   15   20   25   30   35   40   45 PLANS.

A Pair of Eight-room Cottages (semi-detached) Pl.1.

⊲DESIGN FOR A PAIR OF SEMI-DETACHED HOUSES from E. L. Blackburne's *Suburban and Rural Architecture* (1869).
ELEVATION
The houses are in the Classical-Italianate style: the ground floor is stuccoed to suggest stone, the upper floor is plain except for a string course; and the shallow pitched roof is partly concealed with a decorated parapet and overhanging eaves.
LAYOUT
The floor plans are typical of many Victorian 'tunnel-back' houses. Downstairs, the kitchen (marked *g*) has a built-in dresser, while the sink and copper are in the scullery (*h*). There are also built-in cupboards in the bedrooms and on the landing, and no less than three lavatories but no bath. The small room (*m*) would have been a dressing room.

although the lower middle classes might still use the working-class term parlour. (Indeed, the naming of rooms seems to have been the minefield of possible social indiscretion that it is today.) Whatever its name, the main reception room housed the family's best furniture and most valuable belongings, possibly including a piano, yet it was the least used room in the house, only being employed for the formal receiving of guests on Sunday afternoons and for family gatherings, as well as providing somewhere quiet during the week for father to read or study. There is no real equivalent of a room reserved only for formal social functions in modern housing, in which every square inch of space

HOUSE LAYOUT AND APPLIED DECORATION/2

has to be justified on much more practical criteria. Indeed, the waste of space which the Victorian parlour represented in smaller houses aroused much comment from contemporary social observers, including Allen Clarke in *The Effects of the Factory System* (1899):

It is shut up for six days of the week, and is only kept for brag; ostentatious superfluity in the idea of the artisan's wife is, as with those in higher grades of society, a sign of superiority.

The room behind the main reception room, and often connected to it by double doors, was usually the one used most by the family and was the hub of the household. In well-to-do families it was known as the morning room – so called because breakfast was taken there but, confusingly, in upper middle-class houses it might also be referred to as the parlour and be used for family recreation. Ideally, in larger houses, there was also a separate dining room, used for evening meals and the dinner parties that were part of the expected social ritual, but in most houses the functions of morning room and dining room were combined. In houses large enough to accommodate third or fourth reception rooms, it was usual to divide these into 'male' or 'female' territories: a breakfast parlour or day room for the lady of the house or, more usually in an age when the whole house was, strictly speaking, a woman's domain, a study or smoking room where the head of the household could find sanctuary with his chums. Other rooms above ground-floor level were always bedrooms. Boys and girls were segregated, but the idea of one child in each bedroom is relatively new, and two good-sized rooms would suffice quite large families. Servants slept in attics, where in grand houses the nursery was also situated.

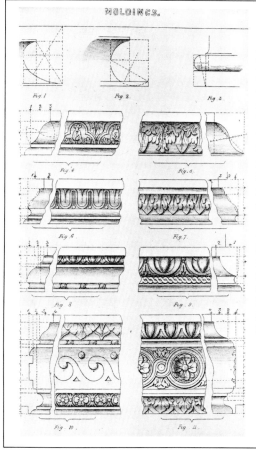

Cornices are often among the first details of houses to be lost or damaged, perhaps through damp penetration, or obliterated under multiple layers of paint. They may also have disappeared with changes in room arrangements and partition walls under successive generations of owners. They can, however, be easily replaced, with fibreglass or plaster reproductions which are readily available; often they provide the essential finishing touch to rooms which otherwise look strangely 'bald'.

◁**Examples of mouldings from E. L. Blackburne's** *Mason's, Bricklayer's, Plasterer's and Decorator's Practical Guide.* **Based on the traditional cable, running dog (Vitruvian scroll), acanthus leaf and egg and dart motifs, these are some of the standard patterns used in the nineteenth century.**

APPLIED DECORATION

Most houses, therefore, employed a strict hierarchy of grandness, from the rooms intended to be seen by guests, through those for family use, down to the servants' quarters; and, generally speaking, the fittings and applied decoration reflected this rigid order. Ideas for these features were drawn from pattern books and building manuals which seem to have been the mainstay of all the speculative builders. A huge variety of individual designs can be found in essentially similar houses, at

first painstakingly hand-made and applied by craftsmen, and later quickly applied from mass-produced selections.

Internal walls were plastered plainly, had deep skirting boards and cornices with varying degrees of moulding, depending on the proposed value of the house and the builder's inclination; a majority had a picture rail. The wall surface might also be broken up by a dado rail with textured paper below it, particularly in the dining room and hall, or wherever the lime-plastered walls

◁ An early Victorian dining room, still very much in the Georgian tradition (except for the elaborately draped curtains which foreshadow the High Victorian style). The restrained decoration of the room is typified by the fireplace with its plain hob grate and fine detailing. Within a few years taste had reacted strongly against the simplicity of this and the applied decoration (cornice and wainscoting) that distinguish this room in favour of rather more ostentatious design, except in the most modest dwellings and in servants' rooms.

needed protection from chairs or the passage of people. This item became increasingly popular in houses built towards the end of the century (see pages 108–9). A particular feature of most houses was a highly ornate ceiling rose, complete with stylized carving of foliage and flowers, or neo-Gothic motifs and scrollwork. Prefabrication methods were developed, and fibrous plaster, a combination of ordinary plaster strengthened with coarse canvas, made it easier to cast whole lengths of cornice or other detail. Many areas of ornamental 'plasterwork' were in fact papier mâché, a cheap, light and very effective method

of creating elaborate patterns. Every room would have had a cornice and skirting boards, if on a more modest scale than those of the principal rooms.

As for the interior joinery, with the exception of the all-important staircase which would be visible to all callers and therefore required a commensurate degree of attention, it was comparatively simple. Skirting boards had plain mouldings and would be painted in dark serviceable colours – possibly maroon or brown – or grained and varnished, or marbled. Interior doors were usually four-panelled, including the large doors which sometimes separated the main

reception rooms, and again had simple mouldings. China finger-plates were placed above and below the handle. In the 1850s and 1860s, internal doors in the hall, kitchen, and bathroom (if there was one) might have decorative coloured glass panels, sometimes etched or painted. (Do-it-yourself 'stained glass' was also popular: 'diaphanie' was one method by which brightly coloured medieval scenes or patterns, obtainable from paint warehouses, could be transferred to glass). Built-in cupboards were a feature of kitchens, sculleries, bedrooms and reception rooms, often on either side of the chimney.

INFLUENCES ON STYLE: A. W. N. Pugin

Augustus Welby Northmore Pugin, architect, designer and antiquarian, was born in 1812 and died insane forty years later, having been converted to Roman Catholicism, thrice married and once shipwrecked. He was short, podgy, energetic to the point of fanaticism, immoderate, and prodigious in his output of work which established medieval Gothic as the quintessential style of the Victorian era.

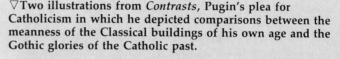

▽**Two illustrations from** *Contrasts*, **Pugin's plea for Catholicism in which he depicted comparisons between the meanness of the Classical buildings of his own age and the Gothic glories of the Catholic past.**

The taste for Gothic ornamentation had been established in the mid-eighteenth century, when Horace Walpole (son of the Prime Minister and author of the Gothic novel *The Castle of Otranto*) transformed his large villa, Strawberry Hill, Twickenham (shown on page 48), using turrets, pointed arches, castellated parapets and other so-called medieval forms. This was very much against the trend for classically inspired Palladian forms which were generally preferred for large mansions throughout the eighteenth century, although picturesque Gothic follies might have been constructed in the grounds. One or two large houses and many more modest villas did, however, adopt Gothic ornamentation, yet this was hardly a major revival, being merely part of a fashion for anything that was considered pretty or exotic. A gentleman wishing to build might choose Tudor, Egyptian, Swiss or even Indian (as in the case of the Prince Regent's Brighton Pavilion), or any one of a dozen or so other fashionable styles which might take his fancy. In his book, *An Apology for the Revival of Christian Architecture* of 1843, Pugin railed against this 'Babel of Confusion':

Private judgement runs riot; every architect has a theory of his own, a beau ideal he has himself created; a disguise with which to invest the building he erects. This is generally the result of his latest travels. One breathes nothing but the Alhambra, another the Parthenon – a third is full of lotus cups and pyramids from the banks of the Nile, a fourth from Rome is all dome and basilica . . . Styles are now *adopted* instead of *generated,* and ornament and design *adapted to,* instead of *originated by,* the edifices themselves.

Pugin's father, an *emigré* from the French Revolution, had worked as a draughtsman for the great Regency architect John Nash and had also in the 1820s published two books on Gothic architecture, drawing inspiration from the magnificent churches of his native Normandy. His son, who became an ardent Catholic, believed that medieval church architecture based upon the pointed arch was the one true style for a Christian country – not the sham Strawberry Hill Gothic of the eighteenth century which merely applied and copied Gothic details, but one in which form and decoration were truthful to the construction and purpose of the building itself. In this sense, Pugin may be described as an early functionalist.

The time was also ripe for a Gothic revival. Thomas Rickman, a minor architect, had laid the foundations in 1817, when he made the first systematic study of English Gothic architecture and coined the four terms Norman, Early English, Decorated and Perpendicular, to describe the progress of the Gothic style, and which we still use today. This period also saw the beginning of the 'Merrie England' myth, a widespread view of the Middle Ages as a more hospitable and charitable era, when the simple pleasures of honest toil and ardent faith were as yet unsullied by the dour post-Reformation Puritan ethic. No doubt the poverty, degradation and social injustice of recently industrialized Britain helped to fuel this myth which, although patently untrue, inspired the imaginations of many great nineteenth-century artists and writers with a love of all things medieval.

Pugin himself was also driven by religious fervour to reject Classical in favour of Gothic architecture. He had converted to Roman Catholicism in 1834, and the life and art of pre-Reformation times were for him a reflection of the one true faith, and he seems to have been at least partly inspired by the hope that buildings in the Gothic style would encourage a return to medieval, that is Catholic, forms of worship.

The burgeoning spirit of medievalism was nicely expressed by Pugin in *Contrasts*, published in 1836, in which he graphically demonstrated his abhorrence of the age in which he lived and his belief in the glories of the medieval past. Pictures of ugly, polluted cities built in severe Classical forms are contrasted with spacious medieval cities dominated by slender Gothic spires. *Contrasts* was of course, rather crude propaganda, but it brought fame and some notoriety to Pugin, and there is no doubting the sincerity of his plea:

What madness, then, while neglecting our own religious and national types of architecture and art, to worship at the revived shrines of ancient corruption and profane temples of the crucified Redeemer by the architecture and emblems of the heathen gods.

Being both Catholic and intemperate tended to make Pugin not quite the respected figure that he might otherwise have been in Victorian society. That he was so influential is perhaps due to his involvement in the rebuilding of the Houses of Parliament. Built to replace the old Palace of Westminster destroyed by fire in 1834, the new Houses were designed by Sir Charles Barry who employed Pugin initially as an assistant, but quickly realized his great ability as a decorator. Their relationship was tempestuous, but eventually the design of the furniture, floors, decoration and internal fittings, even to the ink wells and hat stands, was entrusted to Pugin.

△ **Portrait of Pugin by L. R. Herbert (1845).**

Although he designed a great number of buildings, The Houses of Parliament are his best-known work, and the one which set the official seal of approval on the Gothic Revival which was to eclipse all other styles for a generation. However, the new fashion was often a far cry from the return to truth and honesty in architecture and form which he desired, for apparently anything that could be made, could be made Gothic – from railway stations to telegraph machines. Pugin was highly innovative and always eager to adopt new techniques and materials, but his disappointment at what the commercially minded middle classes in their new suburban villas made of the Revival, which he so fervently espoused, is clear in his description of 'Modern Gothic Furniture and Decoration' in his book *The True Principles of Pointed or Christian Architecture* (1841):

Everything is crocketed with angular projections, innumerable mitres, sharp ornaments, and turreted extremities. A man who remains any length of time in a modern Gothic room, and escapes without being wounded by some of its minutiae, may consider himself extremely fortunate.

By poking fun at the mass-produced domestic artefacts which the new miracle of Victorian industrialism made possible, Pugin was commenting upon a crucial British problem – that manufacturers found it all to easy to adopt styles, or the trappings of styles, without paying attention to good, basic, functional design. The next generation of designers, notably William Morris, who consolidated the Gothic Revival, chose to evade the question altogether by returning to hand-crafting, and the problem has bedevilled British domestic design ever since.

FURNITURE

Among the factors affecting furniture design of the early Victorian period were a taste for novelty, a desire for comfort and a move away from the formality of Georgian furnishing arrangements. The most popular decorative styles were those which both enhanced the symbolic and social value of the family gathered together round the hearth, and gave a good account of their income.

The most important rooms in the house – the dining and drawing rooms in which guests were received – were crowded with bulky and elaborate furniture, heavy draperies and a surfeit of pattern. They would have contained a liberal collection of some, or all, of the following: chairs (at least two easy chairs and eight others), couches and/or sofas, large and small tables (including one large centre table and one dining table), chiffoniers, fancy cabinets, pier glasses and whatnots. Thanks to the rapid development of new manufacturing techniques and the growing interest in 'antique' furniture which was filtering down to the villa dwellers from the upper classes, furniture could be obtained in a great variety of 'period' styles, constructed from an equally large number of different materials. The unifying feature was the quantity of highly ornate decoration which was applied to every available surface, and which served to enhance the apparent value of the pieces. A few items of inherited furniture often added to the eclectic effect.

◁ **A huge variety of materials and a wealth of ingenuity went into the production of Victorian furniture. Papier mâché, the material used to make this 'rococo' chair, was particularly popular for small, highly decorative items. No home was considered complete without at least one example, often a tray, which would have been lacquered and decorated with gilding and floral patterns and commonly featured a painting of a picturesque Gothic ruin or the Queen.**

The period styles most popular with the early suburbanites were, broadly: neo-rococo, Italian renaissance, Elizabethan and, of course, Gothic. These terms are, however, somewhat misleading: the reproductions were by no means accurate and often manufacturers meant different things when describing a piece of furniture as 'renaissance' for example. Individual items such as a chair might include a basic Regency outline with some bits and pieces of Gothic detailing; and the commercial adaptations of styles often bore little relation to the spirit of the original. Some of the more influential household guides, such as John Loudon's *Encyclopaedia* (1833), which is divided into sections on 'Grecian', 'Italianate', 'Gothic', and 'Fat Classical', and variations upon them, and *Cassell's Household Guide* (1869), did little to help clarify matters.

The variety of materials used was equally diverse, and was complicated by the fact that wood was often stained or painted in an effort to make it look like another, more fashionable, variety. Different materials did, however, lend themselves naturally to different styles: oak and mahogany for the solid lumpy chairs and tables with machine-carved high-relief renaissance or Gothic decoration that are so readily recognizable as Victorian; and light wooden frameworks and *papier mâché* for the novel and graceful little neo-rococo chairs and other decorative items that were considered very fashionable for the drawing room or boudoir (these pieces were japanned glossy black, elaborately detailed with mother-of-pearl inlay and often had painted panels in the back which might depict anything from a portrait of the Prince Consort to romantic 'blasted heaths' or ruined castles). Brass and iron were also put to use for the construction of furniture; and many such pieces were displayed at the Great Exhibition, including very elaborate baby cribs and surprisingly modern-looking rocking chairs, but they really only became popular for pub and garden furniture and, more particularly, for beds. Bentwood made its first appearance in 1849, and the classic curvey rocking chairs which are so readily available today were also popular in Victorian homes by the 1860s. One of the unusual items of Victorian household furniture was the folding chair recommended by *Cassell's Guide* as a useful easy chair. This had refreshingly simple outlines and a cane seat and back – *Cassell's* however, recommended that it be 'padded, cushioned and covered in chintz or worsted rep', to give it a truly comfortable appearance.

△This table, its top superbly decorated with complex, brightly coloured inlay and supported by three fowl, is a particularly fine example of just how elaborate much Victorian furniture was.

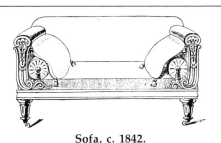

Sofa, c. 1842.

The risk of achieving sterility through stylistic purity need never be a problem for the modern householder seeking authentic furniture for a mid-Victorian home, since the diversity of styles and materials deemed acceptable then means that one can mix styles of different periods as they did. A tour of dealers' auction rooms will help you decide what styles might suit you and your house best, and if you cannot afford to buy there, second-hand shops are a good source of finds.

△Comparatively simple furniture was available, too: the Thonet brothers exhibited their bentwood furniture at the Great Exhibition, and a full range was available in the 1860s and still is today.

The taste for plump, cosy comfort was satisfied, in the 1850s, by coil springing and deep buttoning which were successfully applied to items of drawing-room furniture to produce deeply upholstered easy chairs and overstuffed settees. Highly sprung armchairs (available in 'extra size' as well as the regular bulky version) for the men, and smaller but no less opulent chairs for the ladies (made without arms to aid the discreet arrangement of their own, crinolined, upholstery), soon became *de rigueur* for a fashionable villa drawing room, closely followed by lavishly stuffed sofas, many of them equipped with ingenious hinged arms, and finally by the generous forms of the still popular Chesterfield. Needless to say, all these items were covered in patterned fabrics and generously trimmed. When not lounging amid the ample forms of the upholstered

furniture, the suburban Victorian family was dining, reading, or, in the case of the women, employed in some kind of decorative handiwork. Two or more tables were therefore essential items for the dining and drawing rooms. The most fashionable were circular and of mahogany, balanced on a single, possibly highly carved, pedestal. Some of the more expensive might also have inlay detail in the top, but the average householder would in any event cover tables with heavy chenille cloths in a dark serviceable colour, finished off round the edges with a fringe and tassels. Another essential for either or both rooms was a chiffonier, available in varying degrees of grandeur depending on where it was to be placed. A relatively simple mahogany one could serve as a sideboard in the dining room, while one of rosewood or walnut, with the addi-

tion of glazed doors, would be considered more suitable for the front, or 'superior' room. The remaining essential item was a chimney glass, a large mirror in an ornate frame which was, very precisely, required to be higher than it was broad, and which was placed over the mantelpiece.

With the principal items of furniture in position, it only remained for the ladies of the house to add the homely touches to the family hearth, by turning their hands to any one of a wide variety of decorative arts, detailed instructions for which were included in household guides and ladies' journals. The wax flowers and stuffed birds under glass domes, 'scrap' screens (screens decorated with a collage of bought decorative scraps) and embroidered footstools that so often turn up in junk shops are all examples of the Victorian lady's art.

LIGHTING

For all their fascination with technological advances, most Victorians were remarkably slow to accept innovation into their homes, and lighting was no exception. Gas lighting was not regarded as the norm in suburbia until 1900, and electric lighting, introduced nearly twenty years before, was rarely used until the modern tungsten filament bulb was invented in 1907. Queen Victoria herself spurned both forms, preferring the gentler light of oil lamps for Windsor Castle.

◁ The elegant table lamp in this family scene of about 1860 is, judging from the absence of a reservoir, powered by gas, not oil.
▽ Wall brackets like this one (left) were more effective than ceiling lights for gas, but the dim light from gas jets had to be supplemented by low pendants for reading (right); the picture shows the popular 'vaseline' glass shade on the upper light.

Gas lighting had been used for street and public lighting since 1813, but the reasons for its unpopularity in home use are not hard to find. The simple 'fish-tail' jets did not throw a good light, and gave off a great deal of heat and, worse still, highly poisonous fumes which killed plants (though not the aspidistra), tarnished metal and discoloured furnishings. Where ceiling pendants were used – usually only in the parlour – they were often of the sliding type which could be lowered when lit to make the most of the limited light. In grander suburban homes the elaborate plasterwork of the ceiling roses sometimes concealed grilles connected to the outside air by small ducts which were supposed to carry away some of the fumes. As the upward-pointing flames did not throw much light downwards, wall brackets, with one, two or three branches mounted at a lower level, were more popular. Before the introduction of the gas meter, all homes were subject to restricted supply: the gas companies usually turned the gas on at dusk and off at 11 or 11.30 p.m. Even during the hours of supply, house-holders constantly complained that pressure dropped to unusable levels.

Despite the problems, suburban gas companies sprang up at an astonishing rate and it was not unknown for five or six competing mains to be laid in the same road. Their advantage was a lack of competition from other lighting sources. Tallow candles smelled and wax ones were expensive; and the oil lamps of the day used various animal- and vegetable-

derived fuels which were both smelly and expensive. Gas as a lighting source received a serious challenge, however, when mineral oil (paraffin) was discovered in 1859 as a result of drilling the first oil well in Pennsylvania. The age of the paraffin lamp now began. Encouraged by an oil which did not deteriorate, gave good light, was not explosive, rose up a wick by capillary action alone and did not smell (much), literally thousands of patents for lamps were filed. In 1865 the duplex burner was invented and became very popular. The duplex – two ribbon wicks set very close together, which produce more light than two separate wicks – is the basis of most of the antique and reproduction oil lamps available today in a great variety of designs. Although they have not survived, fabric shades were common on oil lamps, as well as the more familiar etched and coloured glass.

Meanwhile, the gas companies were fighting off the challenge from oil lamps with further technological advances. Governors fitted to lamps automatically increased the flow of gas as the pressure dropped and thus eliminated flickering; and prepayment meters brought gas into more modest suburban homes in the 1880s and 1890s; but it was the invention of the mantle in 1887 that was to transform gas lighting by producing a brighter light from less gas. Mantles were woven from cotton and impregnated with chemical salts. On initial lighting the cotton burnt away, leaving a delicate network of salts which glowed white-hot in the heat of the gas and gave out a greenish light. The actual flame needed was much smaller than for the fish-tail jets, and consequently less heat and fumes were produced. Moreover, the mantles could be suspended upside-down, enabling more efficient ceiling pendants to be designed.

By 1900 simple wall brackets and

SPIERS & POND's STORES QUEEN VICTORIA ST., E.C.

NO TICKETS REQUIRED.

HARDWARE DEPARTMENT.

Price Book No. 52, Published November 1st (1000 Pages), Illustrated of all Departments, Free on Application.

"THE CARLISLE." Copper Body, in Wrought Iron Mounts, with Lining, 37s.

9724 WROUGHT IRON & FLUTED COPPER CONTAINER TABLE-LAMP, 50-Candle Power "Veritas" Burner, 24s. 6d. complete.

834 WROUGHT IRON & COPPER TABLE-LAMP, with 50-Candle Power "Belge" Raiser Burner, 34s. 6d. complete.

POLISHED CAST BRASS FLOOR-LAMP, with Plush Covered Table, 50-Candle Power "Veritas" Burner and Shade complete, £5 13s. 6d.

"THE BRISTOL" COAL-VASE, Wrought Iron and Copper, with Lining, 35s. 9d.

"LOUIS DESIGN" HANDSOME POLISHED CAST BRASS FLOOR-LAMP, with 50-Candle Power "Belge" Burner and Shade complete, £8 19s. 6d.

"THE NORMAN" HAMMERED BRASS COAL-VASE, with Louis Panel, 52s. 6d.

△ The etched, coloured glass shades on the table lamps are familiar today, but not so the fabric shades on the floor lamps. These ornate brass standards were expensive; simpler Arts-and-Craft-inspired lamps of wrought iron and copper would have been cheaper and in better taste.

pendants were very common in suburbia, and gas lighting enjoyed a brief period of mass popularity. Reproduction and original gas lights are readily available today, the former wired for electricity. The need for emergency lighting also means that mantles are still fairly easy to obtain, and can be used with natural or bottled gas, but it is impossible to reproduce the exact quality of light that the Victorians and Edwardians obtained from town gas.

While no one today would want to return to the level of gloom produced by Victorian lighting, authenticity of atmosphere does depend very much on the effect of the lighting. Candle-light is ideal for entertaining purposes; otherwise many period gas and paraffin lamps may successfully be converted to electricity, and there are also many good reproductions available, some of them made using the original casts. Where purely functional, direct lighting is needed, such as in kitchens and bathrooms, it is often better to use modern spotlights recessed in the ceiling than period fittings of any kind.

WALLPAPERS AND FABRICS/1

The wallpapers and furnishing fabrics that were produced during the early Victorian period, particularly in the 1850s and 1860s, amply satisfied the villa-dwellers' taste for elaborate pattern, despite the criticism levelled against it by Henry Cole and his circle (see page 71). With the abolition of wallpaper taxes at about this time, and the first appearance of wallpaper in rolls (as opposed to the expensive strips or 'hangings' which had been more common up to this time), this method of decoration came within the reach of most householders. Fantastically detailed repeat patterns, ranging from exotic birds and flowers surrounded by filigree arbours, to contemporary feats of engineering (such as the pattern described by critic Henry Morley as 'perspective representations of a railway station frequently repeated') were the order of the day. There were, however, simpler patterns available which featured flat, stylized, naturalistic motifs.

◁Some of the Indian designs from Owen Jones's influential design manual *The Grammar of Ornament* (1856). The book (which is now reprinted) illustrates a wide range of patterns including Gothic, Oriental, Moorish and Classical.

Some of the most attractive patterns were designed by Owen Jones, whose famous book *The Grammar of Ornament* (1856) illustrates the great variety of current patterns, and they foreshadowed those that were to be produced by William Morris (see pages 98–9); by the 1860s some of the more self-consciously fashionable homes favoured these styles. Reading between the lines in the household guides, it seems that these papers were very brightly coloured, because they felt it necessary to recommend to their readers that the colours, however bright, should blend, and that the colour of the 'ornament' should be similar in tone to the background.

Furnishing Fabrics

The recently developed jacquard loom and roller-printing techniques meant that the furnishing fabrics of the early Victorians could be as elaborately patterned as their favourite wallpapers. The most popular designs featured birds, flowers and decorative trelliswork. In a fashionably decorated house of the 1840s the predominant colours would be crimson and bottle green, but by the 1860s a new generation of chemical dyes meant that fabric manufacturers could experiment with brighter colours like prussian blue, purple, yellow and green. (A range of embroidery silks in these colours was also available for the decoration of footstools and other items of domestic comfort around the home.)

As with everything else in Victorian furnishing arrangements, a variety of materials was available for different purposes. Heavy patterned wools, velvets or 'rep' (wool, silk or cotton with a corded surface) or possibly damask (especially in combinations of silk and wool or silk and cotton) were used for curtains and upholstery. Chairs were also covered in fabrics woven from horsehair and leather. At a time when spring-cleaning meant a really radical household cleaning session when all the dust and smoke-grimed insulating furnishings were exchanged for summer materials, heavy window draperies would generally be put away in favour of lightweight fabrics such as chintz or cotton.

Furnishing fabrics, however, meant more than simply curtains and upholstery. Much of the impression of oppressive clutter in a Victorian home was a result of the taste for draperies, whether elaborately arranged at the windows and pelmets, as draught-excluders over the doors, or spread over tables and hung across mantelpieces. In some way or other, virtually all the available space in the principal rooms was 'upholstered'. Journals of the time were particularly full of ideas about how to drape curtains and 'dress' pelmets. Typically, it was suggested that pelmets

△For those devoted to the Gothic Revival, this suitably ecclesiastical wallpaper design, c. 1840–50, was available, printed from woodblocks.

△Bright colours were popular with the Victorians, whether in exuberant and elaborate florals interwoven with rococo scrollwork such as the example of c.1860 from Woollams & Co. (left), or in flat, stylized designs such as the rose and leaf wallpaper of c.1852 from Sanderson (top right) which would have been selected by those conscious of the principles of 'good design'. Pale colours and simpler, more delicate florals were considered suitable for bedrooms. The block-printed paper (above right) has a trailing pattern with small flower bunches printed in approximately twenty-four colours. First available from Sanderson in 1870, it is an enduringly popular design.

◁This block-printed cotton chintz of 1850, called 'Victoria and Albert', shows the sort of repeat pattern of realistic flowers that was so popular at the mid-century.

WALLPAPERS AND FABRICS/2

should be covered in the curtain fabric, hung with a valance, and trimmed with braid and tassels – the curtains would then hang behind this. The curtains were to be over-long so that they could be extravagantly looped back, and behind these would hang a machine-lace or muslin curtain – later to become the ubiquitous net of the suburbs.

The excessively ornate arrangements of the curtains were symptomatic of the desire for everything in one's villa to be just a little more than it seemed, and led Charles Eastlake to complain of this in his *Hints on Household Taste* (1868):

The useful and convenient little rod has grown into a large lumbering pole, constructed of metal far too thin in proportion to its diameter. In place of the little finials to prevent rings slipping off are gigantic fuchsias, or other flowers, made of brass, gilt bronze or even china. The curtains are over-long so that they can be looped up in clumsy folds over two large and eccentric-looking metal hooks . . . also the frequent addition of fringes . . .

On a more practical level, however, Victorian homes did use roller blinds and Venetian blinds, which were very popular in drawing-room windows throughout the period. *Cassell's Household Guide* gave instructions on how to construct them, and mentioned that Venetian blinds were also available ready-made in iron, japanned in strong bright colours.

Carpets and Floorcoverings

Early Victorian floorcoverings followed the trend for elaborate pattern and, as a result of the manufacturers' desire to display their expertise and ingenuity, often displayed even more ornate arrangements of naturalistic designs and

scrollwork than other furnishings. Especially popular was a shaded three-dimensional effect, examples of which were displayed in the Great Exhibition. One was described by Henry Morley as having 'a landscape pattern on it, asking you to walk on sky and water' – another as 'drawn to imitate an ornamental ceiling with beams and mouldings'.

The machine-weaving techniques which made these designs possible also brought carpet within the reach of the majority of villa dwellers, with fitted carpets in the wealthier homes. There were two main types: a cut-pile variety (the 'Geneva') which had a velvety appearance, and a looped, uncut pile called the 'Brussels'. Turkey pattern rugs (thick wool carpets with bold, colourful designs) might also be arranged around dining and drawing-room floors. These carpets were still comparatively expen-

△ **Almost every surface in this parlour is covered in elaborately patterned fabric: not only is there opulent flock paper on the walls and an equally obtrusive carpet, but also many examples of the Victorian lady's handiwork.**

sive and elaborate, and would only be used in the main reception rooms. Other rooms were more likely to have carpet or oilcloth squares spread over deal floorboards stained 'mahogany' or given an 'oak' varnish. Another treatment for floorboards, particularly in bedrooms, was to scrub the boards with sand and water to give a smooth, pale finish. All around the house, little rugs would be placed, mainly 'rag' rugs made from scraps of material or trimmings from carpets, to serve as draught excluders.

The stairs and hall posed special problems, being important thoroughfares and liable to more wear and tear than

If the right kinds of fabrics and wallpaper are chosen for a room, a 'period' feel can be given even without the addition of expensive antiques. As far as possible, choose paper and fabric in the same natural materials and made by the same techniques and in the same sorts of colours as they were originally; it is better to choose from the many Victorian designs still being produced today than to opt for a modern imitation in a 'Victorian-style' design. The addition of such trimmings as tassels and fringes also helps to give the right effect.

◁Virtuoso patterns were not restricted to wallpapers and furnishing fabrics: carpets might be even more elaborate. These two disconcertingly naturalistic designs (left and below left) from *Cassell's Household Guide* were machine-made with 'infinite variety in the arrangement of the forms'.

other parts of the house. *Cassell's Household Guide* recommended a 'floor cloth' (oilcloth) for the hall, a type of linoleum made from cork and linseed oil on a hessian backing, which if possible should be the width of the passage. If not, the floor on each side was to be painted the same colour as the background of the pattern on the floorcloth. Alternatively, the hall could be covered with a piece of the stair carpet (usually a plain 'Brussels' or a plain bordered felt). Oilcloths often had geometric designs imitative of the encaustic tiles of grander houses. As the century progressed, interest in decorative tiles increased, and more modest homes would commonly have tiled porches and halls.

◁Flatter patterns were available, too, such as this geometric carpet design, also illustrated in *Cassell's*.

INFLUENCES ON STYLE: *The Great Exhibition*

The Victorian taste for elaborate, heavily ornate furniture and furnishings was nowhere more apparent than in the British exhibits at the Great Exhibition of the Industry of All Nations in 1851. The exhibition, organized within the space of two years through the combined energies of Prince Albert and a team of eminent Victorians led by Sir Henry Cole who was later to found the Victoria and Albert Museum, brought together the manufacturing might of more than half the world under the roof of the Crystal Palace. There had previously been a number of exhibitions concerned with the engineering industry, but this was the first show to include large quantities of the latest in domestic furniture, furnishings and appliances. Thanks to the 'shilling days' and the excursions organized by the railway companies, huge numbers of the British population visited the exhibition and came away with ideas for the decoration of their homes.

The aim of the exhibition was to display the fruits of British manufacturing industry side by side with products from the rest of the world, to show that British goods could stand against the stiffest competition. The manufacturers of Birmingham and Sheffield were particularly adept at applying an enormous amount of superfluous decoration to every conceivable household object: gas lamps were ingeniously disguised as convolvulus plants; children's cribs disappeared beneath a weight of rococo ornament, complete with canopies held aloft by 'guardian angels'; and fabrics and carpets were alive with gardens, animals, birds and exotic flowers. Such excessive decoration was the result of over-enthusiastic applications of the latest manufacturing techniques.

The 'Chamber of Horrors'

After the Great Exhibition, the Government bought a selection of the products that had been shown there to display in the Museum of Manufactures in Pall Mall. The intention was to instruct the public in the principles of good design, and by implication good taste. Unfortunately it was soon apparent that, of the goods selected, the foreign ones displayed more of the 'right principles' that Sir Henry Cole and his colleagues had identified than the British examples, which emphatically displayed the wrong ones: a disregard for structural form and function, a perverse concentration on the superficial aspects of design (all that ornament) and a consistent and unacceptable inclination to 'imitate nature'. Cole responded by setting up a 'Chamber of Horrors' at the museum, itemizing in minute and embarrassing detail why the offending articles – furniture, furnishings, clothing and household goods – were so wrong, despite the fact that almost identical articles could be found in every middle-class dwelling in the country. The outraged response revealed just how accurate an indication of the average household decor Cole's selection was. One visitor to the show, Henry Morley, wrote a piece for *Household Words* (a journal established by Dickens), satirically describing his changed perceptions once he had acquired 'some correct principles of taste':

When we reached the door of Chimborazo Villa . . . I abstained from asking why a Sphinx in brass, with a large wart upon her neck, had been selected as the knocker to a door stained in imitation of rosewood, and why the door stood between two wooden Ionic columns, painted to resemble porphyry.

The debates were to continue, but it was difficult to combat the Victorian taste for conspicuous decoration, especially since many considered it ungentlemanly, even unChristian, not to furnish the home with the degree of ostentation in keeping with one's social position. It was not until the 1870s that the forceful exponents of the Aesthetic Movement began to exert a lightening influence on the decor of the average Victorian home.

△◁**The Great Exhibition and the building that housed it – the Crystal Palace – were major landmarks of their day. The items shown in the Hardware Hall typify the ornate designs of most of the British exhibits.** ◁◁**The roller-printed cotton depicting the Crystal Palace and some of the foreign visitors to it is a fine example of the many souvenirs of the exhibition.** ◁**The organizers hoped that they were showing British design at its best, but this chair, embellished with marquetry, a carved lion, fruit and foliage, and a painted portrait of Prince Albert, shows the reality.**

FIREPLACES

The advent of smoke-control zones in the 1960s and the subsequent popularity of central heating has often made the fireplace a redundant feature in suburbia. This is unfortunate, for as the focal point not only of the room but also of family life the hearth often shows the architectural style of the house at its best.

As in domestic technology generally, the open fire was slow to evolve. Loudon described the increased economy and cleanliness of central heating as early as 1833 in his *Encyclopaedia*, and by the mid-century public buildings and larger houses were commonly heated by hot water circulating in massive cast-iron radiators. In suburbia, however, a deep-seated attachment for open fires remained – after all, both coal and servants were cheap. The suburban Victorians thus incorporated an open fire into nearly every room they built, and many fine examples have survived and can be bought today.

◁This fireplace in a middle-class parlour of 1880 has an arched register grate (the register plate is missing) in a *faux marbre* surround that is almost completely concealed by the fringed mantel valance and other fireplace paraphernalia, as was the custom of the High Victorian period.

Hob Grates

In Georgian and early Victorian suburban homes, the hob grate was the standard form of fireplace. The coal was retained by three or four horizontal bars set between two iron side-plates which were formed into hobs for heating saucepans or kettles. These grates were fixed into the brickwork of rectangular openings that were really miniature versions of the huge wood-burning fireplaces of former times. After the Industrial Revolution, hob grates were mass-produced by many firms, the most famous of which were the Dale Company of Coalbrookdale and the Scottish Carron Company, which employed John Adam as a designer and created mainly neo-classical designs with elegant castings featuring swags and medallions.

Unfortunately, the large rectangular chimney opening, while suitable for wood which burnt on the floor of the hearth, often did not remove sulphurous coal smoke efficiently, and the fire itself was raised too high from the floor for a coal fire to warm the feet. Large, roaring fires created sufficient up-draught to

△This hob grate of about 1850 was probably not used for pans or kettle as the hobs, or side-plates, are quite small, but it has a detachable trivet for a kettle. The surround is plain, decorative detail being provided by the cast-iron fender and the rests for the poker and tongs.

clear the smoke, but also sucked in great draughts of icy air from under door- and window-frames, resulting in frozen backs and scorched faces. Some relief was afforded to the ladies by firescreens placed to shield their cheeks from the heat and thus preserve their complexions (as well as giving them something else to embroider).

Register Grates

The obvious answer to the problem of draughts was to restrict the throat of the chimney by means of a metal plate to create a smaller draught, but one fast enough to ensure efficient smoke removal. These iron plates were called registers, and by 1840 register grates had become the standard fitting, and remained so until the next century.

This form of grate had a back and sides of ironwork completely closing off the chimney save for a small opening in which rested the register plate. On lighting the fire, the plate was swung fully open to allow the smoke to escape easily, but once the chimney was hot and the draught established the plate was closed just enough to suck out the smoke and fumes without losing all the heat up the chimney, and also to prevent some of the cold draughts.

By the mid-century the square form of grate was considered old-fashioned, and arched register grates were becoming increasingly popular and ever more ornate. The sides were splayed to reflect more heat into the room, and firebricks began to be used to line the fire compartment itself. The strong draught still burned coal too quickly, however, and the metal in contact with the hot coals tended to distort and wear out.

Curiously, the answer to many of the problems of English fireplaces had been described in 1797 by the American statesman Count Rumford in an essay. He rejected the register grate and recommended reducing the chimney throat to 10 cm (4 in) to create a good draught, lowering the fire to floor level to prevent this draught from burning coal too quickly and to warm the floor, reducing the depth of the fireplace, and splaying the sides so that more heat could be reflected into the room. He also recommended firebricks, as metal conducts heat away from the fire too quickly, so that its temperature drops and it burns inefficiently. Firebricks retained heat and allowed a very small coal fire to burn well. It took more than a hundred years for his ideas to be fully adopted, although supposedly Rumfordized grates were advertised.

The inventive Victorians experimented with many other types of grate, some designed to reduce pollution, but the essential conservatism regarding the coal fire ensured that designs displayed at the Great Exhibition were still on sale fifty years later.

Fire Surrounds

A typical fire surround of the mid-nineteenth century would be quite simply and elegantly decorated – the side pieces being reeded and having small roundels or brackets at the joint with the mantelpiece. In keeping with its symbolic importance, however, the fire surround would be fairly substantial in size and constructed of marble, or stone painted as marble, or slate, wood or plaster. The mantelpiece would typically be arranged with a rigidly symmetrical array of ornaments which might include a clock in the centre flanked by candlesticks or dried flowers displayed under a glass dome. The almost classical simplicity of the fireplace was, however, lost in most mid-Victorian homes, since it was fashionable to dress the mantelpiece

△ In summer, the enthusiasm for fireplace decoration would be given free rein: the heavy chenille or velvet valance of winter was replaced by lace hangings with curtains draped so that the arrangement looked like a proscenium arch. Flowers – real or artificial – would be used to fill the hearth.

with a valance made from a heavy, possibly embroidered material hung with tassels and fringes. The all-important firescreens were also perfect vehicles for all manner of ornamental excesses, being decorated with feathers, embroidery, paintings or any other handiwork that the ladies of the household were inspired to create. This urge to embellish was given particular scope in the summer months, when the gaping hole in the firegrate would be concealed beneath mounds of folded paper or shredded fabrics, and *Cassell's* recommended putting 'a slight wreath of myrtle on top of the shavings, or carelessly throw a few well-made muslin roses about'.

Towards the end of the century, the fire surrounds themselves began to be more richly decorated. They were also larger than their early Victorian counterparts, with the mantelpiece supported on plain curved brackets set on to the side pieces. Marble was still the favoured material, and was expensive enough not to need any ostentatious decoration. Wooden fire surrounds also became more popular as they could not only be carved in elaborate designs but could also incorporate shelves on which a collection of unusual or exotic artefacts could be displayed.

Since so many suburban Victorian houses have been demolished or converted into flats, there is a vast number of original fireplaces on the market, salvaged by enterprising individuals with shops specializing in such items. Beware of putting a fireplace of the wrong style or period into your house: one way of avoiding this is to look at a neighbouring house with its original features intact and choose one as close as possible in style.

KITCHENS/1

Of all the rooms in a mid-Victorian middle-class household, the kitchen is the one least likely to be reproduced today, for very good reasons. The modern idea of an all-purpose activity room where children can play under the watchful eye of their parents was unknown to the middle classes; the kitchen was solely for the preparation of food and was peopled by servants. Being technically the domain of the cook, the mid-Victorian kitchen was hidden from public view and more than likely to be at least partly below ground level and therefore inadequately lit and poorly ventilated, making the cooking area very hot and stuffy and the ancillary store-rooms and pantries cool but often damp. There is a certain irony, therefore, in the present fashion for converting the basements of early nineteenth-century terraced houses into family/cooking/eating areas, when the mid-Victorian middle classes eventually found them unsuitable even for their servants. As one moved lower down the social scale, the kitchen was of course more and more the hub of family life as it is in many middle-class homes today. In poorer homes separate kitchens were unknown, since only the living room would have been heated; at this open fire all the cooking would have been done.

△ This late Victorian kitchen (actually at Gustav Holst's birthplace, now part of Cheltenham Museum), shows a variety of typical utensils and equipment, including a grill rack hanging to the right of the range, used for cooking chops or steak over the fire and with a small cup to catch the meat juices.

In the nineteenth century, houses were really only shells with doors, windows and fireplaces, and very little of the plumbing, wiring, fixtures and fittings which add so much to the cost of a twentieth-century house (although the elaborate systems of wires which operated the servants' bells can be found in many houses built before the advent of electricity). As suburban houses were nearly all rented rather than owned, the tenants themselves had no desire to build in features which would become part of the landlord's fixtures. The progressing century however, saw more fixtures provided, although nothing like the built-in kitchens of the late twentieth century.

The Range

The most important fitting was the coal range used for cooking. It had been invented in around 1770, and reigned supreme until superseded by gas and electricity 150 years later. Although ranges came in many shapes and sizes, the basic design remained unchanged for more than a century after it first appeared. It consisted of a coal fire contained by the horizontal bars of a grate, the top bar often hinged at each end to fall forward, thereby providing a rest for kettles or saucepans. Hooks, cranes, and swivelling trivets were also employed to hold pots and pans close to the fire which was quite open to the chimney. To one side of the fire was an oven used for baking (not roasting, which was always done in front of the fire). As the oven tended to be hotter on one side, a turntable inside enabled cakes and bread to be rotated by hand during baking. To provide a more even heat, better models had a flue surrounding the oven through which the smoke and hot gases passed before entering the chimney. By opening and closing various dampers and bypass flues, a measure of temperature control was also achieved. On the other side of the fire was a tank to provide hot water. In cheap models this had to be ladled out, but a tap was provided in others. Later in the century a cistern and ball-cock arrangement ensured that the hot tank was topped up with fresh cold water automatically.

Roasting was still done the traditional way, on a spit in front of a bright fire, but the smaller, more economical fires of these ranges presented a problem if the joint of meat was large – and, judging by Mrs Beeton, it often was. Expensive ranges had adjustable side cheeks to the firegrate which, by means of a ratchet, could be moved to create a bigger fire and a greater surface of radiant heat. The meat would be mounted on a horizontal spit with a large tin beneath to catch the dripping. In grander homes smoke jacks used vanes set within the chimney which turned by force of the draught up the flue to rotate the meat by means of gears and pulleys. The average suburban home had to resort to more mundane methods such as the bottle jack, in common use throughout the nineteenth century. This was a clockwork motor housed in a bottle-shaped brass case and often suspended from the mantelpiece. The joint of meat was hung on it and slowly revolved. Being suspended vertically, a smaller fire could be used, with Dutch ovens or 'hasteners'

– semicircular metal reflectors – employed to concentrate the radiant heat of the fire. (Bottle jacks are frequently seen decorating the hearths of country pubs.)

Undoubtedly the almost universal adoption of ranges depended on the railway system to supply the prodigious amounts of coal they consumed. Cheap coal and domestic labour did not encourage economy, but gradually ranges were improved, mainly through the development of the closed range or 'kitchener' in which the fire was enclosed beneath a hot plate and all the hot gases could therefore be forced through flues to heat ovens and boilers rather than going straight up the chimney. The hot plate was good for simmering: it would have circular holes with removable lids so that saucepans could be exposed to the direct heat of the fire if necessary; but the grate

◁The 'Albert Kitchener' was made by Messrs Thomlinson Walker of York in about 1850. The hot-water tank is on the right and pots would have been suspended from the crane. Flues to control temperature were opened and closed by the knobs above the oven door.

KITCHENS/2

was rarely large enough to spit-roast meat and the prejudice against roasting in the oven had to be overcome. To this end a second roasting oven was provided in which the flues were arranged to provide more intense heat from the top and also ventilation to enable the meat to dry slightly and develop a browned surface, as well as remove the smoke from burnt fat which marred the flavour. Some single-oven ranges had complicated flue and damper mechanisms to allow the oven to be used for roasting or baking.

The strong draughts created by the flues caused heavy coal consumption, and the iron parts often wore out from the intense heat. Further refinements, mainly using anthracite, culminated in the Swedish Aga of 1929, but even this could not overcome the problems of inconvenience and dirt that accompany solid-fuel cooking which has, unless social cachet overcomes practical argument, almost died out. So too, therefore, has truly roasted (as opposed to oven-baked) meat, save in a few country pubs.

Kitchen Furniture

The only other item of fitted furniture in the kitchen might be a dresser, which was often set alongside the range in the recess created by the chimney breast. Invariably these simple but solid constructions were of painted wood. (Indeed, very often the whole kitchen was lined with matchboarding which would be painted for ease of cleaning.) Narrow shelves enabled everything on them to be seen, and grooves to retain plates and dozens of cup hooks allowed chinaware to be fully displayed. Beneath these was set a deeper shelf for bulkier items such as a bread bin; it was not a work surface. Under this would be several deep drawers for table linen and, beneath those, cupboards for utensils

▷**A scene from an exhibition at Manchester in 1908 shows the latest electrical gadgetry, including an oven, hotplate, urns, kettle, iron and a griddle, all of which were regarded with suspicion by many.**

that were not kept over the range.

All work was done at the kitchen table – usually of scrubbed deal – set in the middle of the room and as large as possible. It was lower than the modern work surface and therefore more suited to energetic activity such as kneading dough or cake stirring. Usually one or two cutlery drawers were incorporated in it. The need to do lengthy jobs like hulling peas or deseeding sultanas often meant a couple of wooden chairs accompanied the table, at which the servants would also eat their meals.

The sink, in white or brown glazed stoneware with a single cold tap, was relegated to the scullery. Its wooden draining board sometimes had a large plate rack over it. Here, too, was the wash copper (often cast iron) a capacious container set into brickwork over a fire and capped by a wooden lid. Here the weekly wash was done as well as the annual Christmas pudding.

These bulky items have nearly all been removed, but the deep recess for a range can still be seen in many Victorian houses. Contrary to some popular advice, it is not a good idea to put a cooker here: it is usually dark and too low for modern cookers which should also abut a work surface for convenience. Such a recess is better suited to fitted cupboards or even an old range which, blackleaded and burnished, looks attractive and may even be pressed into service for platewarming at Christmas or other festive occasions.

◁**The 1874 advertisement for the Livingstone range (top) also shows a Dutch oven with bottle jack. The scullery (bottom) contains laundry equipment, including a mangle and washing dollies.**

No one would want the inconvenience of a Victorian kitchen today, but it is possible to create something of its atmosphere in a modern kitchen by careful choice of materials and decorations and by incorporating one or two original items such as a rocking chair or set of pans. The effect should be simple and uncluttered, but without the cold clinical look of some modern kitchens. Walls and woodwork should be painted white or cream, with any details perhaps picked out in bottle green or chocolate brown. Keep fitted units to a minimum and, if you have space, do have a table and chairs of simple, sturdy wooden construction. Wall cupboards, if any, should be painted to match the walls, but plenty of open shelves should display crockery, storage jars and utensils, which can become decorative features. A painted dresser of the period is a great asset.

Lighting can be a problem. Simple painted metal wall brackets with glass shades, based on old gas-light designs, may be used to light specific areas such as cooker or sink, but the modern idea of recessed spotlights in the ceiling can be very effective without being obtrusive in a traditional setting. It is quite acceptable to mix the old with the new, but not the old with items pretending to be old.

Where modern standards demand modern products such as easily cleaned work surfaces, stainless-steel draining boards, a mixer tap, cooker and fridge, these should be as simple and functional in design as possible, so as not to detract from any Victorian furniture or other items. Avoid units or fittings with bits of applied filigree or other decorative work, and often described as 'Victorian style'. These usually look cheap, and clash with the real thing.

BEDROOMS

The early Victorian bedroom is perhaps the one room in the house where Victorian and modern taste most closely coincide, and where it would be possible to undertake a near-authentic decorative scheme. Unlike the rest of the house, there seems to have been a consensus amongst the Victorians that bedroom furnishings should be kept simple, for both aesthetic and hygienic reasons.

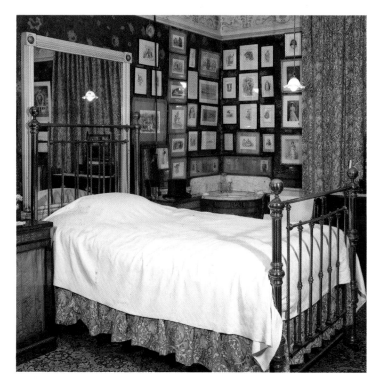

The main feature of the room – the bed – would, in the early part of the period in particular, be a romantic four-poster, or possibly a 'half-tester' which had a canopy at the head of the bed only. By the 1860s, brass beds were gaining in popularity, but were still on a significantly ample scale compared to the modern utilitarian variety. The four-posters and half-testers were decorated with substantial draperies and valances, with most of the household guides recommending pretty concoctions of 'dimmity [a fine, self-patterned cotton fabric] and lace' or 'dimmity with a chintz or coloured cambric border'. White or pale colours were to be used, but care was to be taken over the selection of the colour; as *Cassell's Household Guide* pointed out, for example, 'a pale green will impart the cadaverous hue of sickness'. The structural part of the bed would be of mahogany or, if this could not be afforded, of beechwood (which then had to be painted in imitation of oak); half-testers were also available in iron.

It appears that the remaining furniture was refreshingly simple, if on an inevitably ponderous scale, and consisted of a wardrobe, chest of drawers, washstand and a small chair or two. The copious amounts of applied decoration common in furniture in the rest of the house were considered unsuitable for the bedroom, possibly because of the increased concern with hygiene and the need to keep the room as free from dust as possible. Some indication of status, however, had to be apparent in the scale or type of furniture in the room – for example, the most desirable wardrobes were the 'winged' type, that is, a double ward-

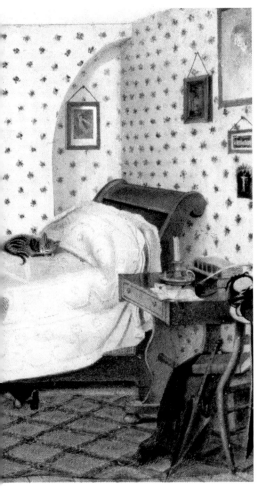

◁ △ **Even relatively grand bedrooms were fairly simple. The bedroom (far left), with its Morris-style wallpaper and curtains, frieze and plain brass bed, is in the Aesthetic taste. The painting of 1861 (left) by Alice Squire depicts a more modest but pretty attic room, while George Scharf's 1868 drawing (above) shows his wrought-iron bed with half-tester.**
▷ **A washstand was an essential item until plumbed-in basins (as shown far left) became more usual.**

robe with a central mirrored section, behind which were drawers and other receptacles. The Victorians were not above employing a little simple do-it-yourself technology in their furnishings, along lines that could be found in any household magazine today. For example, *Cassell's Household Guide* includes instructions on how to make simple 'built-in' wardrobes in the chimney recesses by mounting a pole (a 'bronzed' iron rod) and concealing the hanging clothes by means of dimmity or chintz curtains, or even 'lace over pink cambric'.

Washstands with marble tops and a further small marble slab on a lower shelf were a bit above the average; a more modest version would have a mahogany top, and no marble. The bedroom might also contain a hip bath, a typical type being painted and grained dark brown on the outside, cream on the inside. (Despite the fact that the water had to be carried up and down several flights of stairs, it seems that many early Victorians bathed every day, assisted of course by a long-suffering servant who did the fetching and carrying.) Prettily decorated – with flowers or oriental motifs – pitchers, soap dishes and wash bowls would add a touch of colour. The room would be decorated with a wallpaper of a small floral pattern, and have scrubbed floorboards and rag rugs or carpet squares.

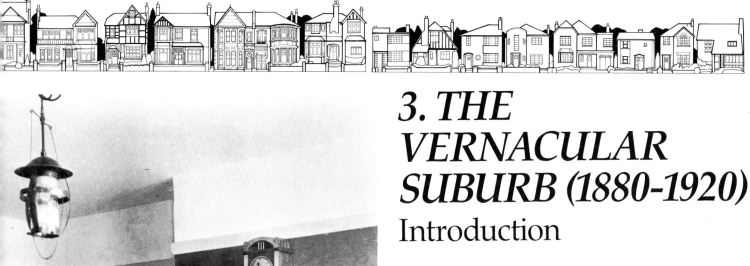

3. THE VERNACULAR SUBURB (1880-1920)

Introduction

The definition of a desirable social position had been a relatively simple one for the first generation of suburbanites: they had merely emulated the gentry. If direction was required, there were numerous descriptions of a gentleman and what his establishment should contain. For the new generation of middle classes, however, establishing their positions in society in the 1880s and 1890s, the question was more complicated. The poet and essayist Matthew Arnold (1822–88) summed up the problem in *Culture and Anarchy*, written in 1869, in which (while not denying the virtues of either) he described the upper classes as barbarians and the upper middle classes as philistines. In his view, the energy and high spirits of the former disguised a boorish and intellectually backward class, more interested in sport than ideas, while the latter were innovative and inventive but narrow-minded, bigoted and self-satisfied, pursuing money for its own sake without knowing what to do with it. Arnold thought that two qualities were missing from these social models: the first was a sense of intellectual curiosity, a thirst for knowledge and the placing of value on education, which Arnold called 'Light'; and the second was an aesthetic spirit, appreciative of beauty and art, which he called 'Sweetness'.

◁**Two very different interiors of the period: a beautifully detailed room in the Aesthetic taste (far left) contrasts with the simple style of an Arts and Crafts interior (left).**

THE VERNACULAR SUBURB/2

Sweetness and Light and the Aesthetic Movement

The Sweetness and Light argument had a deep effect upon many middle-class Victorians, giving them something new to which they could aspire. The desire for enlightenment and the clamour for more educational opportunities fuelled many of the late-Victorian philanthropic organizations, while the interest in art spurred on the Aesthetic Movement: art and beauty were now essential in every home. It was no longer enough to have refined manners and to vote Tory in order to maintain status; one had to be 'artistic' as well.

Taking advantage of this dilemma, a new generation of writers on domestic subjects quickly set about producing guides for the would-be 'aesthetic' home-maker. Unlike their predecessors, these publications were devoted solely to interior decoration and aesthetic matters. It was assumed that the problems which had vexed their parents – the basics of dealing with servants or tradespeople, or arranging a dinner party – were now second nature. Mrs Haweis, in *The Art of Decoration* (1889), described the new mood: 'Most people are now alive to the importance of beauty as a refining influence. The appetite for artistic instruction is now ravenous.' The degree of interest is illustrated by the fact that Mrs Haweis was also able to write a book which simply described the furnishings of a few select homes, much as fashionable colour magazines would do nowadays, in a beautifully presented volume entitled *Beautiful Houses (Being a description of certain well-known artistic houses)*.

Mrs Haweis did not herself give strict guidelines, preferring instead to set out the principles for artistic decorators to create their own milieu. As early as 1868,

Charles Eastlake, in *Hints on Household Taste*, had also given general instructions, recommending that one should collect and cherish examples of rare old porcelain, of ivory carving, of ancient metalwork, of enamels, of Venetian glass, of anything which illustrates good design and skilful workmanship . . . educating the eye to appreciate what really constitutes good taste. An Indian ginger jar, a Flemish beer-jug, a Japanese fan, may each become a valuable lesson in decorative form and colour.

Response to this kind of encouragement was not always as well judged as it might have been. While Eastlake and others, notably William Morris (see pages 98–9), were concerned to increase awareness of the possibilities of good design, the now-legendary cluttered interiors of the 1880s and 1890s were the immediate, simple response. For popular writers like Mrs Panton who wrote *From Kitchen to Garrett* in 1890 (in which she speaks directly to 'Edwin and Angelina', newly arrived in the suburbs), the *appearance* of an 'artistic' and, significantly, an 'oriental' home, was her only aim. Accordingly she urged her readers to decorate their home in 'aesthetic' colours, and to gather about them a liberal sprinkling of the symbols of aestheticism: peacocks' feathers, Japanese fans, ferns, palms, books and drawings.

The Aesthetic Movement at its most extreme was soon an object of ridicule, and its exponents were regularly derided in *Punch* cartoons as rather effete, vapid characters. But their ideas, particularly in combination with those of the Arts and Crafts Movement which had its roots in the same philosophy, had a not entirely superficial effect on the average home. The Arts and Crafts

Movement, in particular, pointed the way to lighter, brighter, more functional interiors, and encouraged a more rational use of space than the previously strict division of rooms – those for show and those 'below stairs' – allowed.

It was also during this period that retailers first arranged their products in room settings in the larger stores and in their catalogues, a move that seems obvious now, but which was another indication of a new sensitivity about the importance of design and presentation. (Many stores, too, were now offering HP terms, enabling consumers to buy complete sets of furniture in the newest styles.) The enthusiasm for 'artistic' interiors prompted the manufacturers of

◁◁**How to be 'artistic' was the new preoccupation for those moving into a Vernacular suburb, and retailers of home furnishings were not slow to exploit this: the 1909 advertisement for Waring and Gillow emphasizes the 'artistic effect' of their products.**

◁**Queen Anne's Gardens, part of Bedford Park, a suburb populated by people of an artistic bent. The houses, many of them designed by Norman Shaw, were in the Queen Anne style, variations of which were later to appear throughout suburbia.**

wallpapers, soft furnishings and furniture to employ architects and artists (the profession of designer as such was not yet properly recognized) to produce designs. This resulted in a general improvement in standards that was an example to the rest of Europe. The theoretical force behind the Arts and Crafts Movement also went to Europe, where it helped to shape the beginnings of the Modern Movement and the 'Machine Age'. In the years leading up to the First World War, however, suburban taste in Britain tended increasingly towards an amalgam of period styles, preferring a simplistic image of a cosy cottage furnished with 'olde worlde' furniture to the rigours of modernism.

◁*The Decoration and Furniture of Town Houses* **by Robert Edis (1881) was an essential work of reference for those seeking guidance on the appropriate furnishings for an artistic home. This print from the book shows items of art furniture including a dining-room sideboard with a collection of oriental ware. The division of the walls into three areas was also desirable.**

THE REVOLUTION IN HOUSE DESIGN, 1880–1914/1

Various Acts of Parliament in the nineteenth century, particularly the Public Health Act of 1875, raised the standard of house building in Britain to unprecedented heights, but only in terms of construction, ventilation and sanitation. The early byelaw streets (see page 56) to be found in every town today, although well built and worthy of care, were aesthetically limited and did tend towards monotony. Ruskin's view that 'existing houses will be none the worse for having little bits of better work fitted to them' was taken up with gusto by building speculators who continued to adorn row upon row of suburban houses with Gothic features until the end of the century.

Ruskin himself hated the suburban sprawl, and while it has always been fashionable to deride it, things did change, and the late Victorian and Edwardian period witnessed a revolution in housing design that was to have a dramatic visual impact on suburbia itself. A succession of brilliant architects created not only practical houses designed to fit the needs of their occupants but also developed and refined new styles to delight the beholder.

Both technically and aesthetically, therefore, Britain soon led the world in housing design. Although most houses built in Britain in the twentieth century have been influenced by this 'Domestic Revival', as it has been called, its legacy has not, however, been properly recognized in Britain. Small-house design is still regarded as lacking in glamour unless practised by foreigners, yet the opposite was once true. For example, from 1896 to 1903 the German government appointed Hermann Muthesius as cultural attaché to the German Embassy in London in order to examine English housing. His book *Das Englische Haus* (Berlin, 1905) is a remarkable survey of English domestic architecture of the late nineteenth and early twentieth century; it clearly had a profound effect upon Continental design and architecture, and made English architects such as C.F.A. Voysey, R. Norman Shaw, Ernest George and Philip Webb famous in Europe. It is perhaps significant that the book was not published in English until 1979.

◁▷ **The main staircase (right) and an exterior view (left) of the Red House in Upton in Kent, designed by Philip Webb for William Morris and built in 1861. The house that began the revolution in domestic architecture, it broke the classical mould and heralded a looser, so-called free style of building: windows, for example, might now be placed to suit the internal layout rather than some notion of regularity. The Red House also paved the way for the Domestic Revival.**

The Red House

Remarkably, the origins of the Domestic Revival can be traced to one building: the Red House at Upton near Bexleyheath in Kent, designed for William Morris by his friend Philip Webb, and built in 1861. At this time the Gothic Revival was in full flood; Morris and Webb had themselves been trained in the practice of the well-known architect George Street, a disciple of the great Gothic church-builder Sir George Gilbert Scott (1811–78). Nevertheless, Morris and Webb wanted a fresh approach. While retaining the Gothic theorists' belief in truth and honesty in art, they sought new themes and inspiration in buildings other than churches. They found it in vernacular architecture, that is, the ordinary, traditionally built, non-architect-designed buildings of England, the styles of which depended largely upon the building materials available locally.

Morris and Webb wanted the Red House to be the most beautiful house in Britain, both in structure and contents, all of which were specially designed, as befitted what was to become the spiritual home of the Arts and Crafts Movement. The result, however, was not the recreation of a medieval manor house that Morris fancied it to be. The fact that it does not look very much out of the ordinary to modern eyes is because of its great influence on succeeding generations of architects and housing designs, for it was the prototype which made vernacular traditions respectable.

The house is built, as its name suggests, of red brick to a roughly L-shaped plan. The steeply pitched roof has red tiles with gables and a turret where the two wings meet. There are some oriel windows, and others with large mid-Victorian panes of glass under gently pointed lintel arches. The placing of the windows in the façade is not symmetrical or falsely regular, but follows the demands made by the internal arrangement of the rooms, so that they form a balanced and rhythmic pattern that was to be the hallmark of much housing built afterwards. A covered well in the courtyard complements what is, in effect, a romantic amalgam of vernacular architecture and a plain Gothic style. The latter seems to have ended with village schools of a decade or so later, but the

▷Suburbia in 1905 displayed many elements of the Domestic Revival: turrets, gables, roof tiles and beams.

THE REVOLUTION IN HOUSE DESIGN, 1880–1914/2

vernacular tradition quickly became the dominant factor in house design.

The Queen Anne Style

Morris soon gave up architecture, and Webb was not particularly prolific, but their influence on the exponents of the late Victorian free style, as the seemingly irregular designs were to be called, was incalculable. The most notable exponent of the free style was the prolific Scots architect R. Norman Shaw (1831–1912) who had also been trained in Street's office. He was acquainted with, if not part of, Morris's circle, and it was he who probably did most to popularize the use of vernacular styles and ultimately change the face of suburbia, through the so-called Queen Anne style which he developed in the 1870s.

The term 'Queen Anne' is in some ways a misnomer, since the new style did not attempt to copy the buildings constructed during her short reign (1702–14). Instead, Shaw, aided and possibly inspired by his friend W. E. Nesfield, developed a style which, while deeply rooted in tradition, was highly original. Spurning the then over-commercialized Gothic forms completely, Shaw and Nesfield found inspiration by touring Kent and Sussex and sketching country cottages and town houses. They came up with a curious but refreshing mixture of characteristics. The vernacu-

1. STONE-BUILT SEMI-DETACHED HOUSE, 1870s. The railways made most building materials available everywhere, but there were still interesting regional variations in domestic architecture. The Dutch gable and the single bay window are fairly typical features of the period, but the creamy stone walls give this house a special quality.

2. RED-BRICK HOUSE IN THE QUEEN ANNE STYLE. The distinctive Dutch roof line of 1 is echoed in this house, whose gable, sections of carved brickwork, classical details and sections of jewel-like glass are all features of the Queen Anne style, which first appeared in suburbia in the 1870s. The rising-sun fanlight motif is Arts-and-Crafts-inspired.

3. SEMI-DETACHED HOUSE IN THE QUEEN ANNE STYLE. This large house incorporates all the elements of the Queen Anne style, but (particularly in the liberal application of white stone dressings) with rather less restraint and success than its neighbour to the left. It is an example of some of the more substantial houses built in the style.

lar influence is evident in many features: tiles hanging on the walls, dominant tiled roofs, usually hipped, massive chimneys, gables, dormer windows, decorative plaster work (an old East Anglian craft known as pargetting), and the constant use of red brick. Also evident is the 'builders' classicism' of the seventeenth-century town house: broken pediments over windows, and doors with six panels under simple canopied or shell-shaped porches; plenty of white stone dressings and white painted woodwork offset the red brick. Dutch gables are another common feature of the style, and the windows are, if anything, Elizabethan in feel: large to let in plenty of light, but without the large panes of mid-Victorian housing; instead they have small panes within white-painted glazing bars or lead strips. The resulting Queen Anne style could so easily have been an awful hotch-potch, but it was, thanks to Shaw, genuinely original, and quickly taken up by a new generation of suburbanites thirsting after the spirit of 'Sweetness and Light', who rejected the gloom of their parents' Gothic for the sunny warmth of Queen Anne.

Sweetness and Light in Bedford Park

The new trend in suburban architectural taste appears to have begun with a development, near Chiswick in west

4. TERRACED HOUSE IN THE AESTHETIC STYLE. This house style was commonly built at the end of the nineteenth and beginning of the twentieth century. The carved brick sunflowers set in the wall between the storeys, the decorative brickwork in the gable and the complex glazing and coloured glass of the windows are emblematic of the Aesthetic Movement.

5, 6. TWO STANDARD BYELAW HOUSES, 1890s. At the same time as Queen Anne and Arts and Crafts detailing began to appear in suburbia, many houses were still being built with Gothic features, like the one on the left, or with an uneasy mix of styles, like the house on the right which combines a tile-hung gable and plaque with an angled bay and plain sashes.

7, 8. HOUSES IN THE EARLY VERNACULAR STYLE. The left-hand house of c.1910 with its elaborate fretwork porch also displays elements of the Domestic Revival and even a hint of mock Tudor, as does its neighbour on the right, a semi-detached villa with stone trim and an elaborate Elizabethan-style window. These features were soon to predominate in suburbia.

THE REVOLUTION IN HOUSE DESIGN, 1880–1914/3

London, known as Bedford Park, started in 1875. Only thirty minutes from the City by underground train, Bedford Park was the brainchild of one Jonathan Carr who owned the land and had the idea of developing a new community for artistic people – painters, poets, authors – complete with church, shops, art school and social club. Because he chose Shaw and other Queen Anne architects to design this 'artistic' suburb, the style of the houses there were associated with the Sweetness and Light Movement and became the natural choice for artistic suburbanites of the late nineteenth century.

The details of Bedford Park – Dutch gables, tile hanging, small panes of glass in white-painted wooden windows, and complex roof patterns – have been copied all over suburbia to a greater or lesser extent ever since, but perhaps even more influential was its atmosphere. Though too cramped to be a true 'garden suburb', it is particularly leafy, and the free design and slightly irregular road plan (designed to preserve existing trees), as well as the apparent variety of house types, creates a homely, welcoming, rather cosy atmosphere which (although examples of the severe byelaw streets of the type now surrounding Bedford Park continued to be built up to the First World War) was to become the hallmark of the Garden City Movement and most of twentieth-century suburbia.

The Arts and Crafts House

The Queen Anne style was hugely influential and survives today not only in houses but also in many pubs, libraries, fire stations, churches, and other smallish public buildings of the 1880s and 1890s. By 1900, however, even the speculative builders of suburbia were abandoning the fussy details of the style in favour of the much simpler and more fundamental vernacular forms

△Dutch gables, extensive tile hanging, red brick with white stone dressings and very large areas of windows composed of small panes of glass set in lead or white-painted glazing bars typify the Queen Anne style, as in these houses designed by George and Peto.
◁The less fussy Arts and Crafts open-plan interior at Letchworth shows such structural elements as ceiling beams and strap hinges on the plain plank door.

which a new generation of architects had developed from the tradition exemplified in the Red House. Undoubtedly the greatest of these was C.F.A. Voysey (1857–1941), who built a succession of country houses famous for their simplicity, respect for materials and craftsmanship. There is none of the applied decoration of Queen Anne, and certainly no copying of any earlier style. To Voysey, the house had to be designed for the needs of the occupant and the conditions of the site, embodying the motto: 'Fitness is the basis for beauty'.

The architects of Arts and Crafts houses usually followed four basic principles. Firstly, the Gothicists' notion of truthfulness was developed further, and no attempt was made to hide the structural details of the building. Thus beams and brickwork were left exposed and simple plank doors with strap hinges and cottage latches were often used – to great effect in Voysey's houses. Secondly, the buildings had to be 'organic' in the sense that they should naturally fit their environment almost as if they had grown from the soil, hence the continued use of local vernacular materials and traditional styles. Bricks and tiles from the clays of Sussex, and timber weatherboards from the wooded areas of the south-east were popular, as was the half-timbering of Herefordshire and Cheshire (which foreshadowed the mock Tudor of the 1930s). Pebbledashed walls (the traditional 'Harling' of Cumbria and Scotland) also came into fashion. Thirdly, simplicity was the keynote. Voysey's houses are typically long and low with horizontal windows,

▷ Voysey's use of horizontal window groupings, using leaded lights set in stone surrounds, is seen in this 1891 house (above). The Orchard, Voysey's own house built in 1900 (below), has the steeply pitched roof and sweeping gables that influenced much inter-war housing.

THE REVOLUTION IN HOUSE DESIGN, 1880–1914/4

and imposing barn-like roofs usually incorporating a single gable sweeping down on one side almost to ground level (a much-copied feature in suburbia). Solid buttresses and massive chimneystacks, and thick walls invariably rough-rendered and whitened give a simple, clean effect which is at the same time strong, distinctive and deceptively difficult to emulate well. The fourth principle behind the building of an Arts and Crafts house was quality of craftsmanship – beauty being in the execution as well as the design of a building or a piece of furniture. For some of the early occupants such strong simple styles demanded simplicity in furnishing too. It is not surprising therefore, that Arts and Crafts architects often designed everything in a house from furniture and wallpaper to the very cutlery. (Voysey's famous heart motif is found on the locks and hinges of his doors and even on the keys.) The wealthy client could thus ensure that every aspect of his domestic arrangements though practical and comfortable, was also properly 'artistic'. Fitting modern devices, even small items such as light switches, into such houses can prove a problem if they are not to seem incongruous. In the average suburban house, however, it is far more likely that certain Arts and Crafts features copied from builders' journals are simply incorporated. These features were, however, often of high-quality workmanship, and are well worth preserving.

Arts and Crafts architects lived in a Britain of unprecedented wealth, in which there was also a 'back to the country' spirit which sparked a boom in

1. HOUSE IN THE BEDFORD PARK STYLE, 1890s. Many ordinary suburban dwellings of the late nineteenth century were built incorporating elements of the houses designed by Norman Shaw and his followers at Bedford Park. This one has a red-tiled roof, wooden balcony and roughcast plaster walls set with small-paned windows in the Queen Anne style.

2. SEMI-DETACHED VERNACULAR VILLA, c.1900. Decorative elements of the Vernacular include the fish-scale slates and ridge tiles on the roof, timber balcony and elaborate plasterwork of the gable and eaves, based on the traditional pargetting of East Anglia. The windows show the typical compromise between the practicality of large panes and the charm of small ones.

3. VERNACULAR MOCK-TUDOR HOUSE, c.1900. The revival of vernacular techniques is seen even more clearly in this late Victorian house of the Domestic Revival: the clay tiled roof and mock beams place it firmly in the mould of traditional rural English buildings; and the sturdy brackets supporting the half-timbering and porch roof are in the Arts and Crafts manner.

country-house building never seen before or since. Muthesius noted that the wealthy were flocking out of the towns and into the country, apparently the very opposite of the German experience. For those who could not afford a country house, a new craze satisfied their pastoral fantasies: the restoration of country cottages. The agricultural depression of the 1870s and the subsequent and continued mechanization of agricultural processes left the countryside littered with redundant buildings. Often ancient and invariably decrepit, these former homes of the farm labourer became highly prized rural retreats for the chic middle classes. The new owners stripped plaster from the outside to reveal the timbering, and put in diamond-pattern leaded windows, thus creating another model for the suburbanites lower down the social scale.

The primitive vernacular style of the Arts and Crafts architects owed much to this country cottage vogue, particular features of which became very popular, notably cosy low-ceilinged rooms complete with inglenooks and window-seats. Many architect-designed houses also featured interesting irregular layouts, with windows on two or more sides of a room, and with glass doors opening directly on to terraces or gardens. Such expansiveness was not possible in suburban houses, but the new desire for brighter, sunnier rooms and garden access was certainly instrumental in seeing the elimination of the gloomy 'back extension', such a criticized feature of much suburbia, in favour of the semi-detached house on a squarer plan.

4. ARTS AND CRAFTS HOUSE, c.1910. **The ornamentation on this detached house is restricted to small areas: the carved brickwork, leaded glass and beamed gable are the only decorative details in a fairly plain façade which has been purposely given the simplicity sought by followers of the Arts and Crafts Movement after the showiness of mid-Victorian styles.**

5, 6. TWO SEMI-DETACHED HOUSES. **Stone mullions were very common in early twentieth-century housing in emulation of the Arts and Crafts style, but in the house on the left this feature and a large vernacular tile-hung gable are combined with a Gothic Revival porch, and it succeeds less well than the more unified style of the house on the right.**

7. DETACHED ARTS AND CRAFTS HOUSE. **This house manages to combine many vernacular features into a coherent and reasonably well-balanced design. The emphasis is on asymmetry, as in the position of the roughcast areas in relation to the brick of the walls; the asymmetrical chimney stack is made into a dominant feature.**

THE GARDEN CITY MOVEMENT/1

As the speculative builders of the mid-nineteenth century enthusiastically developed the suburbs to accommodate the middle classes, a minor revolution in working-class housing was also beginning. In many ways it was this development, culminating in the Garden City Movement at the beginning of the twentieth century, that was to influence the appearance of the suburban environment for the following forty years. The archetypal suburb of the 1920s and 1930s, with each house or semi set in its own garden, owes many of its 'traditional' features to these early housing experiments.

◁New Earswick, York, a model village built by Joseph Rountree for his employees, was notable for the involvement of Unwin and Parker, the architects of Letchworth, the first garden city.
▷A broadsheet advertising Bedford Park, London, the first of the garden suburbs planned in the Utopian tradition. The leafy aspect and varied design of the houses were influential.

◁A row of houses at Port Sunlight, near Liverpool, the village built for employees of Lever Brothers. Begun in 1890, the buildings drew upon different styles of vernacular architecture to give a 'village green' atmosphere.

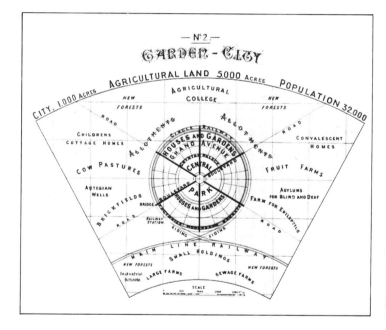

△A diagrammatic plan of Ebenezer Howard's vision of the Garden City, taken from his book *Tomorrow: a Peaceful Path to Real Reform* (1898). The plan shows all the elements Howard felt were essential for these new cities, notably the desired population in relation to the amount of land and the proportion of agricultural land to built-up area. Account is also taken of the need for welfare and transport facilities as well as parkland and allotments.

Driven by a philanthropic concern for their workforce, the wealthy industrialists of the Midlands and North of England began to create 'model villages' to house their employees. The first of these, notably Copley (1849–53) and Ackroyden (1859), both built by a Colonel Ackroyd and Saltaire (1853–63) built by Sir Titus Salt, had little architectural distinction, being for the most part caught up in the 'Battle of the Styles' (see page 52). These developers were agreed that their aim was the creation of a 'medieval village', with all that this

represented in terms of a close-knit, idealized community, symbolically gathered round the village green. The ideal of a medieval village was to be central to future developments on these lines, but an architectural style was also to develop which reflected it more accurately. The real advance in terms of architectural design came with the development in 1890 of Port Sunlight, near Liverpool, for those employed at Lever Brothers, and of Bournville (1898) and New Earswick (1902), created by Cadbury and Rowntree respectively.

The Model Village

The building of Port Sunlight continued under the guidance of a number of different architects until 1913. The houses are arranged in short terraces, each terrace having different architectural features but all drawing upon vernacular traditions in the manner of Norman Shaw. A sense of village community is fostered by the wide expanses of lawn in front of the houses, and by the important inclusion in the plan of a number of community buildings: Hulme Hall, The Lyceum and the village pub The Bridge Inn (which began as a temperance hotel). The houses were of two types: a small cottage comprising scullery, kitchen and three bedrooms; and a larger version which included a parlour and an additional bedroom. The attention to detail in all the houses and the quality of the 'village' as a whole were to attract considerable attention. Muthesius, German propagandist for the modern style, described it with enthusiasm:

Certainly these are only factory workers' houses, but they contain the whole repertoire of contemporary means of expression in such accomplished forms that the estate may be considered the flower of the small modern home in a small space.

Bournville and New Earswick also displayed certain features which were to be influential. At Bournville the estate was laid out with a new emphasis on individual gardens and allotments, and, more significantly, with individual front gardens, the houses being set back from the road by up to 6 m (20 ft). New Earswick was begun by architects Raymond Unwin and Barry Parker, and it features many of their ideas about planning that they were to develop in their work on both Letchworth and Hampstead Garden Suburb: arranging the layout of streets in relation to existing features of the site; having straight main roads and curving subsidiary roads and groups of houses around cul-de-sacs.

Some of these ideas had already been seen at Bedford Park which was a development intended for a middle-class clientele. While its synthesis of Queen Anne classicism and vernacular styles was to have a lasting influence on the development of the external appearance of the average suburban home, the arrangement of the houses in relation to their surroundings, and with an emphasis on gardens, also influenced the Garden City planners. Bedford Park was not planned as such, however: the site had previously belonged to a horticulturalist and was lavishly endowed with trees which it was decided should be preserved. Accordingly, the outline shape of the estate and the lines of the roads were determined by existing boundaries – major roads and railway lines – and by the trees. Because of this, and the fact that the houses were set back from the road with each one (or pair) in its own plot of ground, there is no sense of the straight-line regimentation of many byelaw streets; instead there are interesting leafy views and vistas as streets curve away out of the line of vision.

The First Garden Cities

The ideals behind and the basic plans for a garden city were set out in *Tomorrow: A Peaceful Path to Real Reform*, written by Ebenezer Howard in 1898. Moved by his own experiences of industrial and rural life and inspired by the growing currents of social reformism, as well as the writings of Ruskin and William Morris and the ideals of the Art Workers Guild (not to mention the new enthusiasm for the countryside for its own sake), Howard put together a plan which he hoped would lead to the gradual shrinkage of the cities, and all their attendant miseries, in favour of a move to 'a tightly organized urban centre for 32,000 inhabitants, surrounded by a perpetual

THE GARDEN CITY MOVEMENT/2

green belt of farms and parks' with 'all the advantages of the most energetic and active town life with all the beauty and delight of the country'. The city was to include both industry and agriculture and would have separate areas for housing, factories and municipal buildings. He recommended a site (or sites, for he envisaged many such projects) of 6000 acres in all, with 1000 acres in the centre to be the garden city itself.

Despite the fact that Howard was neither an architect nor a planner (he was a stenographer and inventor of typewriters by trade), his vision struck a chord with a wide variety of people. In 1899 he established the Garden Cities Association (which became the Garden Cities and Town Planning Association in 1907), and conferences and meetings were held throughout the country, including at Port Sunlight and Bournville, to promote interest in his scheme. An influential group of backers was quickly gathered together to set up a company called First Garden City Limited, which by 1903 was in a position to buy land at Letchworth, in the Hertfordshire countryside north of London.

The plans outlined in Howard's book had simply laid down the details of the scale of the development, and of the relationships between buildings and their surroundings, and between industry and the countryside. Raymond Unwin and Barry Parker, the architects chosen to give shape to these principles, shared the ideals of the Arts and Crafts Movement and of William Morris. The first stage was to design the town plan in relation to the distinctive natural features of the site, placing it in a ring of agricultural land. Great attention was paid to the visual and practical features of the roads, with an emphasis being placed on curved roads, in order to provide more interesting views for the inhabitants but without creating (as

◁A striking example of the housing design at Letchworth. Various architects were involved with the project, but it was Unwin and Parker, adhering to the principles of the Arts and Crafts Movement, who gave Ebenezer Howard's basic scheme a shape.
▷A row of cottages in Hampstead Garden Suburb, revealing the arrangement of houses along 'leafy lanes'.

Unwin put it), 'aimlessly wandering' twists and turns just for the sake of it. Unwin expanded on his view in *Town Planning in Practice* (1909):

Rarely will it happen that the site will be so level and so devoid of existing roads, rivers, valleys, woods or other features, as not to provide ample reason for the introduction of many irregular lines; and these irregularities, produced in response to natural conditions following accurately the contours or avoiding obstacles, will be likely, being justified by the requirements and natural lines of the site, to be justified also in appearance.

Perhaps the most important part of Parker and Unwin's design was their concern with housing density (existing by-laws simply regulated the minimum width of streets and minimum amount of space to be left at the back of buildings in relation to their height; there was no restriction on the number of houses per

acre), and they established that the most comfortable ratio (obviously dependent on house size) was ten to twenty per acre. They later settled on twelve, a figure that was to become generally recommended in later planning guides. Within these guidelines the houses themselves were arranged in such a way as to give each one an interesting outlook and as much natural light as possible. By the careful grouping of houses in ways that they had experimented with at New Earswick – that is, around cul-de-sacs or facing gardens and greens – each house was given as attractive a situation as possible. Care was also taken not to intrude upon the natural desire for a degree of privacy and seclusion for each home. Letchworth is also notable for its leafy appearance – an ambitious programme of planting trees was part of the plan – and this feature was also taken up enthusiastically by suburbia.

In keeping with their determination to let the maximum amount of natural light into all the rooms of a dwelling, the

houses at Letchworth did not have back projections or basements. (The decision to do away with the back projection also had an aesthetic basis – Unwin felt they were ugly, and while not visible to the passer-by, people in nearby houses had to see them.) Another way of ensuring maximum light was to introduce an element of 'open planning', in particular to remove the division between the front and back rooms on the ground floor, in favour of a through living room/kitchen with windows at both ends. While this idea was not taken up by suburbia for many years, the notion that the home had to serve a functional purpose, as opposed to being a place divided into rooms for receiving guests and those 'below stairs', with the day-to-day living spaces hidden from general view, was gradually to gain ground.

The Garden Suburb

The opportunity for Parker and Unwin to develop their ideas further came with the project for Hampstead Garden Suburb in London, and in this case there were no constraints in considering the relationship between housing and its economic support. This suburb was the brainchild of Henrietta Barnett, an enthusiastic social reformer, whose aim was both to preserve the Hampstead area from rapidly encroaching suburban developments, and to create housing that would accommodate a socially mixed community in terms of both income and occupation (initially the price range of houses offered was from £425 to £3500). This was something which Unwin also considered essential for the growth of a healthy social environment, but it was something in which Hampstead was to fail. Neither a very mixed nor a very communal community developed, primarily because the houses were very quickly taken up by almost exclusively middle-class buyers, and also because there were no centres where a community atmosphere could develop: shops and pubs were not allowed, and even the bells of the church and chapel which dominate the central square were not permitted to disturb the peace. Visually, however, the development is the epitome of an idealized suburb, containing a variety of vernacular and Domestic Revival architecture, and arranged in curved leafy streets.

In order to have the freedom he required to arrange the streets, paths and gardens of the suburb as he envisaged, Unwin had first to get an Act of Parliament passed to give him local suspension of the 1875 Public Health Act which contained the terms of the byelaw street (see page 56). This allowed Unwin to design intimate village-like streets of less than 165 m (500 ft) long and as narrow as 6 m (20 ft), and where the actual 'carriage drive' might only be about 4.5 m (14 ft) wide. Where roads were made wider than the byelaw requirement of 12 m (40 ft) they were allowed to devote the extra space to grass margins with trees.

Unwin had drawn upon his knowledge of European city squares, town centres and village developments in order to build up an intricately worked out scheme of recommendations for planning. His attention to detail, as seen in *Town Planning in Practice*, was exceptional, and gave form to many ideas that were later to become standard procedure for housing schemes. Unfortunately, much of the speculative-built suburban developments of the 1920s and 1930s simply adopted many of the more obvious visual features of the Garden City and Garden Suburb, leaving much of the subtlety behind. The Garden City Movement itself found new impetus after the First World War, when the push to provide 'Homes for Heroes' necessitated radical measures. By 1919 plans were under way for Welwyn Garden City, the second garden city but of a very different kind.

THE BUNGALOW

In numerous ways bungalows epitomize the problems of suburbia in general: they are not quite socially acceptable, and the term 'bungaloid development' is used to conjure up visions of horror. Nevertheless, they have been, and remain, extremely popular.

The word 'bungalow' seems to have taken on a social meaning beyond its strict definition of a single-storey dwelling. Because bungalows were so often used for leisure and holiday purposes, any second or weekend home, especially those situated by the sea or in rural surroundings, could, at one time, be described as a bungalow, provided it did not have too many floors. Bungalows were associated with a relaxed, outdoor, rather Bohemian way of living that raised suburban eyebrows; such snobbery was misplaced, however, for the bungalow's antecedents, if not impeccable, are eminently respectable.

△ **An Arts-and-Crafts-inspired weekend bungalow designed in 1909. The deckchair is intended to symbolize the leisurely style of bungalow life.**

The word 'bungalow' stems from the Indian word 'bangla', meaning of that area known as Bengal (now Bangladesh). The middle classes who went out to administer the British Raj usually lived in long, low, detached, single-storey dwellings, under high pyramidical roofs which invariably also covered a verandah running around most, if not all, of the building. The spacious and well-ventilated style suited Europeans suffering in the hot climate, and was based on local building traditions, although the *Imperial Dictionary* of 1850 defines the English bungalow as a brick building with thatched or tiled roof, as opposed to the wood and bamboo structure of the native population. It seems that the word bungalow was introduced to Britain before the form, although pattern books showing ornamental single-storey cottages with 'viranda', in the Indian manner, show the colonial influence as early as 1800.

Although bungalows did not become a popular suburban housing form until the 1920s, they existed in the seaside developments of the late Victorian era, when they were built for holidaymakers. Britain's first two bungalows were built, it seems, at Westgate-on-Sea in Kent,

and were part of the great burgeoning of seaside resorts of the last three decades of the nineteenth century. Sea-bathing had, of course, been fashionable since the 1800s when The Prince Regent put Brighton on the map, but it had been exclusive to the upper classes until the 1860s, when the railway boom and the increase in surplus wealth, from which the middle classes benefited particularly, enabled increasing numbers of town-dwellers to seek seaside holidays. Property speculators transformed tiny fishing hamlets into flourishing resorts, all vying for clientele with ever more splendid esplanades, more elegant bandstands, and longer piers. Not all were successful, but Birchington, next to fashionable Westgate, undoubtedly had upper middle-class appeal, and it was here that one John Taylor, in association with the famous Arts and Crafts architect John Seddon, built the first bungalow estate. No one is quite sure why this form was chosen but the Indian connection cannot be ruled out. As Anthony King says in his book *The Bungalow* (1985):

In the 1860s and 1870s, life in the country or hill-station bungalow was

seen as a positive experience, far from the madding crowd and waited on hand and foot. Like other facets of Indian and Anglo-Indian life, it seemed to represent something which had been lost in England, increasingly industrialized and urban, and offering an opportunity to escape from social changes which some people were beginning to deplore. Without the discomforts of actually going to India then, here, in the single-storey simple bungalow, was an institution which, with profit, could be modified and adopted back home.

Taylor's bungalows were not in fact particularly simple: with cellarage, servants' quarters and belvedere towers, they were, at £1000 for the smallest seven-roomed version, aimed at a wealthy market. The social status of the bungalow estate was therefore quickly established. Moreover the health requirements so important to the Vic-

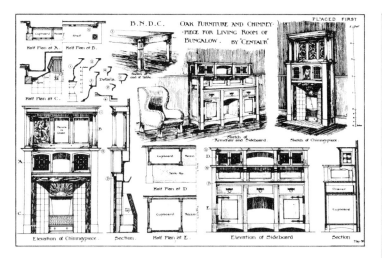

△This 'plain and simple' bungalow furniture of 1898, was, like much Arts and Crafts work, of high quality and expensive.
▷Before long the spread of prefabricated bungalows like this one gave the form a rather less exclusive image.

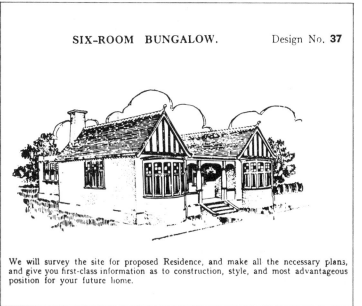

SIX-ROOM BUNGALOW. Design No. **37**

We will survey the site for proposed Residence, and make all the necessary plans, and give you first-class information as to construction, style, and most advantageous position for your future home.

torians also became associated with seaside bungalows when several eminent physicians were among the first purchasers. It was, however, the artistic connection which made bungalows so suited to middle-class taste: they were indubitably Arts and Crafts in character. Simplicity of style was a major feature, as if to reflect the simple country life to be lived there. In 1882 the Pre-Raphaelite artist Dante Gabriel Rossetti stayed, and had the misfortune to die, in one of the bungalows at Birchington, thus confirming the already considerable aesthetic connections that the exclusive little community had developed.

For the next thirty years the seaside resorts grew, catering for a market that moved lower down the social scale as it expanded. Prefabricated bungalows were also produced, originally for the Colonies but soon became the norm in Britain as they could be removed elsewhere when the lease on a plot expired. Their light timber construction and their very impermanence also

helped to create the less serious and altogether less formal way of life that holidaymakers required. The middle classes sought, of course, respectability above all else, but the annual holiday at least was an occasion when the conformity and social rigidity of suburban life might be relaxed a little. The bungalow, with its image of healthy fresh air and a relaxed, slightly Bohemian life-style, seems to have fitted this desire perfectly, and became the standard form in seaside resorts all round the coast of Britain, and particularly in the south-east, where it was quite common for a family to rent a bungalow for a month from which father could still commute to the city.

The increasing use of the countryside for leisure purposes after 1880 also helped to boost the popularity of the bungalow. The habit of 'weekending' in the great houses of the aristocracy was reaching its zenith, and the middle classes also wanted somewhere to go. The architect R. A. Briggs ('Bungalow Briggs' as he became known) sensed this need

and published a best-selling book of plans, *Bungalows and Country Residences*, in which the simplicity of the fashionable Arts and Crafts style was successfully combined with the bungalow form. Thousands of these cheap but sound little dwellings began to appear all over the countryside in the early twentieth century. While providing a means of escape from the city's fumes for many, they angered others; and it was to curb the rash of 'bungaloid growths' that the Council for the Preservation of Rural England was founded in the 1920s.

The social levelling and freedom of life that apparently existed in the larger bungalow developments (the popular press ran stories of loose morals) were seen as a challenge to accepted conventions, and the bungalow itself was therefore regarded with suspicion in conservative suburbia. It was not until after the First World War, when people began to notice a suburb of Los Angeles called Hollywood, that the bungalow, popular in California, gained a glamorous image.

INFLUENCES ON STYLE: *William Morris*

William Morris (1834–96) was an extraordinary combination of characteristics: a romantic, idealistic dreamer, he also embodied the essentially Victorian virtues of practicality, energy and organizational skill. A child of the Gothic Revival, he found inspiration in the medievalism of Pugin and Ruskin, but his influence has been even greater than theirs, for he became the father figure of the Arts and Crafts Movement which radically altered design in the late nineteenth century. Indeed, not only has this influence been felt directly, through his original designs, many of which are still being produced today, but also, and perhaps more importantly, indirectly through the principles of his Movement, which were to be adopted by many of the most significant architects and designers of the twentieth century.

△**Morris in 1884.**

Born of wealthy parents, Morris was apparently a sickly child, but in adulthood he displayed a robust character and rude energy which found expression in many diverse talents. Architecture was perhaps the least of his skills, and as a painter he did not equal the best, but he excelled as a designer, craftsman and entrepreneur. His contemporaries considered him a good enough poet to offer him the professorship of poetry at Oxford, which he declined. He founded the Society for the Protection of Ancient Buildings, still in existence, to fight the Victorian passion for 'restoring' medieval churches. He was also active in politics, being a founder member of the Socialist League.

His best-known political writing, *News from Nowhere* (1891), is a Utopian piece describing an England after the establishment of a socialist commonwealth, when all the towns have been demolished and the population dispersed throughout the countryside to create an environmentally perfect, village-based society. It is a charming, if naive, work, and shows Morris to be as much a medievalist as a socialist, for not only is the wealth shared equally, but the nature of work itself emphasizes craftsmanship, care and pride which have been put back into all occupations, however lowly, and the drudgery of work in industrial Britain seems to have been miraculously abolished. *News From Nowhere* demonstrates the ethos pervading his work: a reaction to the Industrial Revolution and its commercialism.

△**A good example of the wide-ranging influence of William Morris in every aspect of domestic design: the chair, wallpaper, cupboard and carpet are all his designs.**

Craft versus Machine

To most mid-Victorians, the label 'machine made' was still the highest accolade that could be given to an article. Objects for use or beauty that had been produced by the latest industrial processes were considered far superior to those made by hand in the old-fashioned way, and were also much cheaper. Ruskin helped to popularize the growing contempt for machine-made products in *The Stones of Venice* (1851–3), described as the Bible of the Arts and Crafts Movement. He argues that buildings and decoration should show that they are hand-made, since machines can only produce things that are devoid of any human spirit.

Morris also despised the mimicry of so much mid-Victorian taste. Yet, in truth, his artistic values seem sometimes to have been ambiguous. While his friend the painter Edward Burne-Jones (1833–98) said of him: 'all his life he hated the copying of ancient work as unfair to the old and stupid for the present', Morris argued for the form as well as the spirit of architecture to be Gothic. Nor did he utterly despise, as did so many, the regularity and simplicity of Georgian streets, preferring them in some ways to the vulgar styles built for the 'ignorant purse-proud digesting machines' whom he saw in all stations of society. He also mocked the Queen Anne style, but was instrumental in reintroducing the vernacular forms on which it is based.

Morris had met Burne-Jones when they were students at Oxford, and together they formed the nucleus of a small group, known to themselves as 'the brotherhood', to discuss art, theology, history, medieval poetry and the writings of Tennyson and Ruskin. After Oxford, Morris became a pupil architect in the office of George Street, but his friendship with Dante Gabriel

Rossetti and the group of artists known as the pre-Raphaelites (whose mentor was Ruskin) led him to forsake architecture for painting. It was upon his marriage, however, to the beautiful Jane Burden (her face appears in many pre-Raphaelite paintings) that Morris's career as a decorator began in earnest. Using his private wealth, he set about building the Red House at Upton in Kent, the design and furnishing of which was to embody all his principles of decorative art (see page 84). In 1861 a small company was formed, comprising Morris, Rossetti, Philip Webb, Burne-Jones, Madox-Brown, Faulkner and Marshall, under the title Morris, Marshall Faulkner and Co. (later known as Morris & Co.) which undertook church decoration, carving, stained glass, metalwork, wall hangings, chintzes, carpets and furniture. Morris and his friends actually sought to practise the principles of medieval craftsmanship, not merely to imitate its forms or effects.

The Arts and Crafts Guilds

Under Morris's influence a number of guilds and artists' associations sprang up during the 1880s, under the general name of the Arts and Crafts Movement. Several different groups were involved, and stylistic differences began to emerge as their work developed, but as members of the Arts and Crafts Movement they shared a number of principles in common. They all thought that the split between the fine and applied arts was destructive and artificial, and that good design should take into account fitness for purpose, the nature of the materials used and the method of construction. A fundamental belief was that mass-production was anathema to their principles: only under the conditions of hand-craftsmanship could good art and design be produced.

The first of the guilds to be formed was the Century Guild, founded in 1882 by the architect A. H. Mackmurdo (1851–1942) which announced its aim as being 'to render all branches of the arts the sphere no longer of the tradesman but of the artist'. Like the work of other members of the Arts and Crafts Movement, Mackmurdo's swirling designs for both furniture and wallpapers foreshadowed Art Nouveau, though the Guild claimed no connection with that primarily European movement. Other groups, whose work was shown at the Arts and Crafts Exhibition Society exhibitions which began in 1888, included the St George's Art Guild (founded by pupils of Norman Shaw), the Art Workers Guild (a founder member of which was C. F. A. Voysey), and the Guild of Handicrafts founded by C. R. Ashbee. It was this last group that was to maintain Morris's ideals best; in 1902 it moved to

△A cover of *Hobby Horse*, the publication of the Century Guild, the first of many Arts and Crafts guilds, founded in 1882.

the village of Chipping Campden, in the Cotswolds, which to this day has a tradition of being a crafts centre. The Arts and Crafts Society itself was formed in 1893, and its influence on the development of Modernism in Europe was profound. By 1906, however, the Movement was beginning to lose its force in England, and the guilds themselves were beginning to disband. A combination of renewed interest in antique and reproduction furniture and furnishings, and the fact that the ability to purchase Arts and Crafts products had for the most part paradoxically been confined to the wealthy, speeded their demise.

Shortly before his death, Morris made his final contribution to the Movement with the publication of the Kelmscott *Chaucer*, a monumental work designed and printed by hand on his own presses. This is another example of the dilemma that he was never able to resolve: while Morris the socialist believed that art should be shared by all, the comparatively high price of hand-produced goods put them beyond the reach of most. In 1893 *The Studio* magazine reviewed the Arts and Crafts Exhibition Society's annual show, and while welcoming the protest against commercialism in design, described it as 'the work of a few for the few'. Morris in his idealized view wanted to recreate the craftsmanship which the industrial age had stripped from the worker. As he said in 1879, 'real art is the expression by man of his pleasure in labour. He also believed in the ideal of having 'nothing in your house which you do not consider to be beautiful'. But he could not reconcile his beliefs with the practicalities of late nineteenth-century production methods, for the working people had also become mass consumers, and consumption on such a scale could only be satisfied by the mechanical processes he so abhorred.

HOUSE LAYOUT AND APPLIED DECORATION

The period 1880–1920 was very much a transitional one for the design of the average suburban house, in terms of layout and applied decoration. While on the one hand the prototypes of semi-detached suburbia of the 1920s and 1930s could already be seen in individual architect-designed houses and the garden suburbs as early as the 1880s, in the years up to 1900 most new houses were still built on very similar lines to those of their earlier Victorian counterparts.

The narrow back extension of so many Victorian houses, which gave a front-to-back corridor-like effect, continued to be a feature of the standard layout of the late Victorian terrace, but designs arranged on a squarer plan were beginning to appear, as the new interest in vernacular architecture prompted a companion interest in the relationship between house and garden and an increased emphasis on the importance of light and fresh air. Since back extensions tended to reduce the amounts of both reaching rooms at the rear of the house, they were by the end of the century gradually being superseded by squarer layouts which ensured more light in all rooms. For the same reason basements disappeared completely, although more as a result of the Public Health Act of 1875 than because of Art and Crafts fashion. With garden access in mind, many Edwardian dining rooms had French doors, a feature that was to become more or less standard after 1920.

Like earlier Victorian houses, houses built during this period were still quite large compared with those built after the First World War. Not only were the proportions of the rooms more generous, but there were more of them: even quite modest houses had a morning room as well as a sitting and dining room, and the kitchen continued to have an adjoining scullery in a separate room. Important new additions were an internal lavatory and bathroom, which by 1880 were universal in new houses. Particular emphasis was still placed on the hall as the all-important area for 'first impressions', and in the most fashionable houses it would be square, with a turned staircase leading from it. Some Edwardian staircases even incorporated a 'minstrels' gallery – a sort of half-landing up just two or three steps from the hall, which gave the opportunity for another turn of the staircase and thereby added to the pretensions to grandeur that were intended. The idea of making an impression in the hall was taken even further in many of the larger houses built immediately before the First World War: the hall became a 'lounge hall' of generous size with a fireplace, and would be sparsely furnished with one or two casually arranged 'Jacobean' chairs and possibly an ancient-looking chest.

Applied decoration based largely on the ornate Gothic style continued to be

△'A Drawing Room Corner' from Robert Edis's *Decoration and Furniture of Town Houses* (1881) shows the elaborate cornice still popular at this period, with frieze.

popular both inside and outside the house until the end of the century, but the much less elaborate detailing of the Queen Anne style – based, for the exterior, on the interplay of different materials such as tiles, plasterwork, weatherboarding, half-timbering and roughcast rendering – was at the same time quickly gaining ground as builders attempted to follow the trend towards the vernacular that was being set by the architects of the Sweetness and Light Movement. By the beginning of the twentieth century many elements of the vernacular style were firmly established for even the most modest houses, and developed into the standard suburban form of the interwar period. Interior plasterwork followed the same styles that had been popular in earlier Victorian times, and elaborate cornices and ceiling roses were mass produced and used in even the smallest houses. At the end of the Victorian period the larger and more expensive houses built under Arts and Crafts influence might favour Elizabethan or Jacobean styles of plasterwork (the most elaborate examples of which may still be seen in pubs built at the time), using ribbing and stylized motifs such as plants and animals which sometimes covered the entire ceiling, but on the whole surburban houses still had plasterwork in the same patterns as were in use fifty or more years earlier. It was not until after the First World War that plasterwork declined in popularity: cornices slowly became plainer and thinner, and ceiling roses smaller and simpler, following a trend set before the war by the style of more expensive houses.

A HOUSE IN BEDFORD PARK, LONDON, begun in 1875, and often referred to as the first garden suburb. The houses draw their inspiration from Queen Anne Classicism and vernacular architecture.

ELEVATION

The architects' aim was to create an impression of rustic simplicity: all the elements – including the asymmetry of many of the houses – are contrived to suggest a natural, casual development. As a reaction against the opulence and massiveness of the Gothic, inspiration came from the architecture of the early seventeenth century, mixed with Flemish and Dutch elements.

Materials The main materials used were red brick, tiles, weatherboarding, half-timbering and rendering.

Windows A particularly important element of the style was the windows; even quite small houses would have a wide variety of window types.

Roofs and chimneys These were often exaggerated versions of traditional vernacular features: roofs were made steep-pitched and hipped, frequently with gables; chimneys were tall and overstated.

Applied decoration In contrast with the elaborate Gothic style, applied decoration was confined to occasional pilasters or shaped and pedimented doorway surrounds. Interest centred instead on the relationships between the various elements of the façade.

LAYOUT

A notable feature is that there is no basement: the Queen Anne style was intended to bring a light and airy atmosphere to all parts of the house, and basements were dark and considered unhealthy. The layout indicates an attempt to move away from the front-to-back corridor effect of most Victorian houses, and instead to aim for a more rectangular arrangement, allowing a garden view for as many rooms as possible. There was no open planning: each room had its own distinct function.

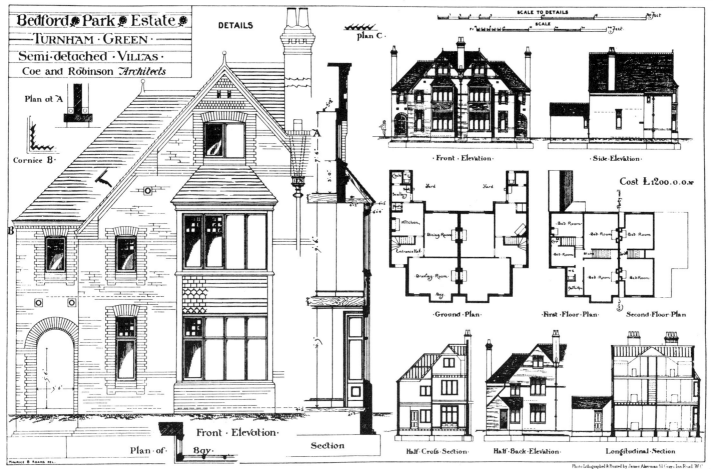

FURNITURE/1

The period 1880–1920 saw the introduction of a number of different themes in English furniture, themes which were to have a lasting effect on its development in the twentieth century. Reaction against the opulence and fake effects of Victorian furniture of the 1850s and 1860s was soon general, but opinion on what should replace it was not so certain. There were three main trends: art furniture, which had its roots in the demands of the 1850s and 1860s for a return to the principles of Gothic architecture and design and which drew on elements of Japanese design; the Arts and Crafts Movement which also looked to the example of the Middle Ages, but which emphasized handcraftsmanship, simple structures and the use of untreated woods; and finally the revival of eighteenth-century English styles of furniture, particularly Chippendale, Sheraton and Adam.

ART FURNITURE

The term 'art furniture' is difficult to define, not least because, as with anything that becomes fashionable very quickly, the term 'art' was haphazardly applied to a wide range of articles in the 1870s and 1880s in an effort to take advantage of its popularity. Art furniture was being talked and written about by many who recommended it for a true 'aesthetic' interior, but with little idea of how it should actually look. By the late 1870s, however, it had taken on a more definite shape: it was commonly made of dark wood – black or ebonized baywood or walnut – and had a light, delicate structure which was often decorated with fine painting, gilding and brass fittings. It is generally agreed that the term first appeared in 1868 in Charles Eastlake's influential book *Hints on Household Taste*, in which he criticized – in the tradition of Sir Henry Cole – prevailing Victorian taste, arguing instead for the 'very plainest and simplest forms of domestic architecture'. The furniture that illustrates the book is in the early-English Gothic style of substantial, decorated structures. Others associated with the design of art

△This artistic morning room at Linley Sambourne House in London shows the late Victorian fashion for the lighter forms of eighteenth-century English furniture, with its painted Sheraton sofa and chairs.
◁Artistic homes might also have some 'art furniture' with a Japanese flavour, the most notable of which was by E. W. Godwin, whose sideboard in ebonized wood has silved-plated fittings and inset panels of embossed Japanese leather paper.

furniture at this time, and also producing highly ornate, solid pieces of furniture, included William Burges, Christopher Dresser and Bruce Talbert. All of them produced a number of designs for commercial firms, something which was to be anathema to the Arts and Crafts designers who shared their regard for the Middle Ages.

It was not until 1877 that the first manufacturer's catalogue bearing the name 'art furniture' appeared. Produced by William Watt, it featured designs by Edward Godwin, the designer of Whistler's house in Chelsea. Godwin's designs strongly reflected the other major characteristic of art furniture – a Japanese influence. Interest in Japanese art and design had been growing steadily for a number of years amongst the avant-garde, and it received a considerable boost at the International Exhibition of 1862, where a stand dedicated to Japanese artefacts had attracted particular notice. Godwin's own furniture, some of which is described as 'Anglo-Japanese' in the catalogue, looks almost precariously insubstantial: constructed mainly from ebonized wood, it has delicate spindly legs, projecting uprights and shelves, and fine detailing including brass handles or hinges and even, occasionally, panels of Japanese leather paper. The structural simplicity of much of Godwin's furniture seems to be before its time, but more commercial versions were soon produced and enthusiastically acquired by buyers for whom the combination of delicate structure and artistic decoration was perfect for their 'aesthetic' interiors.

ARTS AND CRAFTS FURNITURE

Arts and Crafts furniture shared its beginnings with those of art furniture: it, too, was a reaction against the shams of much Victorian commercial design of the 1850s and 1860s, and reflected a wish for a return to pre-industrial principles, specifically to a medieval model. The main tenets of the Movement were an emphasis on handcraftsmanship, the use of untreated wood and simple exposed structures (the furniture is devoid of lumpy, concealing upholstery).

The first pieces of Arts and Crafts furniture to be produced by William Morris's firm, Morris, Marshall Faulkner & Co., appeared at the International Exhibition of 1862. The company produced two types of furniture: there were

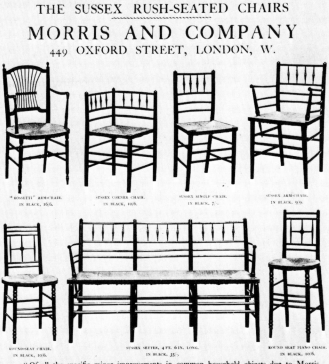

THE SUSSEX RUSH-SEATED CHAIRS

MORRIS AND COMPANY

449 OXFORD STREET, LONDON, W.

"ROSSETTI" ARM-CHAIR. IN BLACK, 16/6.   SUSSEX CORNER CHAIR. IN BLACK, 10/6.   SUSSEX SINGLE CHAIR. IN BLACK, 7/-.   SUSSEX ARM-CHAIR. IN BLACK, 9/9.

ROUND-SEAT CHAIR. IN BLACK, 10/6.   SUSSEX SETTEE, 4 FT. 6 IN. LONG. IN BLACK, 35/-.   ROUND SEAT PIANO CHAIR. IN BLACK, 10/6.

"Of all the specific minor improvements in common household objects due to Morris, the rush-bottomed Sussex chair perhaps takes the first place. It was not his own invention, but was copied with trifling improvements from an old chair of village manufacture picked up in Sussex. With or without modification it has been taken up by all the modern furniture manufacturers, and is in almost universal use. But the Morris pattern of the later type (there were two) still excels all others in simplicity and elegance of proportion."

"Life of William Morris" : By Prof. J. W. Mackail.

63

◁Heal's in London's Tottenham Court Road produced Arts-and-Crafts-influenced furniture, particularly oak bedroom furniture in simple, unfussy outlines and discreet decoration. The wardrobe of c.1905 (above) features a distinctive check border in ebony and boxwood inlay. While much Arts and Crafts furniture was prohibitively expensive for most people, some pieces, such as these Morris 'Sussex' chairs (left), were more commercial. Devised from an original village-manufactured design, they were – and still are – popular items.

FURNITURE/2

simple, functional everyday pieces, the most enduring the 'Morris' chairs by Philip Webb, with ebonized frames and rush seats, versions of which are still available today; and highly ornate items, which had the same simplicity of structure but which were elaborately painted and decorated, often with romantic literary scenes from Chaucer or Walter Scott by artists from the pre-Raphaelite school. The company's output later in the century was primarily of ornate, richly decorated furniture, which was very expensive.

The next generation of designers, members of the Arts and Crafts Guilds which grew up under the influence of Morris, for the most part abandoned the use of elaborate decoration on their furniture. Their designs, which were commonly constructed of untreated oak (or occasionally the more practical 'fumed' oak: wood exposed to the fumes of ammonia after construction to darken the colour), had very simple shapes and made a feature of allowing the methods of construction to be clearly visible. Decoration, if any, consisted of finely detailed metal hinges or handles; loose cushions, rather than sprung upholstery, softened the outlines. Despite the apparent simplicity of this furniture, the emphasis on handcrafting every item made it prohibitively expensive to all except the wealthy. Everyone else had to be content with looking at it at the Arts and Crafts Society exhibitions. It was not until the turn of the century that one or two enlightened retailers began to produce commercial ranges based on the same principles. Perhaps the most famous of these was Heal's, whose ranges of bedroom furniture in particular (designed by Ambrose Heal) were soon very popular. This new well-crafted, honest furniture was particularly appropriate for the garden suburbs beginning to be built at this time.

EIGHTEENTH-CENTURY REVIVALS

Aesthetic households of the 1870s and 1880s demanded furniture of a delicacy suitable for their Queen-Anne style houses, and they found it in English furniture of the eighteenth century. Accordingly, Sheraton, Chippendale and Adam began to emerge from the storerooms to which they had been confined by the previous generation. A number of manufacturers quickly took advantage of the taste, producing vast quantities of reproduction furniture, much of which was difficult to tell from the original. Older firms drew on their own eighteenth-century catalogues for designs, and happily mixed reproductions with originals in their showrooms. Techniques of inlay and wood veneer were revived, and many of the reproductions were of a high standard.

Inevitably, however, modern taste demanded small modifications, and some of the furniture was made with slightly unusual outlines such as flimsy legs in relation to a heavier body. As the taste for the antique gained ground, there were revivals of chinoiserie and eighteenth-century 'Gothik' styles, and some unscrupulous manufacturers employed fake ageing techniques. Up to the First World War period furniture became increasingly popular, and different styles or periods were assigned to different rooms by the home decor writers, who might recommend a 'Jacobean' hall, a 'Chippendale' dining room and an 'Adam' drawing room.

Suburban Synthesis

These eighteenth-century furniture styles were rarely seen outside wealthy homes in their purest form: suburban homes and, indeed, influential writers on the home created their own peculiar synthesis. The majority of critics and home writers were united in their call for a clean sweep of the oppressive furnishings of the 1850s and 1860s, but they were not at all so united in what should replace it, or indeed what they meant by

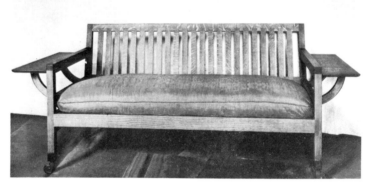

◁◁The drawing room (far left) – actually a set at the Electrical Exhibition held in Manchester in 1908 – reflects the Edwardian taste for eighteenth-century English furniture, in contrast with the photograph of 1905 (centre), an Arts and Crafts arrangement with furniture by Voysey.

◁This artistic 'cosy corner' from Oetzmann's 1896 catalogue, of mahogany upholstered with 'tapestry', was intended for a library, dining room or hall.

◁Voysey's settee in unstained and unpolished oak is a perfect example of the uncompromising lines of most Arts and Crafts furniture.

'artistic interiors' or 'simple honest furniture'. While Eastlake illustrated his ideas with Gothic furniture, R.W. Edis, in his *Decoration and Furniture of Town Houses* (1881), was equally happy to suggest schemes that ranged from a combination of Queen Anne and art furniture to a neo-Adam drawing room. A typical suburban home might feature elements of several different styles.

Mrs Panton's recommendations are perhaps the best gauge of the suburban response to the styles of the 1880s and 1890s. Her books on taste and decoration offer advice mainly for houses of moderate size, and her ideal hall included art furniture ('Liberty has some bamboo settees in black and arm-chairs to match'), together with elements of the most basic Arts and Crafts ('an oak chest with an oaken back is a most valuable possession'), while the rest of the house was ideally liberally sprinkled with reproduction tables and bamboo whatnots, supporting books, plants and other artistic paraphernalia, not to mention a large collection of Japanese fans. She also

recommended built-in furniture – inglenooks or 'cosy corners' in the drawing room, window-seats in the dining room and built-in cupboards in the bedroom – all of which continued to be popular throughout the period.

The derivation and adaptation of built-in or fitted furniture is perhaps one of the best examples of suburban compromise. The leading architects and designers of the Arts and Crafts Movement, notably C.F.A. Voysey, made a particular feature of it in their interiors, in keeping

with their belief in the organic relationship between the inside and outside of the house. The furniture was an integral part of the design of the house as a whole, rather than merely an afterthought. Typically, it was very simple, built of untreated or white-painted wood; it was not referential in any way. By comparison the suburban response was, predictably, less pure: in a Maples catalogue of 1910, those setting up home could find 'cosy corners' in the neo-Adam style, ready for installation.

FURNISHING FABRICS

The development of pattern design for furnishing fabrics followed much the same course as that for wallpapers between 1880 and 1914, when the heavily draped curtains and opulently upholstered furniture of the mid-Victorian period were thrown out in favour of less elaborate effects. Upholstery was slimmed down to more manageable proportions, and curtains, arranged now on simple wooden or brass poles, were recommended to fall only to windowsill or dado level. Light muslin curtains, possibly with lace inserts, hung behind a heavier, patterned main curtain. In addition to William Morris's own and other Morris-inspired fabrics, an important source was Liberty's, who opened their Art Fabrics department in the 1880s. Here the artistic shopper could buy coarse silks and cottons in rich formal patterns based on Indian designs, in russet browns, peacock blues and other 'aesthetic' colours.

The mid-Victorian fashion for draping surfaces with fabrics did not entirely disappear, however. Fireplaces, at least in some homes, continued to be elaborately draped in the 1870s and 1880s, and writers such as Mrs Panton considered it essential to have hall doorways draped with velveteen curtains. Other 'artistic' households with highly developed aesthetic tastes in the late nineteenth century might also do the same for the dining room and possibly the drawing room. In each case the curtain would be hung on a simple wooden or brass pole and looped back for access. Tables would also be covered with heavy cloths, as would one or two other objects, but now with very considered effects in mind. For example, Mrs Panton dictated that an upright piano should have serge worked with bulrushes, irises or grasses covering the back, and a piece of embroidered damask on top; a grand piano could be draped with an Indian shawl, with a collection of sketches 'carelessly' arranged on top, together with a 'big palm in a brass pot on a black stand'.

As fashionable taste moved away from the gloomy cluttered interiors of the 1880s and 1890s in favour of simpler decoration, superfluous draperies gradually disappeared, and pastel-coloured, lightweight fabrics began to predominate. The new taste also dictated a less heavy hand in upholstery; and chintz, previously used merely to protect heavy velvet upholstery, was now often the main covering.

△ This cotton and linen fabric, Crocus by G. C. Haite, is an example of the exuberant patterns and rich colours of wallpapers and fabrics of the 1880s and 1890s.
◁ After 1900 these gave way to more restrained patterns and paler colours, as in this example by G. P. & J. Baker.

▽The Daffodil chintz of c.1892 (below) was one of William Morris's more unusual designs. Morris patterns were so popular that many other designers produced close copies. The 'Lonsdale' chair (bottom), with loose cover of 'Rose Rambler' printed linen or glazed chintz was typical of a type that became popular all year round after 1900 in cottagey interiors.

WILLIAMSON & COLES

SPECIALISTS

FOR

Loose Covers,

Casement Blinds,

Bordered

Curtains,

Etc.

The "Lonsdale" Chair.
With Loose Cover of "Rose Rambler" printed
Linen or Glazed Chintz fast Colours.

CARPETS AND FLOORCOVERINGS

A combination of a concern for hygiene and an inevitable reaction against past fashion led to a movement away from fitted carpets in the 1880s and 1890s, in favour of a more flexible approach to floorcoverings. Artistic taste now dictated that principal rooms should have stained or polished wooden floors or parquet flooring, spread with oriental rugs. Maple & Co., one of the leading suppliers of furnishings, produced a small booklet on the subject entitled *Concerning Carpets and Art Decoration of Floors*, in which they gave the potential purchaser detailed instructions on the suitability of different types of carpet for different rooms, together with price lists, background information, and so on. Particularly recommended were carpets from India, Persia and Turkey, examples of which could be seen in room settings in their showrooms.

As with many other branches of the decorative arts at this time, leading architects and artists were also commissioned to produce designs for carpets. William Morris, C.F.A. Voysey and Walter Crane all designed carpets, the most famous from William Morris being the Hammersmith range of hand-knot-ted designs which were recommended by both Mrs Haweis and Mrs Panton, though both of them also warned of their expense. Many mass-produced designs were imitative of oriental carpets, and in any event flat, stylized naturalistic designs had superseded the realistic depictions of rococo ornament and the elaborately realistic flowers and animals of mid-Victorian fashion.

Alternatives to parquet or good wooden flooring were felt or rush matting. Felt was available in a wide range of colours, (as well as very much less fashionable patterns) and served as a suitable background for a few smaller rugs. Rush matting, either Japanese or Indian, was also very popular, particularly where a fresh and healthy effect was required, for example in bedrooms; this, too, would have a number of small rugs scattered over it.

For the really hard-working floors of the hall, stairs and kitchen or scullery areas, oilcloths or linoleum were the practical choice. Typical designs would feature imitations of medieval or Minton tiles, while others reproduced Persian carpet patterns or the ubiquitous Greek key design.

◁Lily carpet by William Morris. Carpets designed by Morris had flat, stylized patterns and were recommended for 'artistic' homes, although they were expensive. Oriental carpets were also popular at this period.

WALLPAPERS AND WALLCOVERINGS/1

The aesthetic fashion for dividing walls into three areas of dado at the bottom, a central filling and a frieze below the ceiling, separated by a wooden dado rail and picture rail, became the standard treatment in suburban homes in the 1880s and 1890s, and was considered essential in any house with a pretension to artistic taste. As H.J. Jenning was to point out in *Our Homes and How to Beautify Them* (1902), the dado in particular came to signify membership of this elite cultured group, and was in consequence the butt of satirical jokes and songs, including one set to the tune of Campdown Races:

Oh sweet adornment for the cottage wall
Dado dado
Oh poverty's sure solace whatso'er befall

After 1900 suburban taste began to move towards simpler effects, and wall treatments became considerably lighter and plainer, although the dado and picture rails were to survive, at least in dining rooms and halls, into the 1930s and beyond. For drawing rooms, plain walls without a dado but with a highly decorative frieze became fashionable, and light-coloured period styles soon began to dominate wallpaper patterns. The growing popularity of period styles was also reflected in the vogue for wood-panelled ('Jacobean') walls, notably in dining rooms, with a small shelf running round at picture-rail height for displaying collections of plates.

Dado, Filling and Frieze

A considerable variety of materials was available for the decoration of the dado: wood panelling, washable, varnished 'sanitary' papers, 'leather' papers and even fabric and matting. A wooden or matting dado would be painted in the dark background colour of the wallpaper selected for the filling. Sanitary papers were often supplied with embossed surfaces imitating carved panelling or tiling. Wealthier homes favoured leather paper, another type of embossed paper which had, as its name suggests, a tex-

Dado dado da;
To dream of thee all night, to gaze on thee by day
Is the proletarian's supreme delight;
Dado dado da.

The three areas gave considerable scope for decorative effects, as each section could have a different treatment. Many wallpaper designers produced related patterns, particularly for the filling and frieze, as is shown, for example, in *The Silver Studio Collection* exhibition catalogue (1980), which illustrates patterns produced by this design studio for many of the leading retailers of the period. Favourite aesthetic colours were green, peacock blue, terracotta, and warm reds and golds. The desired effect was dark, mysterious and faintly exotic.

tured, leather-like surface. Many of these were in designs based on Spanish leather, while others were imported from Japan and had strong exotic patterns incorporating birds, fruit and foliage. Mrs Panton in particular recommended that those decorating their homes should try to use leather papers in some part of their schemes. For example, for the dining room she suggests, 'for those who can afford it, a plain gold Japanese leather paper (for the filling) with a bold red and gold leather paper as a dado; red paint. Ceiling papered in yellow and white.' Anaglypta was also used for dados as well as for ceilings and friezes, and had the distinction of having a number of patterns designed by leading architects such as C. F. A. Voysey.

For the most part the filling and frieze areas were given over to densely patterned wallpapers, and in fashionable houses the papers selected would be in designs by William Morris & Co., or by other companies producing patterns in direct imitation of his work. William Morris had started to produce wallpaper designs in the 1860s – relatively simple, stylized naturalistic patterns reminiscent of Owen Jones, but the designs that were to prove enduringly popular were the rich, densely patterned designs of the 1870s and 1880s which had their inspiration in Renaissance tapestries. (Morris, like many other designers, had studied the collection of historic textiles housed in the museum at South Kensington; this was one of the collections begun by Henry Cole after the disasters of the Great Exhibition, to give some indication of the 'right principles of design'.) Morris himself favoured the use of real

◁◁This design for a wallpaper frieze is among the huge number of Morris-inspired designs that were produced at this period. This example, dated 1897, is by Harry Napper of the Silver Studio, one of the leading commercial design studios of the day. The studio produced many coordinating designs for the fashionable dado, filling and frieze wall arrangement.

◁A sitting room of 1910 in the Aesthetic style. The fashion-conscious owners have decorated the room with a plain dado and used flat, stylized Morris and Morris-influenced patterns for the wallpaper filling, carpet and chair fabric.

WALLPAPERS AND WALLCOVERINGS/2

tapestries for covering walls, obviously not a feasible proposition for the suburban householder, who could, however, use Morris or Morris-style wallpapers to achieve the desired richness of effect. For the most part, the lesson had been learned that pattern should be flat and not an attempt at garish or disarmingly realistic representations of nature. Even so, heavy naturalistic designs, along the lines of those that had been so popular with the earlier Victorians, were still produced, and a number of period styles were also still available.

Wallcoverings after 1900

The dark, luxuriant colours and designs of the 1880s and 1890s continued to be popular in some suburban homes at the beginning of the new century, but reaction was inevitable, and new influences were beginning to make themselves felt. The Arts and Crafts Movement had pointed the way to a simpler, lighter feel, away from the self-conscious 'artiness' of the Aesthetic Movement, and chose plainly decorated interiors to complement unfussy, natural oak furniture. On the other hand, a growing taste for eighteenth-century furniture created a demand for decorative schemes of a similar period.

The taste for dividing the wall area into dado, filling and frieze continued to be popular, particularly in the hall and dining room. Other rooms were gradually moving towards less elaborate treatment, abandoning the dado in favour of plainer pastel-coloured walls, but still favouring a decorative frieze. If anything

◁For those with very advanced tastes, the dado, filling and frieze arrangement was soon passé for most rooms, and decorative treatments stencilled by hand, like this example dated 1887, became a popular alternative.

◁Heavily embossed wallpapers, or leather papers, like this example (top left) incorporating high-relief dragon-like fish amid spiralling foliage, were a fashionable choice for dados in the late nineteenth century. Portman (bottom left), a 1903 design from Sanderson, is a good example of the Regency-style wallpapers which began to appear after 1900, when fashion favoured furnishing schemes based on English eighteenth-century styles. Blackthorn (left) was one of Morris's most popular papers.

▽C. F. A. Voysey was one of the many architects commissioned by wallpaper manufacturers anxious to respond to demands from the newly design-conscious public. His block-printed paper for Sanderson of 1897, called Glade, is a refreshingly simple design of stylized tulips, marigolds and butterflies in three colours on a buff ground.

the frieze became more important, with companies producing elaborate landscapes, Japanese-influenced scenes, as well as decoratively embossed papers. The Arts and Crafts Movement influenced the production of plainer patterned papers, notably from architects and designers such as Voysey, who in their turn influenced a number of imitators. Voysey produced a number of designs for papers which were stencil-like in their simplicity; they still featured stylized versions of flowers, foliage, birds and animals, but in light colours on pale backgrounds and with none of the luxuriant depth of the designs of the 1880s and 1890s. A strict Arts and Crafts decorating scheme would leave out wallpaper altogether, in favour of plain, painted walls or white-painted wood panelling. Voysey, along with Mackmurdo and Godwin, were commissioned to produce designs for Jeffrey & Co., one of the first companies to take the influential step of employing architects and designers.

At the same time, period styles never quite disappeared and the vogue for eighteenth-century furniture increased the demand for traditional patterns with birds, vines and flowers on chintz, neo-Adam and rococo-type patterns, all in pastel colours. Their production effectively eclipsed the more forward-looking developments of the Arts and Crafts Movement. It was these designs that were to dominate the years up to and immediately after the First World War.

FIREPLACES

Despite myriad technical experiments, the vast majority of them total failures, the open fire remained almost the only method of domestic heating during this period. The fire had considerable symbolic value, as noted by Muthesius in his survey of English housing:

> The fire as symbol of home is to the Englishman the central idea both of the living room and of the whole house; the fireplace is the domestic altar before which, daily and hourly he sacrifices to the household Gods . . . In England the fireplace remains and always will remain.

It is hardly surprising, therefore, to find that the need to glorify so sacred a place often went beyond the bounds of good taste. The simple marble surrounds and elegant cast-iron arched grates of the mid-century gave way to very elaborate pieces, often made entirely of cast-iron with ornate overmantels in wood or iron, and invariably with inset tiles flanking the grate. Many shops restore and sell such fireplaces today, usually sandblasted to reveal the blue-grey metal, although the surrounds were always painted originally, and the actual grates were blackleaded daily.

△ **Turn-of-the-century fireplaces were often very elaborate, incorporating shelves, mirrors and even small cupboards. The columns, ribbons, swags and bows on this piece mark it as part of the Adam Revival.**

The Arts and Crafts Movement had a profound effect upon fireplace decoration towards the end of the century, and there was a reversion to much simpler forms. Fireplaces in the 'artistic' homes of the 1890s and 1900s were smaller and less dominant, often with a simple painted wooden frame encasing plain or mottled blue or brown tiles in which was a plain rectangular fireplace opening. The ornate brass and iron fenders of the Victorians were also replaced by simpler versions. The Adam revival of the 1880s, however, led to a fashion for eighteenth-century dog grates – or at least sham andirons – which were seen in some houses for the next twenty years.

The 'country cottage' revival of Voysey and his colleagues was to have an even greater and more lasting effect on fireplace design. The inglenook now became the ideal in suburban drawing rooms – a cosy room within a room with built-in seats and small porthole windows. In larger Arts-and-Crafts-

◁ **In stark contrast to the scene above, this fireplace of the same period is in the simpler Arts and Crafts style, based upon the traditional cottage inglenook with fitted seats and peephole windows. The planished copper canopy and attention to detail, such as in the fuel cupboard hinges, mantel shelf and tiling, perfectly match the simplicity of the room.**

designed houses, bare red or whitened brick and wooden beams were the usual materials, and an inverted cone of planished copper to carry away the smoke and conduct heat into the room became a fashion which exists to this day. Suburbia took to the inglenook like a duck to water, and if space or design did not permit one, high-backed settles placed by the fire to create a recess where none existed were the next best thing. Numerous manufactured red-brick fireplaces, often with little inset shelves and possibly hearths raised at the sides to form uncomfortable seats were also introduced in imitation of a supposedly 'cottagey' style, and were popular in suburbia for many years. In deference to the new style the more traditional cast-iron fireplaces were also often given brass or copper inset hoods, and at the same time the very un-English Art Nouveau style seems to have had an influence, particularly on smaller fireplaces designed for bedrooms.

Above the mantel-shelf, the large mirrors previously favoured were replaced in the 1870s by 'display overmantels'. This fashion, popularized by influential writers such as Edis and Eastlake, provided shelves on which to display the blue and white china or *Japonnerie* which every 'artistic' household was supposed to collect. By the turn of the century, however, the overmantel had disappeared from the most fashionable homes, and even the mantel-shelf itself was done away with in some of the plainest fireplaces. It was more usual, though, to want the chimneypiece to be as grand as possible, and in many houses, the fashion for chimneypieces with little cupboards, mirrors, shelves, and even 'bookcase fireplaces' persisted well into the twentieth century.

Technically, the fireplaces of the new century were a great advance, and at last realized Count Rumford's theories of the 1770s. The fire compartments themselves were made of fireclay, angled forward at the back, and with splayed sides to reflect heat into the room. The absence of metal in contact with the coal, and the heat-retaining qualities of the tiles, also meant that the fire burned more efficiently, while the narrow fixed throat cured the worst of the draughts, although chimney cowls to aid smoke extraction were usually still essential. The fire was also set much closer to the floor and it became standard to fit a cover with holes over the ashpit, to regulate the flow of air under the fire and thus slow down combustion. In short, by 1900 the pattern of open-fire design was set for the next sixty years.

Gas and Electric Fires

Gas was not a very popular heating medium before the First World War. Like closed stoves, gas fires were said – incorrectly – to dry the air. Reasonably efficient gas fires had been produced since 1856, when it was shown that fireclay tubes heated by the blue, smokeless flame of a gas-air mixture glowed red-hot and sent out radiant heat. In 1882, the Smoke Abatement Exhibition featured many gas fires designed to fit into existing grates with imitation coal made from asbestos, on an identical principle to the imitation coal fires produced today, and just as wasteful of heat. Gas at that time cost about four times as much as coal, and most gas fires were installed in bedrooms where convenient, instantaneous but sporadic heating was required.

Electric fires only became a practical proposition just before the outbreak of war, when nickel elements were introduced. Prior to that, elements had been sealed in sausage-shaped glass tubes to protect the wires from the oxidizing effect of the air. Belling produced the first modern electric fire in 1912, complete with kettle and toast rack. By 1921 the first imitation coal-effect fire had been produced by the same firm, and imitation has dogged the design of both coal and gas fires ever since. It is a pity that designers have not heeded the words of Muthesius, writing in 1905:

It is true here and there, especially in the houses of the small men, the Philistines, one sees imitation coal and log fires, constructed of clay and asbestos and made to glow by gas flames designed to simulate the image of the fire in the hearth, but cultivated Englishmen with their sound good sense rightly resist this substitute. Imitation fireplaces have as yet gained no ground . . . an honest gas fire is quite unexceptional in itself, but why make it simulate an open fireplace?

△ **The first modern electric fire, made by Bellings in 1912, complete with kettle and toast rack. Such honest design soon gave way to imitation coal or log effects.**

TILES

Tiles, which Victorian builders increasingly incorporated into their houses, fulfilled many Victorian requirements: they were permanent and durable, and available in a vast number of bold patterns and forms to enable artistic whim to be pandered to; moreover, the easily cleaned glazed surfaces satisfied the increasing public desire for hygiene. Tiles began to be used not only on floors but also on walls in kitchens, bathrooms, halls and entrance porches, and they were also set into fireplaces and furniture such as washstands. Their hygienic image made them particularly popular in the new shops springing up to serve suburbia, and butchers and dairies, in particular, often had fully tiled walls depicting elaborate if romanticized pastoral scenes appropriate to the products sold. Some of these have survived today and are wisely preserved by their current owners, as they are some of the finest examples of the Victorian tilemakers' art.

◁▽ Shakespearian and mythological scenes were popular with Victorian tile makers, as were stylized flowers. ▷The most famous Victorian tile designer was William de Morgan. His work, being hand-made, was expensive, but inspired patterns on mass-produced tiles.

Encaustic Floor Tiles

The practice of tile-making had all but died out in Britain when Herbert Minton managed to perfect the commercial production of inlaid, or encaustic, tiles in 1840. These are basically tiles moulded from one clay, usually red, with an indented pattern into which was poured clay of a different colour, usually white. On being fired the two clays fused together. This technique had been used in medieval times to decorate churches, and its reinvention using mechanical processes coincided with the Gothic Revival of the 1840s and 1850s. Pugin himself (see pages 60–61) advocated encaustic tiles in Gothic fleur-de-lis or trefoil patterns for the floors of the many churches of the Gothic Revival being built in suburbia. Soon encaustic tiles were being used to floor the hallways of many suburban homes, both large and small, and, unless damaged, they provide an attractive, practical surface that cannot be bettered. Repairs can be made, and antique shops are increasingly stocking Victorian tiles, and it is even possible to find whole floors salvaged from demolished buildings.

Wall Tiles

After 1870 many tile-making firms were established to cater for an almost insatiable demand that was to last until the popularity of tiles began to wane shortly before the First World War. Many of these firms produced thinner wall tiles decorated by transfer print, a process which allowed more elaborate patterns and finer detailing than on encaustic tiles. The range of patterns and the avail-

ability of styles was, as with many other products of Victorian design, almost limitless. The early Gothic forms remained popular, as did Greek and Roman patterns, and the traditional blue and white Delft tiles depicting Dutch scenes were imported as well as made in Britain. Landscapes and views ranging from the Highlands to the Bay of Naples were common, but the most popular motifs were flowers and birds in both naturalistic and highly stylized forms. Later in the century human figures

became increasingly popular, often in medieval or Elizabethan costume and sometimes enacting scenes from stories or plays.

The Arts and Crafts Movement was an important influence on tile design, and the most famous of such tiles were produced by William de Morgan, a friend of William Morris and clearly influenced by him. True to Arts and Crafts philosophy, his exquisitely designed and vividly coloured tiles – often depicting peacocks – were made entirely by hand. Expensive then, like most Arts and Crafts products, they are collectable but very expensive today.

The other major influence on tile design, the Art Nouveau Movement of the 1890s, offers more hope to the impecunious purchaser. The bold, highly stylized, floral forms and long, flowing, mellifluous lines were usually further emphasized by using relief, and lustrous glazes add an exotic feel to the rather sombre greens and browns that were favoured. Although Art Nouveau was never as popular in England as on the Continent, its bold lines did appeal to the tile-makers, and many thousands of lower middle-class and artisans' dwellings, particularly in northern cities, incorporated them in fireplaces and porches – hence their relative availability today.

Modern plain white tiles can be used in kitchens and bathrooms, but remember that plain tiles used at this period were not only larger than most modern types but were hung in a brickwork fashion, not 'square on' as is usual today. Border tiles, either patterned or in relief, are also usually necessary to recreate the correct effect, and authentic-looking designs are once again being manufactured and becoming widely available.

LIGHTING

Late Victorian and Edwardian homes were lit by gas, electricity and oil, as well as by candles. Muthesius claimed that electricity was the most popular lighting method, even in remote parts, and that gas was reserved only for halls and kitchens, but he was probably referring to fairly grand houses; suburbia was more likely to have been lit by a combination of all four methods. Electric lamps became more efficient after 1900, but their light was still relatively dim, and it was usual for ceiling pendants to be suspended from quite complicated systems of pulleys so that they might be lowered when in use to make the most of the light.

The great advantage of electricity, of course, was that it could be switched on and off instantly, with switches fixed conveniently by the door to a room. Gaslight manufacturers, having achieved technical superiority for a while with their inverted incandescent mantles, tried to compete by introducing 'switched systems' in which lights were connected to switches mounted near doors either by tiny pneumatic tubes or by cables rather like brake cables on a modern bicycle. The gas valve could thus be operated by remote control, and, unless the pilot light had blown out, the room lit without the need to fumble for matches in the dark. The connecting pipes and cables could be sunk into the plaster of the wall just like electric wires. Oil lamps too, were in widespread use throughout this period, and their portability made them particularly useful as standard lamps, which were very common. Usually made of wrought iron, they had a mechanism for adjusting the height of the lamp so that the light could be concentrated on a person's book or needlework.

The design of oil lamps seems to have been influenced by the Arts and Craft Movement, and many designs in brass and copper with plain opaque glass shades were now produced, in reaction to the heavily ornate lamps with etched and coloured glass shades of previous decades, which continued to find favour with some. Gas lights, on the other hand, seem to have been more influenced by the Art Nouveau style, possibly because the pipes and brackets could readily be transformed into the sensuous fronds and tendrils of that style.

◁▷ The only similar items in these two early twentieth-century dining rooms are the electric pendant lamps. The one in the Adam-style room (which lacks the restraint of the original) has wrought-iron scrollwork and is complemented by shaded electric 'candlesticks', and the one in the no-nonsense Arts and Crafts room is of brass and copper and has the heart motif first used by Voysey. Both have a fabric valance which was typical of the period, whatever the style of one's house.

It was the design of electric lamps, however, which most excited Muthesius. He was particularly enthusiastic about the work of the architect W.A.S. Benson, who designed lamps in the Arts and Crafts manner in the 1880s:

[Benson] created lamps that were to have a revolutionary effect on all our metalware. Benson was the first to develop his design directly out of the purpose and character of the metal as material. Form was paramount to him. He abandoned ornament at a time when, generally speaking, even the new movement was fond of ornament.

Benson is also credited with introducing shades of shiny metal which reflected the light downwards and prevented the dazzling glare of a bare electric lamp suspended over the dining table that so many early users seem to have endured. For all lights, however, whether gas, oil, or electricity, silk shades were still preferable, and those sold by Liberty, the London store, were particularly renowned. Muthesius notes that 'England introduced a strange adjunct to the light appliance in the form of the material shade', and remarks upon the complete absence of American 'mosiac glass' shades, although reproductions of these are sold today in Britain as supposed Edwardiana.

△Mass-produced gas brackets such as these from a catalogue of 1913, *Art and Utility in Gas Fittings*, lent themselves to designs with curving leaves and tendrils inspired by Art Nouveau, but lacked the subtlety of handcrafted work such as that by W. A. S. Benson, most famous of the Arts and Crafts metalworkers.
▷Benson's Art Nouveau electric table lamp of 1904 has a 'Ceonix' glass shade.

STAINED GLASS

The Victorians were fascinated by glass, the price of which fell considerably during the nineteenth century as manufacturing techniques improved and excise duties were discontinued. In addition, given the interest in all things medieval which accompanied the Gothic Revival, the ancient craft of stained-glass work, which for centuries had been confined to churches, quickly found a place in civic and domestic architecture. Its Victorian virtues were obvious: it let in light but retained privacy, and at the same time could be as showy as cost, if not good taste, would allow. Builders' merchants supplied complete windows in which coloured and painted pieces of glass were set into strips of lead called cames.

▽This remarkable window is in the drawing room of Linley Sambourne House in west London, built between 1868 and 1874. The sunflowers in blue 'art' pots are evidence that the owners subscribed to the Aesthetic Movement. Although the central lights with their formal grid pattern of family crests show the influence of Morris's style, the exuberance and free-flowing lines of the lead in the upper panels are typical of Arts and Crafts work of the 1890s, which was to influence leaded glass design for the next fifty years. In particular, the rising sun motif was to be exactly reproduced, complete with swifts, on the windows of hundreds of 1930s semis.

Since stained-glass windows were relatively expensive it was desirable that they be placed in a prominent position, and the front door was the obvious choice. For this reason, the Georgian tradition of a solid wooden door with two full-length, or four or six panels, surmounted by an opening fanlight of delicate tracery, was superseded in the mid-nineteenth century by the practice of actually incorporating the glass into the door itself. Normally only the two upper panels were glazed, either in a sand-blasted and etched floral design or by coloured pieces set in lead. The size of the glazed area was increased until by the 1880s the whole of the top half of the door might contain several leaded panels holding dozens of pieces of differently coloured glass, in a variety of shapes and sizes. Designs displaying such Victorian exuberance were common right up to the First World War.

The early Arts and Crafts Movement, under the influence of William Morris, had done much to revive and popularize this ancient craft. Many famous windows in churches and other public buildings were constructed at this time, those by Edward Burne-Jones being particularly well known. Scenes from legend and mythology were favourite themes, but such elaborate work was too expensive for most middle-class homes. Simpler designs, such as the ubiquitous peacock's feathers and sunflowers, symbols of the Aesthetic Movement, were more usual, and stylized flowers and foliage and medieval motifs were commonly found painted directly on the glass. A favourite medieval theme was heraldry. Shields with suitably unattributable heraldic devices, sometimes even with fictitious family mottoes, lent an air of nobility to many a suburban porch, or at least hinted at good family connections and pandered to the notion of dispossessed country gentlefolk that suburbanites imagined themselves to be.

In Queen Anne and Arts and Crafts houses, window designs were a reaction against the mid-Victorian fashion for large panes of glass that were practical but rather stark-looking, without returning to the tiny panes and light-restricting glazing bars of the Georgian tradition. The usual compromise was to retain a single sheet of glass in the lower sash of each window, but to glaze the upper sash with several panes held by glazing bars arranged in highly individualized geometric patterns. In 'artistic' homes these small panes were often a mix of pale amber, pink or green occluded glass, in a pattern often repeated on the fanlight (usually no longer fan-shaped) over the front door, into which the house number might be inserted.

△ A stained-glass panel by William Morris. Morris helped to revive this medieval craft, creating designs by decorating the glass rather than by the leading.

◁Transfer-printed glass in the form of roundels (left) or front-door panels (above left) was mass-produced in the late nineteenth century.

BATHROOMS AND PLUMBING/1

Before 1870 almost all houses were built without bathrooms. Although obsessed with cleanliness, the early Victorians had a suspicion of hot water; and hot lounge baths, of similar shape to our own, were used mainly for rather vague therapeutic purposes, bathers being referred to as patients. Many commentators advocated daily cold baths, though few surely indulged in such masochistic pleasures. Even in the 1890s, the delicate were still being warned to sponge down in tepid water rather than hot with its attendant, if unspecified, risks. Yet the suspicion of hot water was rapidly overcome by a desire for personal hygiene, encouraged by the mid-century cholera epidemics and a new recognition of how such diseases spread. Cleanliness became an essential element of respectability and although the new suburbanites may not have had fixed baths, they did have enough servants to maintain regular labour-intensive bathing rituals.

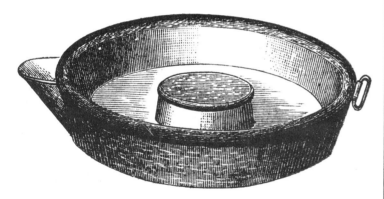

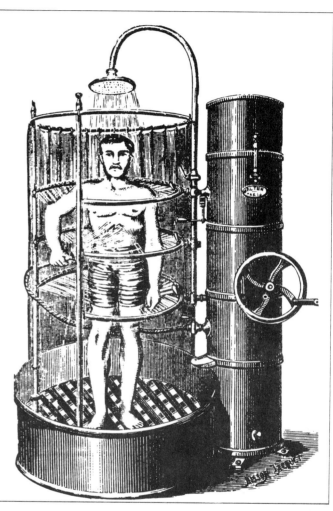

△The simple sponge bath was an effective if rather chilly way of washing the whole body.
▷At the other extreme, elaborate combined 'needle douche and shower baths' such as this French model of 1889 were available.

Portable Bathing Equipment

Before the introduction of bathrooms, the simplest way to wash all over was to stand in a shallow dish about 1 m (3 ft) in diameter and sponge oneself down. Such sponge baths were a common and effective way of getting clean, but did not provide the therapeutic effect which the Victorians wanted. A more elaborate and invigorating system was the portable shower, which resembled a miniature Roman tent set up by a servant in the bedroom or dressing room. A tank at the top was filled with water which, at the pull of a cord, cascaded over the bather to be caught in a tray below. It seems, however, that then, as now, many preferred the more relaxing effect of a bath, and the most common method of bathing was the hip-bath. With or without a wooden seat, this was usually made of iron painted to resemble marble inside, and brown on the outside, and had a high sloping back to support the neck and shoulders. Although one's legs flopped over the end below knee level, it was possible to submerge most of the body in a minimum of hot water. Sometimes a small separate foot-bath was used as well, and both baths would be topped up by a servant from time to time. Such an arrangement was by no means uncomfortable, and the luxury of bathing in front of a roaring fire in one's own bedroom continued to be enjoyed by many ladies long after the advent of fixed baths into their homes.

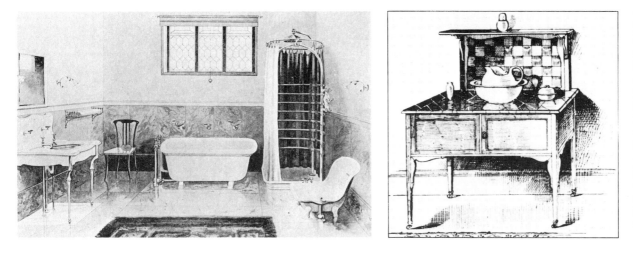

◁◁This turn-of-the-century fixed bathroom displays all the simplicity of the best bathroom design, although the cost of such fittings restricted them to the wealthiest households.
◁The less well off had a washstand, with a marble top and tiled back, like this one dating from 1905.

VICTORIAN FIXED BATHROOMS

A simple technological development, the circulatory hot-water system, made fixed bathrooms possible for the first time, and after 1870 a separate bathroom became a necessary status symbol in every new middle-class home. Baths with gas and even coal-fired boilers built into them had been tried, but the normal practice had been for water heated on the kitchen range to be carried to bedrooms in ewers or special hot-water cans (reproductions of which are often sold as watering cans today). With the new system a water tank, usually housed in an airing cupboard on the same floor as the bedrooms, could be heated by the kitchen range below, and the water piped almost anywhere in the house. The first gas-fired geysers mounted over the bath were apparently a safety hazard but, after 1880 improved designs made them very common. The new technology posed a dilemma: the Victorian philosophy of segregating all functions insisted on a separate bathroom for washing, but the idea of performing such personal activities in a place common to all was distasteful. As few people

could afford more than one bathroom, the usual solution was for everyone to use the bathroom except the lady of the house, who would not only bathe in her bedroom but retained her washstand there also, for daily ablutions. Marble-topped washstands, invariably with tiled splashbacks, continued to be sold, usually with matching dressing tables, well into the twentieth century.

In wealthy homes, rectangular 'Roman' baths of glazed fireclay might be found, but cast-iron baths, which appeared after 1880, soon became the norm. With rounded backs, and often having elaborately ornamental feet, they were sometimes sharply tapered towards the tap end in order to save water. Hip baths or sitz baths (small baths with a fixed seat) were also sometimes plumbed in to save on water and space. Because the enamel made at the time was thin and chipped easily, a protective rail of hardwood might be fixed to the rim of the bath, which might also be encased completely in wooden panelling. After the Edwardians developed tough 'porcelain enamel' baths,

they tended to do away with these wooden surrounds in favour of free-standing baths which were easier to keep clean. The combination of white porcelain and polished mahogany in bathrooms is popular today, however, and quite in keeping with Victorian and Edwardian designs.

Fixed washbasins either stood on metal legs or were suspended from the wall on ornamental iron brackets, and were generally much bigger than their present-day counterparts and thus prevented splashing more effectively. Occasionally basins were plumbed into existing marble-topped washstands, rather like those built into vanity units today, and provided convenient space for the soap dish, sponge basin, dentifrice and toothbrush holder, tumbler, scents, pomades, brushes, and the ever-increasing paraphernalia demanded by the Victorian toilette, both male and female.

Exposed metal was usually brass, or of more expensive nickel plate, and cross-head taps seem to have been universal. Some plumbing arrangements could be

BATHROOMS AND PLUMBING/2

very elaborate, and wealthy homes might boast combined bath and shower units that provided horizontal 'needle' sprays as well as the usual overhead *douche*. The sturdy construction of such magnificent pieces meant that many are still extant, if in need of re-enamelling.

Decoration and Design

Victorian bathrooms were elaborate and cosy by present-day standards; after all, they had developed from bedrooms and dressing rooms. A fireplace was considered essential for ventilation although apparently rarely used for heating. Wallpapers, such as were to be found in any other room, might also be used, with a coat of varnish applied to protect them from the effects of condensation. Heavy patterns were recommended to help conceal any drip runs. The boom in tile production at this period (see page 114) probably owes much to their widespread use in the new bathrooms. Tiled splashbacks for basins and baths were essential, even if a tiled dado for the whole room was beyond the pocket. Homemakers' books also stress the value of tiled floors, but most suburban bathrooms seem to have made do with linoleum or 'cork carpet', either plain or patterned, with mats or cork boards to warm the feet and soak up water. If space permitted, there was also a great deal of freestanding furniture and equipment. The washstand may have found its way into the bathroom from the bedroom, and a chair, often with a cane or rush seat, was usual. Freestanding wooden towel rails were very common, and originals are still available in junk shops today. Linen curtains, small tables, pictures and mirrors all helped to create a more homely, less functional atmosphere than the streamlined look of a more modern bathroom.

The smaller, purpose-built bathrooms

of later Victorian times were, however, prone to condensation problems, so that hard, shiny, impervious surfaces which are not so easily damaged had to be used, and this led to a more clinical look. The new streamlined functional bathrooms delighted Muthesius, who declared that Britain led Europe in the design of bathrooms and sanitary fittings. Hard walls and floors, good hot-water systems with heated towel rails, and, above all, simple but efficient metal and ceramic fittings, received his fulsome praise. He points out that, although the catalogues of the day show WCs and bidets in model bathrooms, WCs were always housed in a separate room, and bidets were never actually seen at all, although 'one may take it for certain that a later culture will regard it as

△**The Victorians used the word lavatory correctly, to mean a washing place, and not as a euphemism. Basins in this style are being reproduced today.**

an inescapable necessity in the water closet'.

Muthesius's praise of the style of early twentieth-century English bathrooms captures the essence of all he admired in good design, which was to influence Europe for the rest of the century, but which England, an unwitting pioneer, was so sadly to neglect. He describes the British bathroom as fundamentally modest and unpretentious, a simple, plain room dictated by need and with none of the conspicuous opulence of continental luxury bathrooms:

It is so genuine and will endure because it has developed strictly logically and ignores sentimentality or studied atmospheric qualities. A modern bathroom of this kind is like a piece of scientific apparatus, in which technique of a high intellectual order rules, and if any 'art' were dragged in it would merely have a disturbing effect. Form which has evolved exclusively out of purpose is in itself so ingenious and expressive that it brings an aesthetic satisfaction that differs not at all from artistic enjoyment. We have here an entirely new art that requires no propaganda to win acceptance, an art based on actual modern conditions and modern achievements that perhaps, one day, when all the fashions that parade as modern movements in art have passed away, will be regarded as the most eloquent expression of our age.

The WC

The problem of human waste disposal is a tale of inventiveness and technology blocked by bureaucratic delay and political ill will. Water-flushing WC pans had been invented in the reign of Queen Elizabeth I, and many efficient types existed in Victorian Britain. What were lacking, however, were a main drainage system to carry away the waste and a fresh water supply that could cope with the demand. The situation varied enormously from town to town: those near the sea or large rivers had main drains, while others had outdated byelaws actually requiring disease-creating middens to be constructed long after their dangers were recognized. Most towns employed dustmen (dust literally meant excrement in those days) to empty privies and provide fertilizer for the market gardens surrounding the growing conurbations. The effect of such primitive arrangements on the middle classes was that they had their chamber pots and commodes emptied by servants, which obviated the need to visit the stinking privy in the garden. For the rising new middle classes, whose only servant might not cope with a large family's needs, suburbia, with its main drainage and flush lavatories, was most attractive.

Lower middle-class Victorian homes featured the rather inefficient hopper-type pan, which was an inverted cone with a U-bend trap at the bottom to keep out sewer gas. To flush it, water was let into a hole at the side and swirled around the hopper, sweeping (if you were lucky) the contents through the trap. Higher up the social scale, the Bramah WC was generally used. Invented by Joseph Bramah in 1777 and in use throughout the nineteenth century, it had a pan closed at the bottom by a valve or small flap, and when the handle was pulled to flush it a complex system of levers opened the flap, let in water to clear the contents, and closed the valve, retaining just enough water in the pan to keep out noxious gases. Although Bramah pans are still in use in some old houses today, nobody would wish to install one in their home now. Many people do, however, recreate the

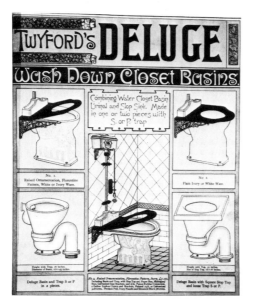

△ **Twyford and Doulton manufactured washdown water closets, some with ornate decoration. Twyford's Unitas one-piece pan made public-health history.**

standard Victorian practice of concealing the pan beneath a built-in wooden bench with a panelled front. These benches were very often handsome pieces in polished mahogany, but the fixed seats meant that they were difficult to keep clean.

By 1890, the two types of pan had been combined into the standard modern washdown type, with trapped pan and flushing rim. Models of the period are still acceptable today, and many firms make exact reproductions. After plain white, and white inside and beige outside, blue floral designs were most popular; and some patterns were even more elaborately coloured and depicted landscape scenes both inside and outside the pan. Wooden lavatory seats, however, were essential. They were normally mounted on cast-iron brackets fixed to the wall rather than directly on to the pan, and many reasonable reproductions can be bought today. Unfortunately, the new pans needed rather ugly high-level cast-iron cisterns to increase the water pressure into the bowl, and these were very noisy. The porcelain handle to be found at the end of the chain usually had the word 'pull' written on it, to save the embarrassment of the house guest who had not come across such a novelty before. These, too, are often seen in shops selling bric-a-brac and are now being reproduced.

The basic design of the washdown pan remained unchanged into the twentieth century, except that the 'lowdown' suite, introduced in 1895, became more common. In this type, the cistern was positioned at the top of the pan to reduce the noise of rushing water, and to make up for the pressure loss its capacity was increased; the feed pipe into the cistern was also lowered to stop it splashing. The siphonic closet was even quieter, but was rarely used until the 1930s, and then only in better-quality houses.

4. 'BY-PASS VARIEGATED' (1920-1960)
Introduction

The inter-war period saw an unprecedented increase in the number of houses built in Britain: the eight million homes fit for occupation in 1919 had been transformed into twelve million by 1939. This spate of house construction expanded the suburbs into the countryside surrounding towns and cities with alarming voracity, and the houses of this period, built mostly in semi-detached pairs, have become the epitome of what is usually meant by suburbia. It is a place which inspires fond emotions in some and derisory comments from others, not only about the appearance of the houses but also the supposed values of their occupants.

Whereas the main aim of the Victorians in suburbia was to emulate the gentry, and of the Edwardians to reflect an artistic sensibility, the new generation of suburbanites had a more complex set of aspirations. The suburban semi-detached house, now mostly owned rather than rented, had to express a degree of individuality without being too different from its neighbours. Even more importantly, it had to be easily distinguishable from its local-authority counterpart (about a quarter of the houses built in this period were council-owned). Ideally, the internal and external decoration was intended to evoke an 'olde worlde' cosy cottage image, since the suburban dweller craved a 'rural idyll' full of traditional values.

◁**Sunday morning in suburbia just before the Second World War – note the newly planted saplings and the gas lamp.**

The Rise of the Semi

It was this rejection of the uncompromising images of the neo-Georgian and Modernist styles favoured by the architectural establishment that provoked the most acute criticism. While suburban architecture had hitherto usually followed – albeit late and in diluted form – the styles preached and practised by the great architects of the day, with Gothic, Italianate and Arts and Crafts styles all adopted in their turn by speculative builders, the predominant style of the 1920s and 1930s (while having its origins in the Arts and Crafts Movement and vernacular revival) created a building type peculiar to itself. The haphazard combination of architectural details – mock beams, lattice windows, weatherboarding, pebble-dash and fancy brickwork – created, in Osbert Lancaster's words, an 'infernal amalgam' of the 'least attractive materials and building devices known in the past', a view shared by the architectural profession and social commentators alike.

Not only did the aspirations of the new suburbanites differ from those of their predecessors, but so also did their whole way of living. The new houses were considerably smaller than those of the Edwardians and Victorians, and generally servantless, and these two factors encouraged a new attitude to the use and arrangement of the home. Reception rooms were no longer segregated into formal reception areas and those for family use; guests would be entertained in the family's sitting room or living room (now sometimes called the lounge), and the family as a whole found shared amusement in new gadgets such as the gramophone and the wireless. Children in particular played a more visible role in the household, and as much attention was given to their comfort and recreation as to the adults'.

The increasing informality of domestic life led the architects of the Modern Movement confidently to predict that a functional open-plan living space would become the norm, but although some gestures were made in this direction during the 1930s, it was not until the 1950s that people really began to look at the layout and arrangement of their homes in a fundamentally different way.

'BY-PASS VARIEGATED'/2

The Moderne Approach

While the Modern Movement had little visible effect on the suburbs except for the pockets of 'suntrap' housing that sprang up here and there, it did become fashionable to be modern in some way. For example, the *Complete Home Book* of 1937, in describing itself as 'concerned with labour and space-saving features to make it [the home] ideal for its purpose', echoed the 'fitness for purpose' arguments of designers of the Modern Movement. In common with other books and magazines of the period concerned with the home, it gave tips on instant modernizing, such as adding a moulding to bisect window sashes to give the horizontal effect of the 'moderne' home and recommending that doors be flush-panelled with hardboard. Another fashionable preoccupation was with the sun and its health-giving properties. Those who lived in moderne semis could sunbathe on their flat roofs, the scientific bought themselves sunlamps, while others were encouraged to have the new 'Vitalite' windows fitted, since 'Vita' glass let through the ultra-violet stopped by ordinary glass and 'lets health flood into your home – whether the windows face north, south, east or west'.

The period also saw an increase in Government attempts to influence public – and manufacturers' – taste in the appreciation of good design. Exhibitions of industrial design, and the Government's own housing policies, all furthered the cause, but with marked lack of success. The Utility programme introduced during the Second World War (see page 146) seemed a perfect opportunity to impose 'good design' on the public, but unfortunately, just as they did not want their homes to look like council houses, suburban home-owners disliked the potential uniformity of Utility furniture, not to mention its understated, unreferential simplicity.

Utility represented only austerity, and by the 1950s home-owners were enthusiastically opting instead for colour, pattern and quirky furniture. There was, however, a general renewed interest in the possibilities of design and, in particular, the joys of homemaking, not least because it was considered important to get wives back into the home and away from the 'men's work' they had undertaken during the war. The *News of the World Better Homes Book* of 1954 reflects this popular view:

> The art of homemaking was sadly neglected during the war . . . The home has always been the backbone of the British way of family life. A tastefully planned home provides a wife with a graceful background and a haven for the husband, where business worries can be temporarily banished.

And where better to establish it than in the standard suburban house?

THE TUDOR WALTERS REPORT AND ITS INFLUENCE

The Tudor Walters Report of 1918 was based upon a very wide consultation process and, in its efforts to get things right, examined the experience of the numerous model suburbs of the late nineteenth and early twentieth centuries. The intention of its recommendations was to improve the design of all housing, not only that built by councils for rent but also that built by private developers for owner-occupiers. The report thus became an important guide for the inter-war planners, and its practical approach to costings appealed directly to speculative builders. Unfortunately, much of its influence on design was negative, as private developers took pains to avoid any hint of the council estate.

Some recommendations were almost universally adopted, such as the twelve houses per acre density norm, which, when combined with cul-de-sac road layouts actually became more cost-effective than the standard pre-war terrace. But the differences between council and private suburbia are obvious to the most casual of observers, suggesting that the recommendations were, to say the least, open to interpretation. Possibly the report itself was ambiguous: while stressing the need to standardize elevations and create an overall sense of order, it also warned against the creation of monotonous uniformity. Naturally enough, the local-authority architects, striving to create supposedly egalitarian communities, stressed an overall sense of order, while developers, anxious to pander to middle-class individualism, tended to heed the warning against monotony.

So powerful was this fundamental difference in housing philosophy that simmering resentment of nearby council estates by owner-occupiers erupted into something near open hostility in the late 1930s. The inhabitants of several private estates arranged for high walls to be built across roads where they ran into council estates to prevent the encroachment of the hoi-polloi (and their children and dogs) into their more 'select' domain. Although owners and council tenants were often from similar social backgrounds, it took twenty years of legal battles to remove the walls, which gives a clear indication of the concerns of the private owner – the need to rejoice in one's individuality, and the inability to accept anything that does not conform to middle-class norms and which might 'lower the tone' of the area and with it property values. Thus the very design of council estates, no matter how good, was rejected by the middle classes as having the wrong associations. The good intentions of the Tudor Walters Report therefore backfired somewhat.

Housing specification in the report included a number of interesting features. Although access to rear gardens was universally accepted as desirable, council estates tended to adopt short terraces with access to gardens via tunnels which, although costing more to build, preserved the unity of style of the front elevation, as did the inner-city terraces of a hundred years before. To enhance this effect, horizontal bands, string courses and long continuous roofs were also preferred, to link the whole group, and it is sometimes difficult to tell where one house begins and another ends. Tudor Walters had praised the American open garden system (experimented with again in the 1960s) but, recognizing the public's desire for private gardens, most council estates achieved uniformity by means of a continuous, neatly clipped privet hedge. Public open spaces were, however, deliberately incorporated into most estates to emulate the greens of village communities. Shops and other amenities were often lacking, however, unless warranted by the market forces created by very large estates.

The style commonly used for the council suburbs of the 1920s (which was that used for the drawings accompanying the Tudor Walters Report) is the neo-Georgian popularized by Louis de Soissons at Welwyn Garden City, and epitomized by almost any inter-war Post Office. Its order and regularity appealed to the architects' own sense of taste and, as the houses were designed to need the

◁Although the 'Coronation Room' at York Castle Museum captures a particular moment in 1953, it was typical of suburban front rooms of the time in bringing together earlier styles: for example, the picture rail, border paper and brown woodwork date from the 1930s, as does the carpet; and the three-piece suite still has the antimacassars popularized in the Victorian period.

minimum of maintenance, there was little the tenants could actually do, even if they had the financial incentive, to render their homes more individual.

No such restrictions held back the owner-occupier or the developer trying to woo him. The council estate, which so many hoped would educate the masses in matters of architectural taste, actually had the opposite effect. The obstinate preference shown by the middle classes for the picturesque, rural, vernacular style can be largely accounted for simply because it was not the ordered neo-Georgian of the council estates. Indeed, only when council housing became functionalist modern after 1950 did the mock-Georgian style become fashionable in the private sector.

Cost-conscious builders only incorporated public open spaces on the most expensive private estates, the emphasis generally being on private gardens, and similar price considerations dictated the form of the houses. The ideal was detached, but the cheaper semi became the standard form.

'No two houses the same' was the proud claim of many estate developers advertising in the 1930s, and yet that was not strictly true, for although gables, half-timbering, porches, leaded windows and other details were added and subtracted in infinite permutations, each pair of semis was usually identical, as symmetry was used to give weight and importance to the whole structure.

Important as such detailing was for reasons of social status, both council and private housing tended to be essentially conservative in design. The council architects needed to work within strict cost yardsticks and meet egalitarian principles which forced them to produce houses almost exclusively aimed at the needs of the 'average family' as effectively as any market-oriented developer. The private owner, who may have wanted to sell his house one day, and, perhaps more importantly, the building society who needed safe, saleable collateral, frowned upon anything that strayed too radically from tried and tested designs.

ARCHITECTURAL STYLES BETWEEN THE WARS/1

The four million homes built between the wars in the huge belts of leafy suburb encircling towns and cities, and often extending far into the countryside, probably represent our most powerful image of suburbia, and much that has been vilified ever since. The houses of this time fall into two quite different stylistic categories. First was the picturesque 'cottage style' based on the Arts and Crafts vernacular and the Edwardian rural revival. Often called mock Tudor, it used styles and motifs from the times of Queen Elizabeth and King James I, hence the other usually derisory name 'Jacobethan'. In contrast, a less popular style, inspired by the starkly functional Modern Movement, also made its impact on suburbia. Both these styles were highly modified and given distinctly suburban characteristics of their own.

JACOBETHAN

The Jacobethan or cottage vernacular style, once much derided, is enjoying something of a revival today. It is typified by half-timbering, herringbone brickwork, leaded windows, gabled porches, and red-brick or pebble-dashed walls. Inside, the theme would be continued by the use of oak panelling, false beams and, in large houses, inglenooks. Cosy images of traditional vernacular rural architecture were combined in endless permutation, and provided the semi or, more correctly, pair of semis with individual characteristics that were nevertheless well within strictly defined norms. In the conservative suburbs individualism could not be allowed to get out of hand, and even detached houses were often just like semis in every way except that they were without their other half.

A porch was essential. At its simplest, the porch might be a plain canopy suspended by two ornamental wrought-iron bars from hooks on the wall above, very much in the earlier Arts and Crafts manner. More elaborate porches had timbered gables and red-tiled roofs supported on oak posts. Also popular was the recessed porch reminiscent of late-

Victorian suburbia. The steps were of brick or quarry tiles, to which was applied a rich patina of 'Cardinal' red. By day, striped awnings were sometimes used to keep the sun from the door, and at night an electric pendant, usually a 'rustic lantern', made a welcome glow. Porches were never fully enclosed. The storm porches frequently added today look quite out of place on inter-war housing because they conceal the front door, whereas the original intention was to frame and emphasize it.

The front door itself was ideally of oak studded with false nail-heads and strap hinges, and sturdy enough to give an impression of solidity and cosiness. Most houses, however, had a painted front door, the top third of which was invariably glazed, usually with six small panes arranged in a rectangular or oval pattern. It was also usual for the hall to be lit by an extra window, either adjacent to or close by the front door and often in the form of a small oriel or porthole glazed with stained glass.

The two-storey bay, whose windows served the front reception room and bedroom was possibly the most standard feature of inter-war speculative housing.

The stone mullions copied by Edwardian suburbanites from Voysey's houses gave way almost entirely to wooden frames, with the casements themselves constructed of metal or wood. Lead lights were very common: coloured glass in the Edwardian manner was incorporated into the top lights of bay windows, but tended to be applied more sparingly in the parts people looked through. Circular windows were sometimes set into chimneystacks in order to light inglenooks, and these and large staircase windows were glazed in stained or at least occluded amber glass. Since these windows often faced the house next door, complete stained glazing avoided invasions of privacy and maintained the illusion of being secluded. On houses which took the mock-Tudor style as far as emulating the 'jettied' framing (an overhanging upper storey), it was also common to recreate the Elizabethan solar window, in which the central casement is formed into a rounded arch taller than its neighbours. (The original solars were rooms with large windows designed to catch the light and usually on the upper floor.) Sliding sashes with small panes and wooden glazing bars

◁These suburban houses photographed in 1938 have probably changed almost beyond recognition by now, under a plethora of misguided additions and so-called improvements.

▷The page from the *Daily Telegraph* of 1935 clearly shows a twentieth-century Battle of the Styles, between the clean modern lines favoured by Laings and New Age Homes, and the Olde Englishe style of Messrs Curton and O'Sullivan, which in the latter case even extends to the typography. Significantly, however, all of them stress the involvement of architects in the design of their houses.

were used only in council housing and on architect-designed neo-Georgian houses built in the 1920s for the chic few.

The walls of Jacobethan houses epitomize the suburban genius for compromise. The favoured material was red brick, both for its warmth and for its Tudor connotations. But large expanses of brick were not liked, and a variety of vernacular materials was also used. Pebble-dash, favourite of the Arts and Crafts builders, was very popular in the 1920s but declined thereafter. Plain rendering and tile hanging were also widespread, although the former was often confined to the upper floor and the latter, used by the Edwardians on the entire upper floor, was now restricted to gables and bays. Creosoted weatherboarding, 'rusticated' beyond all recognition of its Wealden ancestry, was another favourite on gable ends; and expensive houses might incorporate some stone-work in their brick walls, or even contrive ancient 'repair work'.

Whether rendered, dashed or brick, walls invariably had half-inch-thick timber planks to suggest timber framing. It is important to note that it was only rarely and in large (often architect-designed) houses that this feature was actually an attempt to copy medieval timber-framed houses: the timbering of

ARCHITECTURAL STYLES BETWEEN THE WARS/2

most suburban housing, like its herringbone brickwork, had a symbolic function only, as a link with another age.

The overall impression of the Jacobethan elevation, then, is one of cosy clutter, and this is continued at roof level. Red tiles were the standard material, but gables and large overhanging eaves supported on brick corbels or wooden brackets gave an otherwise plain hipped roof the interest and mass of an old Sussex cottage. A very common practice was to continue the gable over the bay window down almost to ground level, forming a porch over the front door on its way; this technique is obviously a vestige of the great sweeping gables of the Voysey tradition. The Arts and Crafts treatment of chimneys can also still be clearly seen. Chimneystacks on outside walls were made into features, although the tall, ornate, and elaborately carved brickwork chimneys which the Victorians sometimes copied from Elizabethan manor houses were too difficult and expensive for speculators to reproduce. Instead, flues were grouped into solid, sturdy stacks with stubby, unobtrusive pots, which, protruding through the ridge of a steeply pitched roof, are suggestive of massive (but non-existent) inglenooks below.

MODERNE

The Jacobethan style remained popular throughout the inter-war period, but after about 1930 the Modern Movement began to make its distinctive, and to many minds alien, mark even on deepest suburbia. As house prices fell in the 1930s, the myriad house-building companies which had jealously competed for the market began to amalgamate, and several large firms such as New Ideal Homesteads and Laing emerged to dominate the industry. As a result of the stiff competi-

1. SMALL TERRACED HOUSE, c.1920. **This simple, well-detailed house displays many features of the Vernacular style, including tile-hanging, scallop-edged lead work on the bay and pebble-dash on the well-proportioned gable. The restrained use of leaded glass in the downstairs windows and front door is particularly effective, and the impression of the whole façade is harmonious.**

2. DETACHED ARTS AND CRAFTS HOUSE. **The porch is a modern addition to this somewhat grander house, but is quite in keeping with the Arts and Crafts mood. The horizontal cottagey windows, fine detailing on the gable and complex roof pattern with only minimal use of mock beams typify much early twentieth-century suburbia. Compare this house with the one in the poster on page 6.**

3, 4. SEMI-DETACHED HOUSES WITH DOUBLE BAYS. **This pair of houses (in reality the pairs were nearly always identical) show how windows could be used to give character to an otherwise quite ordinary house. Those on the left are inspired by the huge solar windows seen on some Elizabethan buildings, while the right-hand house uses the ubiquitous sunray motif. Unfortunately replacement windows have ruined many such houses.**

tion and narrowed profit margins they tended to produce less picturesque, plainer houses, although they still relied heavily on vernacular detailing. Perhaps in response to the continuing criticism of this housing style by the architectural profession, which was dominated by adherents of the Modern Movement, some developers also built homes based on the International Style of these architects, many examples of which had been built in Europe in the 1920s. Thus small pockets of 'moderne' or suntrap housing, as it has come to be known, sprang up in the suburbs in uneasy neighbourliness with the more usual Jacobethan.

Many of the basic tenets of the Modern Movement had their origins in the English Arts and Crafts Movement, but they had been developed further in Europe, particularly at the Bauhaus School of Design in Germany. The school, formally opened in 1919, was headed for many years by architect and designer Walter Gropius, who emphasized the value of acquiring crafts skills, but as a necessary prelude to designing for the industrial process, and not as an end in itself. The exploitation of modern manufacturing methods, the derivation of the form of an object from its function ('form follows function') and the eradica-

tion of all unnecessary decoration were the central principles of the Bauhaus and the Modern Movement in general. The architecture, as represented by the houses built by Gropius himself as well as Mies van der Rohe and Le Corbusier in the 1920s, was stark and functional: houses had flat roofs, sheer white walls (generally concrete) large, completely plain windows, and open-plan living areas; they were devoid of all decorative referential details.

The house was, in Corbusier's words, simply 'a machine for living in'. Corbusier's first houses, however, included details reminiscent of ocean liners; these

5, 6. SEMI-DETACHED HOUSES WITH SWEPT GABLES. The low sweeping gable common on suburban semis was inspired by Voysey, who used it frequently. The pebble-dashed walls, exposed roof timbers and gable vent on the left-hand house, together with the massive chimney stack and ornamental pots, are also in the Arts and Crafts tradition, while the house on the right is less sure of its stylistic origins: the corner window is a moderne touch.

7. HOUSE WITH INTEGRAL GARAGE. By the late 1930s car ownership was common enough for garages to be built into larger houses. This bow-fronted villa has the oak front door, porch, sunray motifs in window and garage doors, and deep overhanging eaves that were all typical of that time.

8. MOCK-TUDOR HOUSE, 1930s. The jettied (overhanging) upper storey of this detached house shows the exuberance which the mock-Tudor style sometimes inspired. The upper-storey windows are particularly distinctive, and it would be impossible to make any modern 'improvements' to the façade such as picture windows without making a house with such a style of its own look ridiculous.

ARCHITECTURAL STYLES BETWEEN THE WARS/3

and other symbols of the 'machine age', such as cars and aeroplanes, were used as references for decoration by those who found the pure functionalism of the style a little hard to take. Such streamlining effects became popular in all areas of design (see Art Deco, page 138), and it was this pseudo-modernism which found considerable success when used for public buildings in England – for example Broadcasting House in London's Langham Place – and for the new factories then being built, especially those for the new electrically based industries which were actually built in the suburbs.

Moderne housing, however, was less well received, with the exception of the few private homes that were specially commissioned. The first example of the International Style in England, a private house appropriately called New Ways, was designed by German architect Peter Behrens in 1925, but it was some years before the first tentative developments in the style appeared in more modest houses. The most famous of these were at Silver End near Braintree in Essex, for the workers of Crittall's metal-window factory. Since metal windows were an essential element of the style, the company was no doubt attempting to influence public taste rather than reflect it (and not very successfully: the houses are still considered 'weird' by the locals). Other examples were the 'sunspan' types built by Wells Coates and Pleydell-Bouverie, which featured huge expanses of curved glass to catch as much sunlight as possible. Wells Coates was one of the greatest critics of the suburban Jacobethan style, and yet the layout of his moderne-style houses and estates differed little from that of their more usual or traditional neighbours.

The typical moderne house of the suburbs has a cuboid shape and a flat roof; in place of concrete, the walls are

△This house at Silver End, near Braintree in Essex, on an estate built by the Crittall metal window company for their staff, is one of the few estates built in the uncompromisingly functionalist International Style. ◁The stark outlines of the International Style proved unpalatable in suburbia, where a compromise form became common, called moderne or 'suntrap', because of the curved windows designed to receive as much sunlight as possible.

rendered brick painted white, and the windows have black-painted metal frames and horizontal glazing bars, possibly exaggerated by a motif of horizontal bands on the walls between the windows. The windows themselves may go round the corners of the house in the rounded 'suntrap' style. The only relief permitted to the horizontal effect might be a small window light with chevron glazing bars; the facade might be further enlivened by a recessed porch and front door with full-length inset window, while the more austere versions had a plain cantilevered porch over a flush-panelled black-painted front door, which might have a small porthole or diamond-shaped window.

Internally, there was usually little difference between the moderne house and its Jacobethan neighbour, other than the appearance of the windows. The open-plan designs of the avant-garde architects seem to have had little, if any, effect on the standard layout.

The first functionalist houses were not a great success with home buyers, and were rapidly modified by the developers to suit the customers' more conventional tastes. This usually meant the addition of a pitched roof, albeit in green or blue rather than red tiles. These, of course, are actually more functional in the English climate than the sunbathing area on the roof which many architects advocated. In this form, starkly modern houses were scattered among cottage-style semis on many suburban estates and, as estate agents will confirm, still remain less popular with buyers today.

The reasons for this lack of popularity were probably to some extent practical: the white rendering was prone to cracking and needed constant and expensive repainting, while the metal windows

▷**Another example of suntrap housing at Southgate, north London.**

III OAK LODGE ESTATE

CHASE ROAD
SOUTHGATE N.14.

Houses may be viewed at any time including Saturdays and Sundays.

BUILDERS ALLEN FAIRHEAD & SONS LTD.,

CHAMBERLAIN & WILLOWS,
ALDERMAN'S HILL PALMERS GREEN, N.13
Auctioneers, Surveyors, HOUSE & ESTATE AGENTS,
Telephone PALMERS GREEN 4471/2.

**ESTATE OFFICE
CHASE ROAD
SOUTHGATE N.14**
Telephone Palmers Green 2925

ARCHITECTURAL STYLES BETWEEN THE WARS/4

(though galvanized) rusted fast, cracking the panes of glass; they were the first to merit the attentions of the window replacement salesmen in the 1960s and 1970s. Another reason could be that these houses tended to date rather faster than their cottage-style neighbours which were designed to a timeless formula. The most important reason, however, was probably emotional: for many people, strictly functional design was the style of the world of work, be it the office or the factory. At home, the suburbanite wanted to inhabit another world entirely. In *The Social History of Housing*, John Burnett says that people did not want Corbusier's 'machine for living in' so much as a 'vehicle for living out a fantasy'.

△For 18/– a week you could buy a cross between a house and a bungalow.

BUNGALOWS

After the First World War, people's perception of the bungalow, previously seen merely as a temporary holiday house, began to change, partly through being seen in films emanating from Hollywood where it was the standard building form; and during the inter-war period this housing style achieved both its greatest popularity and notoriety. Many of the outer suburbs of this time were being built on relatively cheap land which could accommodate low-density housing and still provide an adequate return to the developer. Entire estates of bungalows, detached and semi-detached, were constructed.

1. MODERNE SEMI-DETACHED HOUSE, c.1930. The moderne or International Style flowered briefly in the 1930s, its trademark a horizontal effect created by a flat roof and bands of white rendering. The horizontality here is further enhanced by the lines in the black 'marble' of the porch which extend the lines of the glazing bars on the curved suntrap windows.

2. SMALL DETACHED JACOBETHAN HOUSE, 1930s. Every trick in the builder's repertoire of Jacobethan styling has been used to make this house seem as much like a country cottage as possible: the sweeping gable, tall chimneys, half-timbering and leaded lights in the windows are all suggestive of the rural vernacular tradition. The stones of the garden wall are made from waste-products of blast furnaces, and were commonly used to create a rustic effect.

3, 4. RESTRAINED MODERNISM, late 1930s. The suntrap house on the left is the simplest version of suburbia's response to the International Style. It has compromised on a number of features, notably the roof, which is pitched to appeal to the conventional tastes of most buyers. The house on the right is also an attempt to escape the referential and symbolic clutter of the standard semi, but with more success. Brick rather than rendered walls are sympathetic to the British climate, while the façade is an original touch.

Before long a compromise form of bungalow – the chalet style – was commonly seen. Based on several large country houses built by various Arts and Crafts architects around the turn of the century, suburban chalets usually incorporated an extra bedroom or two under the roof. The necessary dormer windows, or, on expensive properties, 'eyebrow' windows, helped to create the highly desirable cottage look, but the overall appearance was marred on many semi-detached chalets by placing the front doors at the sides of the building. True suburbanites have always shunned this practice, preferring to make visible to the world the entrance to their domain, with all its symbolic connotations.

There were several reasons for the upsurge in popularity of bungalows with both speculators and purchasers. The seaside holiday connection helped to make them popular with retired people, and then, as now, builders pushed the convenience factor hard in their advertisements. The higher prices charged relative to conventional houses have traditionally been blamed on the extra land and roofing materials necessary, but in fact the real reason was related more to the spending power of the potential purchasers – older people, with some accumulated capital and fewer outgoings with their children gone, and therefore more money to spend. This factor tended to have an overall inflationary effect upon the bungalow market.

A second financial inducement existed in the 1920s. The state housing subsidy, which the government introduced in 1919 to stimulate the house-building industry, paid the same amount for houses as for bungalows but allowed the latter to have a much smaller overall floor area, which made the subsidy more valuable. Many townspeople saw ownership of a cheap subsidized bungalow as their key to the countryside, and they quickly became a major new feature of rural areas. The appearance of little bungalows on the edge of towns often heralded the imminent encroachment of suburbia proper, and perhaps it was for this reason that bungalows have borne the brunt of the criticism made of suburbia at the time.

5. HOLLYWOOD MODERNE, late 1930s. **Just before the Second World War a new form of the moderne style, incorporating Mexican or Mediterranean influences, reached Britain via California, or – more precisely – Hollywood. Elements of the style included white rendering and a pantiled roof in either green, as here, or blue.**

6. NEO-GEORGIAN HOUSE, c.1950. **The post-war rebuilding programme, while marred somewhat by a shortage of materials, was distinguished by a desire to return to the simplicity of Georgian architecture and away from the ornamentation and clutter of the preceding century. This house is a typical example of the housing built during the new mood of planned development as the ideal.**

7. NEO-GEORGIAN HOUSE, 1950s. **A good example of the neo-Georgian of the 1950s, with sliding sash windows, dainty glazing bars and simple porch. Variations on the style were favoured for most new building projects, and were rather more restrained than those seen in new houses today.**
8. 'CONTEMPORARY'-STYLE HOUSE, c.1960. **At first sight the unusual window arrangement makes this house seem novel, but the 'cat-slide' roof with dormer and rustic brickwork are, of course, references to the vernacular tradition.**

POST-WAR HOUSING

Some idea of the differences between post-war housing and that built between the wars can be gained from the Parker Morris Report of 1961. This was a fundamental examination of the way people used their houses, and what provisions should be made for housing in a modern, affluent society. Its recommendations, intended for both the public and private sectors, provide a clear picture of the perceived needs of the time and of what was generally provided.

▽ The semi-detached form of the pre-war period was often retained in the 1950s but given an entirely new treatment. Instead of bay windows, stained glass and other elements of the vernacular tradition beloved of inter-war builders, the façade has a simplicity that owes more to the Georgian style of 125 years earlier than to anything else. The metal window frames with horizontal glazing bars low down and set in deep concrete-lined recesses are typical of the period.

The main recommendations of the report were for more living and circulation space and for better heating; the design of the kitchen was seen as fundamental to the layout of the whole house. Two living spaces were invisaged, one for private or quiet activity, and the other for eating, but the latter could quite easily be part of an enlarged kitchen rather than a separate dining room, a practice unthinkable before the war. A parlour or room 'saved for best' was no longer even considered. The kitchen area itself was to be extensively fitted to provide copious storage space, with the famous 'work sequence standard' of work surface/cooker/work surface/sink/work surface as the norm. Plenty of power points and provision for electrical equipment were to be supplied as labour-saving gadgetry became affordable by almost every household. Minimum room sizes were specified, generally larger than had been the norm, and built-in wardrobes in bedrooms were to be standard, to replace the cumbersome 'suite'. Circulation space was also given greater consideration: independent access to each living room – formerly a standard suburban requirement – was no longer regarded as essential. Experiments in complete open planning, on the American apartment model, were not regarded, however, as likely to be popular in Britain.

Extra heating, to supplement the traditional open fire in the living room and the coke boiler in the kitchen, was envisaged, to ensure that bedrooms

could be fully utilized for study or recreation by the children of the family rather than used for simply sleeping and dressing. This idea was warmly welcomed, and by the mid-1960s part, if not full, central heating was a feature of every new home, and rapidly being installed in older ones.

Parker Morris recommended very high minimum standards which have never been mandatory for private housing (although they were for a while required of new council housing), but

their effects can be seen in every town and city in Britain. The typical housing of the 1950s and early 1960s, although often still semi-detached, was increasingly built in terraces of two or three storeys, with tiny gardens and integral garages. The shallow pitched roofs have possibly one, but usually no chimney at all. Large picture windows occupy much of each elevation, and it was usual to apply cladding to at least part of the walls. Vertical strips of cedarwood were popular for a while, in emulation of the Scandinavian

▽The Georgian influence may be seen even more clearly in these terraced houses of 1954: the idea of a wall pierced at regular intervals by window and door openings, the lack of differentiation between the houses, and the parapet wall concealing roof and guttering are all references to the Georgian style. Only the porch is utterly 'contemporary'.

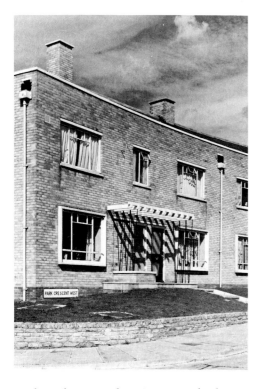

styling that was then in vogue for large, architect-designed houses; but brick, tile, or plastic 'weatherboarding' was a better sop to the local vernacular. Such houses could be and were built almost anywhere; it was often difficult to tell private housing from local-authority work, and traditional regional differences were disregarded.

In the private house of the late 1950s, there were several small but significant differences from earlier houses. Sink units in enamel or pressed steel, avail-able since shortly after the war, became common, and so did coloured bathroom suites in pale pink, blue, yellow or green – called Coraline, Claire de Lune blue, Ivoire de Medici and Ming green by one manufacturer. The living room might be dominated by a 'feature fireplace', often with a chimney breast in 'York' stone tapering towards the ceiling, and sometimes acting as a room divider. The grate itself incorporated the latest technology: draughts were eliminated by an underfloor air supply and a deep ashpit needed to be emptied only once a week; its back boiler would also heat the water and a radiator or two. The 'fireside set' was still present, frequently in the form of a lustreware knight in armour.

Another feature of many living rooms at this time was a cocktail bar fitted in one corner. Usually padded at the front, with glass display shelves and complete with two tall stools, this attempt to recreate the 'local' at home was met with horror in some quarters. Wickerwork bars were slightly more acceptable, but in general they were thought in poor taste. A far better social asset, and a more practical one now that eating in the kitchen was common, was a utility room – in effect the old scullery reborn – to house the latest white goods.

Generally speaking, the interior fixtures of such houses were plainer than earlier styles. Picture rails and cornices tended to disappear completely, and the minute skirting boards, sometimes only 5 cm (2 in) high, left large expanses of unadorned wall relieved only by picture windows. Painted flush-panelled doors (that is, no panels at all) became standard, although a curious fashion for reeded glass doors ensured little privacy and was positively dangerous for young children. Front doors were also commonly fully glazed in the 1950s, usually with an inset of scrolled wrought iron with stylized ivy leaves.

Perhaps the most drastic changes in post-war housing were in the features that were now hidden from view: the huge increase in services meant that even the most basic houses concealed a complex network of pipes and cables. Houses had now to a certain extent indeed become 'machines for living in'. Certainly, their general styling did not even approach the flights of fancy that pre-war suburbia had managed so well, even though people now had higher expectations of the functions their houses should fulfil. Parker Morris was aware of this: as well as fulfilling basic requirements, the house had to be 'something of which [people] can feel proud, and in which they must be able to express the fullness of their lives'.

For a while the styles of public and private housing seemed almost to converge, as the middle classes rediscovered terraced houses, small gardens and urban living. Indeed, a study in 1966 showed that many houses for sale were smaller and had less extensively (although better-quality) fitted kitchens than comparative Parker Morris council homes. What had actually happened was that the all important symbols of status had shifted away from the house onto moveable objects, particularly gadgets replacing servants. Washing machines became status-enhancing possessions and mass car-ownership and package holidays abroad meant that one's standing could be expressed in new ways. The era of the simple, unadorned house was, however, short-lived; developers found they could offer the buyer the opportunity to proclaim owner-occupation by adopting a style that local-authority architects could never condone: the mock Georgian, which, by its symbolic and inaccurate reference to an earlier age, became by the 1960s the equivalent of mock Tudor forty years earlier.

INFLUENCES ON STYLE: Art Deco/1

▷▷**The Art Deco style incorporated many influences, including a taste for the exotic, for surrealism, and for classicism (seen in the column-shaped powder boxes).**
▽**The pottery of Clarisse Cliffe epitomizes the style.**

During the 1920s the suburban taste for reproduction Jacobean furniture and a vaguely 'olde English' style began to change, and a quite new and startlingly different style became fashionable, and remained so throughout the 1930s and 1940s. The style has become known as Art Deco (after a famous exhibition held in Paris in 1925, the Exposition Internationale des Arts Décoratifs et Industriels Modernes), and it was all-pervasive, appearing in artefacts as diverse as furniture, jewellery, poster design, lighting, pottery and ceramics, fabrics and clothes, book bindings and typography, as well as in architecture.

For most of the 1950s and 1960s the style was utterly despised, possibly because it had no obvious philosophical basis or underlying set of principles which had given intellectual respectability to the Gothic Revival and the Arts and Crafts Movement; similarly, no really great names are associated with it, as Ruskin and Morris were with earlier styles. Design commentators, well versed in the Arts and Crafts tradition of hand-crafting, tended to dismiss Art Deco as mere tasteless kitsch, mainly because many of the materials used – chrome, plastic and bakelite, for example – were new and cheap, and ideal for mass production and consumption. Nevertheless, they lent themselves readily to the new idiom.

Themes and Motifs

Several themes and motifs characterize the style across the whole range of products to which it was applied. One was undoubtedly the influence of Cubism and Futurism, and the jagged shapes, zigzag lines and straight-sided geometrical designs which typify the style reflect this (as, for example, in the conical cups with triangular handles designed by Clarisse Cliffe), and immediately distinguish it from the long, flowing, organic lines of Art Nouveau. Another influence was Ancient Egypt, interest in which was dramatically revived by the discovery of the tomb of King Tutankhamun by Lord Carnaervon in 1922. Unlike the 'Regency Egyptian' seen in early nineteenth-century England after Nelson's victory at the Battle of the Nile, this Egyptian Revival did not merely copy sphinxes and obelisks (although the scarab did become a popular design for jewellery), but absorbed the forms and outlines of Egyptian shapes into a thoroughly modern style. The Pyramids themselves

were often thought to have been a source of Art Deco inspiration, but Bevis Hillier argues in *The World of Art Deco* exhibition catalogue (1971) that the true influence for the stepped shapes found on such items as standard lamps (and New York skyscrapers) was the stepped pyramid temples of the South American and Mexican Indians and the Aztec and Mayan art of that region. When Socialist governments were in power in Mexico, they embarked upon massive public building schemes (notably of schools) in which the Spanish Colonial style was rejected in favour of a modern, rational, functionalist approach which drew heavily on the native Indian architectural heritage; the many Mexican revolutions of the early twentieth century kept that country well in the public eye, and the style undoubtedly found its way in the USA and thence to the Modern Movement.

If there is any philosophical basis for Art Deco it is the style of the 'machine age'. Faith in machines as the answer to all human problems was prevalent; but the mood then was the very antithesis of the low-technology approach that is becoming fashionable today. Streamlined forms, in emulation of the car, the boat or the 'plane were seen everywhere, and although the clean lines of many Art Deco objects were pleasing

INFLUENCES ON STYLE: *Art Deco/2*

there was a logical error in their application, as Bevis Hillier pointed out:

There came a point where streamlining had more to do with aesthetics than with function; where glass bricks, vitaglass, vitriolite and bakelite were used not for their structural superiority but for modernistic chic; the machine's importance had become symbolic not real. Streamlining was applied to many kinds of object never intended for speed: radios, refrigerators, accordions, fans, irons, vacuum-cleaners, sales registers, alarm clocks, tractors, toasters, Chinese restaurants, and underwear.

Even if largely rejected as an architectural form, Modernism found its way into every suburban home in the form of Art Deco objects. Such objects were particularly associated with three new customs imported from abroad. Firstly, the 1920s saw the introduction of cocktail drinking into Britain from America. At first confined to chic hotel bars in the West End of London, the habit quickly spread, and every home that professed to be 'with it' had to have a cocktail cabinet which was invariably Art Deco in style (there being no precedent). It might be lined with pink mirrors and chrome detailing, and opening the doors often operated a concealed light. Glasses made of frosted glass with geometrical motifs in the favourite Art Deco combination of green, black and orange would be displayed, along with an array of strainers, swizzle sticks, ice buckets and other paraphernalia except, more often than not, the necessary spirits. Unlike Americans, British suburbanites tended to drink outside the home except on special occasions, and never mixed anything more complicated than a gin and tonic.

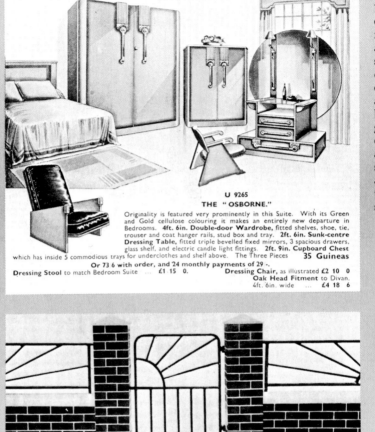

U 9265
THE "OSBORNE."

Originality is featured very prominently in this Suite. With its Green and Gold cellulose colouring it makes an entirely new departure in Bedrooms. 4ft. 6in. Double-door Wardrobe, fitted shelves, shoe, tie, trouser and coat hanger rails, stud box and tray. 2ft. 6in. Sunk-centre Dressing Table, fitted triple bevelled fixed mirrors, 3 spacious drawers, glass shelf, and electric candle light fittings. 2ft. 9in. Cupboard Chest which has inside 5 commodious trays for underclothes and shelf above. The Three Pieces **35 Guineas**
Or 73 6 with order, and 24 monthly payments of 29 -.
Dressing Stool to match Bedroom Suite ... £1 15 0. Dressing Chair, as illustrated £2 10 0
Oak Head Fitment to Divan. 4ft. 6in. wide ... £4 18 6

◁This bedroom suite from the early 1930s adopts a form of Art Deco styling in its attempt to appeal to those seeking something different. Its originality is, we are told, enhanced by its 'green and gold cellulose colouring', although similar styling also appeared on more traditional wooden suites.

◁The sunray pattern on a garden gate: Art Deco's most popular motif.

The second habit to be taken up after the First World War suffered no such restriction: cigarette smoking became a mass habit, and was considered chic among the smart set. Most homes catered for this with an array of ashtrays, often on pedestals, cigarette boxes and smokers' companion sets which were often Art Deco in style.

The third cult, if it can be called that, which Britain took to in the 1920s, was that of the sun. The Art Deco motif of the rising sun appears to have won a special place in the hearts of suburbanites, and it

spread its rays on front gates, garage doors, gable ends, chinaware, the fretwork screens of wireless sets and countless other places. It has been suggested that its popularity stemmed from the fact that the two ancient cultures that influenced Art Deco – Egyptian and Central American – were sun-worshipping, but the real reason is probably that sunbathing actually became the thing to do. The Victorians and Edwardians had kept their skins pale, but now exposure to the sun was thought to be beneficial, and a tan became fashionable.

Art Deco Revival

Although some Art Deco architecture, notably that of cinemas, has survived, enormous numbers of Art Deco objects were thrown away, not only because they represented the taste of the previous generation but also because the very materials used – bakelite, chrome and plaster – were not in themselves valuable enough to keep (ebony and ivory objects have generally had a happier fate). In the 1950s and 1960s the style was seen as 'flashy tat' by connoisseurs of art and antiques: chromium candlesticks, bakelite door-handles, plaster figures restraining wild beasts or holding orbs in their outstretched arms, low dressing tables with enormous round mirrors, armchairs with tassels, 'cut' glass scent sprays with silk-covered rubber bulbs, and innumerable other artefacts typical of the style were discarded as worthless.

Today, the fact that much of it is 'trashy' does not seem to have diminished its collectability or value. Indeed, therein lies much of its charm, for it reflects the age that produced it, an age of insecurity in which the fun, the exuberance and the feverishness of many aspects of life at the time reflected a desire for escape and led it to be described as the Jazz Age. The Cut-Glass Age and the Aspirin Age are, however, perhaps better epithets for a society trying to gloss over its problems. As the economic depression deepened and world war loomed once again, the fun of Art Deco seemed as attractive as the cosy, romantic cottage style of much of suburbia, reflecting as it did the desire to live life for the present with little time for introspection. As such it captures the spirit of its age as perfectly as the Gothicists or Arts and Crafts practitioners did theirs.

◁The ability to surprise or even shock was seen as an essential part of the Art Deco style. Here the traditional long case (grandfather) clock has been treated with a typical lack of reverence, by being used the basis for a concealed cocktail cabinet. The stepped base is a common feature of much Art Deco furniture, as are the built-in mirrors and concealed light.

HOUSE LAYOUT AND ELEVATION

The plan of the standard semi built during the 1920s and 1930s varied little: rectangular in shape, it had two main rooms, a hall and kitchen downstairs, and two bedrooms, a boxroom, a bathroom and separate WC upstairs. Larger houses might have two additional rooms – a study downstairs and an extra bedroom upstairs.

The entrance hall was still important as a display area and for giving the right first impression to the visitor, and ideally was wide enough to allow the stairs to turn at the bottom to display newel posts and balusters. The most fashionable decorations were hardwood parquet flooring and oak-panelled walls, completed with a chair and 'olde worlde' chest; more modest halls might feature a 'Delft rack' on which to display knick-knacks picked up in seaside gift shops.

Separate access to each room was still considered essential, and access from one reception room to the garden through French doors was usual. A side door into the house was also standard, from the driveway into the kitchen.

It was not until after the Second World War that the layout of houses came to be reconsidered.

The loss of servants saw the Victorian dinner party habit decline somewhat after the First World War (not to be revived until the 1960s), but a separate dining room was steadfastly retained. Although now generally smaller than the sitting room, it might easily double for general family use if the larger room were kept for 'best', a hangover from the previous generation's desire for formality. The Victorian practice of providing large folding doors between reception rooms, to create greater flexibility of use, disappeared completely.

Open fires were found in each reception room, although few troubled with the extravagance (in cost and labour) of two fires on anything but high days and holidays. The space actually available for winter use was therefore considerably curtailed, although electric and gas heaters did compensate somewhat for the almost total lack of central heating.

Upstairs, the trend towards smaller and fewer rooms but greater functionalism was continued. Most houses now had only three or four bedrooms, one of which was likely to be little more than a boxroom. Open fireplaces would be provided where a chimney-breast from the ground floor passed through a room, but usually served only for ventilation. Electric or gas fires provided heating, and were usually freestanding. If fitted, they were set into tiled surrounds.

Bathrooms and WCs continued to display the functionalism so admired by Hermann Muthesius thirty years earlier. A tiled dado was usual, at least around the bath and wash basin. The bath itself would be boxed in, and would have chromium rather than nickel-plated taps, with possibly a hand-shower attachment. A streamlined pedestal wash basin and chromium towel rail heated by the flow pipe to the hot-water cylinder would be described as 'luxury fittings' in estate agents' jargon, but were common enough. The decorations also reflected this functionalism: even in Jacobethan houses the rustic-cottage image of the rest of the house had no place here, and even the windows would often have practical occluded glass rather than leaded lights, and the floor in both the bathroom and the WC would probably be covered in abstract Art Deco linoleum rather than anything floral or 'pretty'.

The basically rectangular two-storey layout continued to be the most usual one for houses built up to 1960, after which time the town house approach began to appear, in which houses might be split into three floors. The main difference in housing layout after the Second World War merely reflected the more flexible attitudes of the inhabitants to the use of the available space. There was a move away from the formality which had still characterized the houses of the interwar period, and bedrooms were more likely to double up as playrooms or studies. Fitted or unit furniture became more common, and the formal dining room was ousted in favour of another, everyday type of family room. The only real physical difference in the layout of houses built at this time was in the disappearance of the separate WC, which became integral to the bathroom.

A SEMI-DETACHED HOUSE OF THE INTER-WAR
PERIOD in the cottage vernacular style.

ELEVATION

Materials The tiled roofs and gables, red
brick and plain oak of Costain's
'Oakwood' home (left) place it firmly in
the English vernacular tradition.
The Form The influential Tudor Walters
Report of 1918, recognizing that the
semi-detached form was gaining
popularity, had recommended that the
centre of the pair be stressed to give
visual balance to the building as a whole.
In practice, however, builders emphasized
the individuality of each house by *not*
stressing the centre, and placing focal
points at the sides, with front doors as far
apart as possible. Acoustically it makes
sense to keep the reception rooms apart,
and estate agents now advertise 'halls

adjoining' in houses with some glee.
Windows The two-storey bay, either
angled or curved, was now an absolute
essential, and also emphasized each house
rather than the pair, especially when
viewed from along the road.

LAYOUT

The layout of the Oakwood home is
typical of the great mass of 1920s and
1930s housing, being a standard semi with
the addition of a garage and extra
bedroom to one side. The hall, although
far from large, incorporates a staircase
with two quarter turns, and the landing is
narrowed to accommodate a miniscule
'gallery'. Such effects were symbolically
important vestiges of baronial halls, and
denoted a house not built to strictly
utilitarian standards. This is less true
elsewhere in the house: space is rather

short in the fourth bedroom and, more
importantly, in the kitchen. The cooker
and sink are crammed into corners, and
although there are built-in cabinets, room
has to be found for a coke boiler and
three doorways. With no space for a table,
a drop-down flap presumably provided
the only other work surface.

Although the plans differentiate the
dining room from the pretentiously named
drawing room, the formal usage of rooms
according to function was by now
breaking down somewhat, and was to
lead in the 1950s to new houses being
built with a combined dining and sitting
room on the open plan.

The family as a whole found shared
amusement in new gadgets such as the
wireless or gramophone, and children
were less segregated in the middle-class
household than previously.

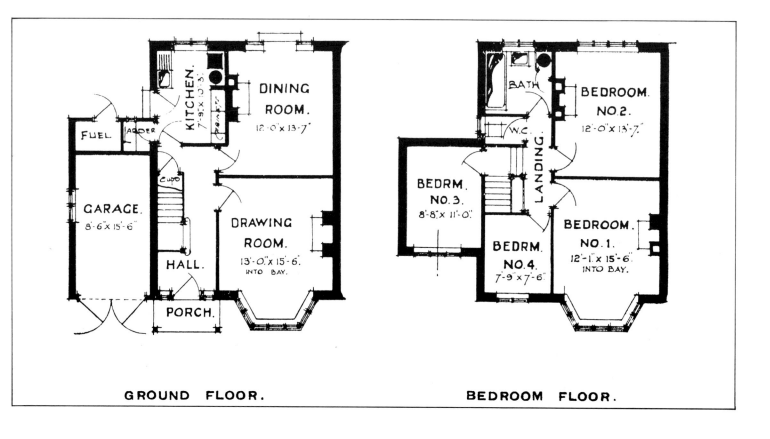

GROUND FLOOR.

BEDROOM FLOOR.

FURNITURE/1

The years between the two world wars formed a period of extremes in household furniture design. On the one hand, 'period' and cottagey furniture became even more important as adjuncts to the Jacobethan semis springing up in suburbia; on the other, new designs based mostly on the functionalist ideas of the European avant-garde opened up the possibilities of a modern style using new forms and materials.

It was at this time that practical considerations also became more important. Furniture had to be chosen to fit into the smaller houses being built after the First World War, and the lack of servants made people more conscious of the need to create rooms that were easily and speedily cleaned. Built-in and unit furniture began to appear, and was particularly popular with those whose tastes veered towards moderne. It was not until after the Second World War, however, that practical considerations became paramount and that modern, or contemporary as it was then termed, furniture assumed the predominant position in the average home.

△A suburban dining room of 1934, furnished with a combination of real and reproduction antique furniture. The Delft rack round the walls for displaying ornaments and the curtains with Tudor motifs are the more fashionable elements.

The Suburban 'Cottage'

A typical decorative theme for a suburban semi in the 1920s was that of the country cottage, in the form of a cosy haven of chintz-covered easy chairs and Tudor, Jacobean or Georgian-style accompanying furniture. The settees and easy chairs had a fairly slim outline, but sideboards, dining tables and chairs and other cupboards were of imposing proportions. Much of the furniture was available on hire purchase from companies such as the Tudor Manufacturing Company, which in 1930 was offering substantial pieces 'carved in the fifteenth-century manner'; those who could afford it selected genuine antiques. The fashion for period (or, more accurately, reproduction period) furnishings continued into the 1930s but with subtle changes of emphasis: baroque and Regency furniture now joined Tudor and Georgian, and modern concepts such as the cocktail cabinet and unit pieces were often available in Jacobean as well as contemporary styles. Victorian and Edwardian furniture also

Now Ready, Post free, Book C.373, illustrating, in colour, all the rooms of

HAMPTONS' six-roomed HOME £235
FURNISHED THROUGHOUT complete with Carpets & Curtains, for

This Specimen House shows, by actual examples selected from stock and ready for immediate delivery, how, for only £235, a Home can be furnished substantially and in a manner which shall be a source of constant pleasure and satisfaction to the owner.

For example:
THE DINING
ROOM

HAMPTONS' No. C. 13988. 5 ft. Carved Oak Sideboard; top drawer lined Baize and divided for Cutlery.

£15 : 18 : 6

HAMPTONS' No. C. 14313. Carved Oak pull-out Dining Table. Size, when extended, 5 ft. x 3 ft.

£6 : 15 : 0

HAMPTONS' No. S. 13506. Carved Oak Small Chair, loose seat, covered Peganoid.

£1 : 10 : 0

HAMPTONS' No. S. 13507. Carved Oak Arm Chair to match.

£2 : 5 : 0

(All as illustrated herewith.)

DEFERRED PAYMENTS : Terms on application

HAMPTONS
Decorators · Furnishers

Pall Mall East
LONDON, S.W. 1

Hamptons pay carriage to any Railway Station in Great Britain

◁ ◁ **Streamlined shape and modernist fabric were an appropriate choice of three-piece suite for this suntrap house (the house also shown on page 132), even if it is partly disguised by traditional chintz armcovers.**
◁ **To more conservative tastes, the solid Jacobethan oak dining suite of 1926 had appeal.**

made something of a comeback, if only out of necessity, but it was recommended that it be ruthlessly stripped down and fitted to modern taste, as described in *The Complete Home Book* (1937):

A suite of Edwardian Chippendale furniture for the dining room . . . could be painted, or as an alternative stripped and cellulose lacquered. If painted a medium green or blue, furniture of this kind can look extremely well against a modern background.

The Moderne Touch

Although the 'olde worlde' or cottage styles continued to be popular, some element of the Moderne soon became essential if a home – whether suntrap or Jacobethan – was to be fashionable. The simplest solution was to buy one of the new boxy three-piece suites, which were considerably bulkier than their counterparts of the 1920s and seemed to be styled along racing-car lines. In one *Ideal Home* magazine advertisement of 1930 for this kind of suite, its modern credibility was stressed: 'a modernesque three-piece suite . . . the last word in modern furniture, art and comfort covered in exquisite futurist design fabric'. Cubist and futurist-based designs for autumn-coloured tweedy upholstery were all the rage, even though they might well be covered with lacy antimacassars in many a suburban parlour. Other instant modernizing tricks were to flush-panel the doors with hardboard or box in the fireplace and balusters, or possibly to build in cupboards under window bays.

The streamlining approach was also applied to dining and bedroom furniture, and angular and occasionally asymmetrical shapes began to appear. These items also had unusual decorative features which had a practical as well as a fashionable basis. As a result of timber shortages during the 1920s, plywood was increasingly used for furniture construction, veneered with exotic wood such as walnut, ebony and rosewood or with contrasting bands of different woods, and the resulting decorative effects owed much to Art Deco and 'jazz' ideas. Curved or stepped surfaces and decorative applied details appeared on furniture everywhere, and even those with limited budgets were encouraged to purchase more decorative veneered suites for their bedrooms instead of plain solid oak.

This type of 1930s Art Deco was of course a kind of pseudo-modernism that had more to do with Hollywood and the lavish proportions and decorations of Odeon cinemas than with the avant-garde theorists of Europe, but the more austere modernism of the International Style was also beginning to make itself felt. Designers working at the Bauhaus School in Germany (see page 131) had experimented with tubular steel for furniture, and produced a number of undecorated functional items for mass production. Other European designers, notably in France, were also beginning to produce designs for plain, functional furniture. Such furniture caught the imagination of public and retailers alike, and by the mid-1930s designs by Marcel Breuer and Mies van der Rohe (or versions of their designs) were being mass-produced by such companies as Thonet (the pioneers of bentwood furniture production in the nineteenth century) and PEL (Practical Equipment Ltd.) in England.

Tubular steel furniture began to appear in the British high street, at first only in the most prestigious stores and then very soon afterwards virtually everywhere. Chairs and beds seem to have been the most readily accepted items in the average home, although the construction methods were applied to whole suites of furniture, and provoked considerable mirth in some quarters. For example, Heath Robinson cartoons appeared in which full sets of dining furniture were constructed from one apparently endless piece of tubular steel. Modern bent plywood furniture also began to appear in the shops, this time

FURNITURE/2

by Finnish designer Alvar Aalto, but despite its comparative cheapness it had little success with the average suburban householder.

The inter-war years were therefore something of a hotchpotch in terms of domestic furnishings, with new ideas jostling for space alongside more traditional pieces. The arrival of the Second World War, however, introduced new priorities, and its end heralded a determined look to the future in design.

The Utility Furniture Scheme

The Utility scheme for furniture came into effect at the beginning of 1943, and ended ten years later in 1952. The scheme was devised to meet a specified need in the face of extreme shortage, and to protect the public from profiteers. The brief for the scheme was 'to ensure a supply of furniture of the best quality available at controlled prices to meet a real need'. For many of those involved it was also an opportunity to influence the design of post-war furniture: as Lord Forres of the Board of Trade pointed out, there were hopes that they might succeed in 'influencing popular taste towards good construction in simple, agreeable designs to the benefit of our after-the-war homes'.

There had been a gradual imposition of restrictions on furniture manufacture from the beginning of the war. In an effort to meet the demands of those whose homes had been bombed, the Government introduced the Standard Emergency Furniture Scheme, together with an insurance scheme to assist with purchase. This furniture, made by companies already engaged in war work, was extremely basic and designed to meet the immediate emergency only. Where they could get supplies, other manufacturers were continuing along the lines of their pre-war production.

◁Strict standards of materials and workmanship ensured that Utility furniture was built to last. The clarity of form and fine detailing of the oak dining suite also show the attention to design that characterized the furniture.

▽This dining suite is an example of the 'Diversified' range, introduced in 1948 when restrictions on design were lifted.

This scheme was followed by another measure which limited all production to twenty specified items and, while not dictating design, laid down guidelines on the maximum amount of raw materials that could be used.

By June 1942 proposals for Utility furniture had been drawn up. They confirmed the limit on production to twenty specified items, but further recommended that both price and – for the first time – design be standardized. A number of designers were asked to submit proposals from which three were selected. By October sufficient pieces (available only to those whose homes had been bombed and to newly-weds, and free of purchase tax) had been produced to stage an exhibition, and by the end of the year the scheme was instituted. No other furniture was to be made, and the Utility range itself was made only under a licence. The first catalogue was published in 1943, offering basic items for living rooms, bedrooms, the kitchen and the nursery.

The furniture had to be of 'sound construction in simple but agreeable designs and at reasonable prices', and the selected designs perfectly fulfilled the brief. It was intended that the furniture be built to last, and so it was solidly constructed from oak or mahogany, with veneered hardboard panels and strongly morticed or pegged joints. It was plain and functional, but with a notable attention to both practical and decorative detail. For example, fireside chairs were available with adjustable backs and kitchen cupboards and tables used every available space for storage. All the pieces were finely proportioned, and panelling on cupboards and grooved borders on the tables were perfectly finished.

In many ways Utility furniture is reminiscent of the later work of those connected with the Arts and Crafts Movement, particularly the finely

◁ **This Utility kitchen furniture of 1947 reveals the emphasis on clean lines and practicality that distinguished the range as a whole.**

▽ **As soon as restrictions were lifted, more decorative pieces in other woods began to appear, like this unit furniture in Australian walnut. Made in 1949 (at first for export only), the range was, significantly, for the new combined living-dining room layout.**

FURNITURE/3

detailed fumed oak pieces produced by Heal's and other manufacturers (see page 103). The connection with the Arts and Crafts Movement was also apparent in the work of Gordon Russell, a member of the Advisory Committee. Russell's own furniture company had its base in Broadway in the Cotswolds, surrounded by workshops that maintained the crafts traditions established by the Arts and Crafts guilds which had moved there at the beginning of the century, and he absorbed their general aim of raising the standard of furniture design; his own furniture displays a structural honesty and decorative simplicity that was widely praised. Russell seized the opportunity presented by the expediencies of war to try to educate public taste, and wrote:

I felt that to raise the whole standard of furniture for the mass of the people was not a bad war job. And it had always seemed sound to me, when in doubt as to people's requirements, to aim at giving them something better than they might be expected to demand.

Russell's desire to see the design work continue, and to influence the manufacture of furniture after the war, led him to suggest that a Design Panel be set up. Hugh Dalton, President of the Board of Trade, recommended that Russell should head it. The Panel oversaw the production of the existing range and worked on new designs and prototypes for additions to it and to post-war production. 'Chiltern' and 'Cotswold' were two ranges that went into production in 1946, but by the end of the following year plans were well in hand for their withdrawal and the gradual introduction of freedom in design, which in fact took place in 1948. In the same way as it started, the scheme was gradually dismantled until its end in 1952, despite

a considerable amount of support for its continuation.

After the Festival

Through the Festival of Britain in 1951 (see page 162), the public had been alerted to new possibilities in furnishings and decor, and were glad to see the end of the wartime restrictions. As the House and Garden pavilion demonstrated, the post-war situation required a complete reappraisal of the arrangement and decoration of the home. Questions of economy, the efficient use of space and the new priority given to labour-saving features, which had arisen in the 1930s, became paramount. Flexible (and portable) units and space-saving built-in furniture now played an important part in the furnishing of many homes, particu-

△ The new 'contemporary' styling was not everyone's choice, or within their reach financially: this room photographed in 1953 is furnished in the style of the 1930s.

larly where rooms served dual purposes: concepts like the kitchen/diner, the bed-sitting room and the all-purpose living room began to be regularly featured in home furnishing magazines. The new furniture was lightweight and unassuming; even the traditional three-piece suite had a new, slimmer profile. Easy chairs, cupboards, settees, tables and even wardrobes were all perched on slim, splayed, tapered legs, 'like a ballet dancer on her points' as a writer in the *Ideal Home Book* for 1951–2 noted, also stating that the purpose of this 'off-the-floor-feeling' was to give a sense of a 'wider floorspace in small rooms –

△ **Scandinavian-influenced furniture (left) was typical of the 1950s; and experiments with aluminium produced the phenomenally successful BA chair by Ernest Race (right).**

floating the designers call it'.

Scandinavia was the primary source of this new furniture, specifically Denmark, where research undertaken in the 1940s into cramped housing conditions there had indicated the need for a completely new approach to furnishings. A team of designers produced a range of furniture consisting of lightweight pieces that were easy to clean and, while not actually a 'suite' or even matching each other, could be successfully combined. Other distinguishing features were the use of pale wood such as birch and beech and minimal upholstery. The furniture was an immediate success at home and abroad, achieving record export sales and inspiring a rash of copies including G-plan furniture in Britain. The new furniture was not all sensible functionalism, however: no

home was complete without an unusually shaped coffee table; according to *The Ideal Home Book* these were 'called after clouds, boomerangs, palettes, or just down to earth kidneys. Many of these are planned to fit around the sides of armchairs, where they look just like shy tots cleaving to a well-upholstered mum.'

The development of unusual materials for the construction of furniture continued during the 1950s, when the armament and aircraft industries opened up the possibilities of aluminium, in the same way that tubular steel was developed in the 1930s. The shortage of more traditional materials immediately after the war prompted Ernest Race to develop an aluminium chair, the BA, a basic dining chair which was first shown at the 'Britain can Make It' exhibition of

1946. It was so successful that it stayed in production for twenty-three years. Other companies experimenting with aluminium included Heal's, which produced a range of 'Plymet' furniture in which aluminium sheet was veneered with figured ash or rosewood to form a plywood with a metal core, which was then curved to form seats and backs and bonded to a structural frame of steel. Both Race and Heal's produced complete ranges using these methods, but there seems to have been only limited public acceptance for anything other than their basic chairs.

WALLPAPER AND FABRICS/1

As with architectural styles in the 1920s and 1930s, a number of different themes in furnishing design were available to the suburban householder. The main distinguishing features of both wallpapers and soft furnishings during the 1920s were their strong colour – blues, yellows and purples on dark or even black backgrounds – and exotic patterns. The most popular designs were of oriental landscapes, plumed birds and unusual flowers; and the Chinese lantern was a recurring motif. Inspiration for the designs was also often drawn from the cinema, particularly the smouldering Valentino films which prompted a vogue for palm trees and desert scenes. Any kind of novelty was rigorously exploited by designers and manufacturers who, for example, quickly transformed the discovery of the tomb of Tutankhamun in 1922 into textile and wallpaper designs featuring Egyptian friezes complete with Isis, chariots and mummies.

The better-off suburban home-owner favoured a slightly more subdued 'olde Englishe' approach, and sought out Jacobethan designs for curtains and upholstery. These designs, also brightly coloured, were based on Tudor or Stuart embroidery and tapestries, and often had trellis-work patterns intertwined with stylized flowers. It was fashionable to keep walls plain or if possible wood-panelled, and wallpapers made to look like wood panelling were available: Lincrusta Walton papers came in oak and mahogany as well as leather, silk and tile effects. It was also possible to buy Anaglypta in patterns imitating Tudor and Jacobean plasterwork for the cornice and ceiling. There was at the same time a continuing market for traditional chintz and floral designs for fabrics, particularly among those who preferred to create a country-cottage effect in their mock-Tudor semi, as advised by magazines such as *House and Garden*.

FUTURIST PATTERN FOR THE MODERNE HOME

△ An example from Sanderson of the textured wallpapers with decorative coordinating borders and corners that were popular during the 1930s.

By the end of the 1920s the European avant-garde was beginning to make itself felt, and 'futurist' and 'Cubist' (terms applied to anything vaguely abstract) patterns started to appear. French design had always been a source of inspiration for British furnishing companies, and the Paris Exhibition of Decorative Arts of 1925, combined with the influence of home furnishing magazines featuring modern designers, ensured a new interest in more abstract design. *Ideal Home*, for example, began regularly to include the work of the new generation of designers in the 1930s, initially alongside illustrations of 'Tudor chintz' interiors (which never quite went out of fashion), but later more prominently as abstract designs found increasing favour, possibly because they were especially appropriate for the new generation of 'suntrap' homes with their emphasis on light and air. In his introduction to *The Silver Studio Collection* catalogue (1980), Mark Turner notes that modernist designs were becoming increasingly popular in the early 1930s, albeit in somewhat toned-down versions

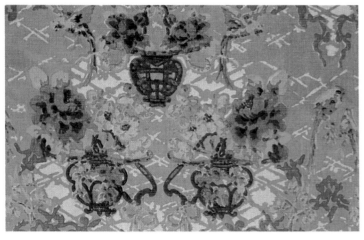

◁◁This wallpaper design from G. P. & J. Baker, appropriately called Manchu, is an example of the dark colours and oriental motifs fashionable for both papers and furnishing fabrics in the 1920s.
◁These soon gave way, however, to more severe patterns and lighter colours, as in this wallpaper of 1928 by Sanderson.

to suit the suburban taste: 'cubism became fashionable in subdued colours, but with the severity of such designs modified by the addition of such disparate motifs as stylized or naturalistic flowers.' The most popular colour range was shades of brown with orange and some green, often referred to as the 'Autumn tints'. By this time most suburban homes had followed the fashionable example and opted for plain walls, using textured wallpapers in shades of cream or beige. Decorative elements might be added in the form of borders, friezes or wallpaper corners (which were patterned papers used at the corners of the room); these last two were available in modified cubist designs. It also became fashionable to 'step' the wallpaper borders, to give a large geometric shape over the wall as a whole. The idea was also applied to pelmets, which now became strong visual features. Companies such as Sanderson produced wallpaper borders to match their furnishing fabrics.

The Importance of Texture

During the 1930s designers began to experiment with texture and woven

◁This is the 'Epson' decoration from a builder's catalogue of 1934, comprising 'an effective corner which can be used with any simple stile', that is, wallpaper panel and border as shown here. It reflects the fashion for subdued colours and plainer decorations along with a taste for more abstract designs influenced by Cubism.

WALLPAPER AND FABRICS/2

designs, combining different threads – wool, linen and Rayon which gave a shiny effect – to produce geometric self patterns in subtle shades. The assortment of fibres available, and the variety of effects they were capable of producing, attracted a number of fine artists to the applied arts, most notably Ben Nicholson and Barbara Hepworth. These woven fabrics, with their soft appearance and understated patterns, were a particularly good foil for the fairly austere interiors of the new semis. They also complemented the modern furniture of the period, which included simple bentwood designs by the Finn Alvar Aalto and the tubular steel furniture of Bauhaus designer Marcel Breuer which was becoming readily available in the more adventurous furniture stores.

For the most part, however, the flirtation with the modern was short-lived. Suburban taste never really came to terms with the austere, ascetic interiors advocated by the Modern Movement, and throughout the 1930s Jacobean, Tudor and cottagey designs continued to be available to, and popular with, the suburban householder.

WALLPAPER AND FABRICS AFTER 1940

With the onset of war, supplies of wallpapers and furnishing fabrics gradually dried up, as many manufacturers were forced to devote their production lines to war work. Furnishing fabrics were still required by the Utility scheme, but by 1943 were also in short supply. Time constraints meant that patterns for new batches of fabric had to be selected from existing ranges, but nevertheless a number of designs, specifically for cotton upholstery fabrics, were produced by Enid Marx who had been appointed to the Utility Design Panel (see page 148). Her freedom both in the creation of designs and the selection of colours was severely limited, primarily by considerations of supply and cost. As complicated repeat patterns would have involved fabric wastage when used to cover chairs, the majority of her designs were small, formal, geometric patterns – although she did produce one or two floral designs – and were in the Utility colours of rust, blue, green and natural.

Wallpaper manufacturers, worried by the low profile their product was inevitably assuming in the public imagination during the war, introduced 'reminder' advertising in the popular press, and mounted a promotional exhibition in 1945. The show included historic wallpapers and a large selection of patterns that it was planned would be available after the war. The 'Britain Can Make It' exhibition held at the Victoria and Albert Museum in 1946 also included a selection of wallpapers in room settings as part of a general survey of current trends in British industrial design. (Unfortunately, much of what was on display was as yet unavailable to the general public, or was destined for export, earning the exhibition the alternative title of 'Britain Can't Have It'.) For a number of years after the war promotional exhibitions such as these were particularly important, as no pattern books were available.

The Festival and Afterwards

The wallpaper manufacturers need not have been concerned, however: within a

◁After some years the Utility furniture scheme was extended to furnishing fabrics, as demand increased for upholstery material for the furniture being produced. A number of designs including these two were commissioned from Enid Marx in 1948. Constraints on both cost and time meant that the fabrics featured simple, formal and fairly small repeat patterns, using the weave of the cloth to add texture, and softened in these two instances by the use of floral motifs.

few years of the eventual lifting of Utility restrictions, and inspired by the Festival of Britain (see page 162), manufacturers and consumers alike were given the opportunity to indulge their starved taste for colour and pattern. Wallpapers and furnishing fabrics with a new emphasis on distinctive, lively designs and vibrant, even clashing colour, slowly began to appear in the shops. The fashionable catchword for interiors was now 'contemporary', which replaced the 1930s' 'modern' and stood for all that was up to the minute. Fabric and wallpaper designs which could be described as contemporary had a very wide range of sources of inspiration – from a micro-

scope's view of crystal or atomic structures which had been seen at the Festival of Britain, to 'cuckoo-clock naive', with interpretations of Scandinavian folk art and classical themes in between – but all were distinguished by their flat pattern. Each motif in the pattern would be isolated in its own rectangular 'medallion' or irregularly shaped space, the motif itself often having the quality of a line drawing.

It was felt that the new pale furniture, which usually had plain upholstery, required the contrast of plenty of pattern to set it off adequately. The *Ideal Home Book* of 1951–2 pointed out that patterned wallpaper did not by any means preclude pattern elsewhere in the room: 'Several patterns can lie down together like the ideal lamb with the ideal lion without one eating up the other. Indeed with the simplicity of furniture plenty of pattern and of colour are almost a necessity.'

In addition to contrasting wallpapers and curtains, it also became fashionable to have different papers for walls in the same room, and many manufacturers began to produce matching sets. Further devices to enliven the interior included using strongly patterned papers to highlight certain areas, such as the alcoves on either side of a chimney breast or the wall area behind shelves. *Trompe l'oeil* designs such as wood panelling or swags of silk were particularly popular for this sort of use.

WALLPAPER AND FABRICS/3

◁▽Contrasts of both colour and pattern were the predominant feature of house furnishings in the 1950s, as is shown by these two examples from the *Daily Mail Ideal Home Book* of 1951–2. The room setting (left) in fashionable lime-green and maroon by Liberty shows wallpaper in 'the popular stripe and pattern combination', with the same pattern in different colourings used to mark off the dining corner from the rest of the room. Sanderson fabric and Heal's wallpaper (below) show one pattern happily combined with another.

Contrast was also a priority when it came to the choice of colour, favourite combinations in the early 1950s being citrus lemon or lime with wine or plum or grey; turquoise, pink or brown might then be added to give the accent or 'vitality' to a room. The sort of effects to be aimed at are described in the *Ideal Home Book* which illustrates a 'Dining room in Nile green, sugar pink and plum', and for a 'sophisticated' room with contemporary furniture recommends:

Walls and ceiling geranium pink; paintwork matt white; doors geranium with white handles and finger plates; sofa in regency striped chintz, the same pink and white; other chairs in deep plum upholstery; carpet also plum, over surrounds painted with turquoise blue lino paint; curtains turquoise.

For those with more traditional tastes, period designs were still readily available, including the still-popular William Morris patterns, but now in new 'contemporary' colour schemes in which there might be 'a combination of long-ago motifs and loud elementary colours'! There was also a particular fashion for neo-Regency styles, ranging from whimsical and rather theatrical swags and swains to more restrained classical Regency stripes.

CARPETS AND FLOORCOVERINGS

The Edwardian taste for parquet flooring and oriental rugs continued to be popular well into the 1920s and early 1930s. Cheaper alternatives were also available: for example, cork tiling, in parquet-like patterns, was often used for halls and landings and possibly in reception rooms; alternatively, linoleum could be used for all the rooms. In both cases carpet squares or rugs would be spread on top. Linoleum was available in a variety of moderne designs along the lines of those available in the wallpaper and fabric ranges of the 1930s, and in subdued colours, and there was also a growing fashion for moderne designs in rugs; a number of chic designers were producing abstract patterned rugs that complemented the tubular steel and pale wood furniture of the avant-garde, and the more commercial manufacturers began to produce copies for the ordinary home, as the fashion for both Art Deco and the moderne took hold.

After the war and during the 1950s, taste turned to pale-coloured 'sculptured' carpets which were plain apart from raised and textured self patterns. The taste for rugs continued, the range available now being augmented by lively new abstract designs with a Scandinavian feel.

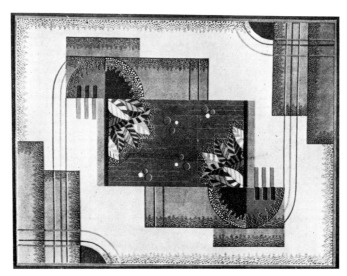

△The rugs designed by avant-garde designers Serge Chermayeff and E. McKnight-Kauffer (above and above left) are of the type considered to be essential in fashionable homes of the 1930s.
◁The taste for abstract geometric designs soon spread to suburbia, albeit with slightly softened lines, as in this example from a 1930s' catalogue.

GAS, ELECTRICITY AND GADGETS

Of particular help to the middle-class lady of the household who found herself to be a 'housewife' after the First World War was the coming of electricity into the home, and the concomitant plethora of gadgets to make household chores easier. Mains electricity was not yet universal, although the number of houses connected to the supply rose from two per cent in 1910 to seventy-five per cent in 1939. Gas, too, met the challenge from rival energy sources, and soon manufacturing companies were marketing new gadgets run by gas or electricity through the showrooms which sprang up all over suburbia.

Electric Fires with Tile Surrounds
Please state voltage required

No. W.F.3

A gas or electric refrigerator, described as essential in a modern cellarless house by one writer in the 1930s, was actually something of a luxury because of its price. Almost every house, however, had a wash-boiler, a large enamelled drum on legs with a lid and a tap at the bottom, heated either by gas or electricity. According to the *Complete Home Book* (1937) it was rather more versatile than its coal-fired predecessor: besides boiling the clothes and heating water for baths, it was also suitable for boiling Christmas puddings and for hams, 'or it

may be used as an urn for a large party or social with a tea bag dangling in the water'.

Many washtubs were simply small galvanized barrels with ribbed sides in which the clothes were agitated either by a dolly, an implement looking like a small three-legged stool on a stick, or by a vacuum plunger, a copper cone on the end of a pole, a time-honoured and back-breaking practice. The latest wringers, however, had rubber rollers and could be converted into a small kitchen table when not in use. Before long, these

separate elements became combined into the washing machine. This was essentially a boiler with a wringer and a set of agitator paddles worked by a crank handle on the lid. The addition of an electric motor to drive the crank was an inevitable improvement. The *Complete Home Book* described the electric washing machine as an expensive item which would nevertheless soon become universal: 'It saves more housewife's time than any other piece of domestic apparatus.' Clothes-drying cabinets resembling tall changing-room lockers could be warmed by gas or electricity, but they were not as widespread as the airers or drying racks suspended on pulleys from the high ceilings of pre-war kitchens which had relied on the constant heat of the range.

Various hand-pumped suction cleaning machines had been available since the nineteenth century, but their operation required either several servants or considerable dexterity and physical coordination. The first electrically driven vacuum cleaner was produced in 1917; by the 1930s the latest thing in household technology was backed up by the latest thing in American hard-sell techniques; the jingle 'it beats as it sweeps as it cleans' became as familiar as it was again to be thirty years later, and by 1939 a third of all households possessed a vacuum cleaner. The *Complete Home Book* recommends that thought be given to the cylinder rather than the upright type, as 'too little attention is given to the large variety of some of the odd jobs that can be done with some of the cleaning attachments – grooming the dog, putting feathers from one pillow case to another are just two suggestions.'

Electricity Takes Over

Electricity, with its motor as well as heating power, gradually superseded gas as the main energy supply for the up-to-date home. By the outbreak of war, warming plates, toasters, coffee percolators, waffle irons and egg boilers, as well as copper electric kettles, might be seen in almost any suburban kitchen. The *Complete Home Book* also records 'kitchen motors', which will do 'merely at the touch of a switch, many of the irksome little jobs of the kitchen' such as whisking, beating or chopping; and 'Stokes' Table Cooker' is described as an omelette pan with a heating element that cooks food on the plate on which it is

A few of the many "Beta" quality electrical and domestic products – every one made to the highest standards of design, performance and service-in-use. Ask to see "Beta" products at the better shops.

◁◁**By the late 1930s the arrival of electricity into most households was making a big difference to domestic comfort. Fitted electric fires (far left) began to replace open fireplaces – which were never lit – in bedrooms. The tiled surrounds 'slabbed with best English mottled tiles' in assorted colours, and reminiscent of an open fireplace surround, were retained.**

◁**Of the myriad electrical gadgets advertised as the new status symbols (left and centre) and sold to relieve the servantless housewife of her chores, none was marketed so keenly as the vacuum cleaner.**

served. Elsewhere in the home, electrical goods were rapidly finding favour. Electrically heated towel rails, and even electric shaving mugs, appeared in the bathroom, while bedrooms might boast an electric blanket, hair dryer, sun lamp, and even an exerciser or 'agitator'. Lethal-looking 'home perm' sets in which tiny heated rollers were connected to a mains transformer by dozens of tiny wires were used, although the frequency of burned scalps apparently rather marred the enjoyable use of this device.

The sales techniques used to persuade the new middle classes to buy these devices acknowledge that gadgets had replaced servants as the status symbol in many families. Even today, names like Butler and Tweeny (a type of Victorian servant) are given to coffee pots and waste-disposers. Awful puns such as 'Teasmaid' are also employed, and pander to a class that still regards servants as the norm even if it has never employed any and its own forebears came from the wrong side of the green baize door.

KITCHENS

◁ △ **The 1930s' kitchen (above) had built-in cupboards and a central table. The continuous worktop (left) appeared after the war.**

In the newly servantless house of the 1920s, adjacent to the dining room, and connected to it by a hatch, was the kitchen. It was here that most changes in housing design occurred. The kitchen was no longer the domain of employees but of the housewife herself, and she demanded much higher standards for what was to be seen as her 'workshop'. Although still a far cry from the fitted kitchen of today, it was undoubtedly lighter and more convenient than its Edwardian counterpart, but a lot smaller. At least one speculative builder of 1919 built kitchens the old way, with high windows to ensure that the servants could not pry on the family in the garden, only to be forced to insert larger windows so that the housewife could watch her children while washing up.

The newly built kitchen of this period was usually half-tiled in white with a narrow border of black and white checkered tiles; in the 1930s cream tiles were also used. The coal range might have gone, but the gas or electric cooker would often be housed very inconveniently in a recess. In one corner, a black or enamelled 'Ideal' coke boiler stood on a quarry-tiled base to heat the kitchen and circulate hot water to a copper or galvanized cylinder in the airing cupboard above it. (An immersion heater for summer use was usual with such a system.)

It was not until after the First World War that gas and electric cookers became popular, although they had been manufactured in a variety of forms since the nineteenth century. It had been felt that servants would not understand their complexity (but probably the cannier servants chose not to, as coal ranges at least kept their quarters warm all day). By the end of the nineteenth century many massive cast-iron gas cookers were in use, in which meat was supended from hooks on the oven over the flames. Practical electric saucepans were demonstrated as early as 1887, but were reported to give the meals an 'electrical flavour'. Electric cookers became

available after 1900, mainly converted from gas, but they presented no threat to the reign of the range.

All this was to change after 1920. Although ranges continued to be improved and sold (the current Aga dates from 1929), the clouds of greasy ash which they produced was still a problem. The modern middle-class housewife, finding herself in the kitchen for perhaps the first time, sparked an intense campaign for scientific and planned kitchens in which the range was an early casualty.

The *Complete Home Book* (1937) recommended gas or electric cookers, provided they did not have dust or dirt traps. They were generally all similar in appearance, having a green or grey speckled enamel casing and a white enamelled oven door, with a large iron latch which gave way to a bakelite handle. Electric cookers tended to be slow to heat up and cool down but many provided a radiant ring for fast boiling pans, which could then be moved to the slower enclosed rings. These and the oven could be switched off before cooking was finished to allow residual heat to complete the process, and thus save electricity. This may seem a cumbersome practice but not to those used to coal ranges, and was certainly far cleaner.

◁This kitchen of 1955 is a fashionable kitchen/diner, with only vertical panels and shelving dividing the two areas. It is described as having a 'welcoming farmhouse appearance' and as 'a workable friendly place where the family can eat in comfort and where the cooking can be carried out with practical efficiency'. It does not, however, have a continuous work surface – only the dresser with its drop-down flap would have served this purpose – a situation that was to seem intolerable only ten years later.

THE SCIENTIFICALLY PLANNED KITCHEN

The *Complete Home Book* stressed the need for proper planning in a modern kitchen. The 'three centres' of activity – table, sink and stove – needed to be positioned to minimize walking and effort. The table was to have either an enamel top, to do away with the scrubbing that Victorian deal tables needed or, failing that, linoleum, which might be wiped clean. Its proper height was 'nine inches below the worker's elbow'. (The ambiguous term 'worker' was used to pander to a society in which everybody was still supposed to have a servant but fewer and fewer people actually did; and the section in the book on household law devotes considerable coverage to 'servant and master' matters.) The sink itself was usually the deep white glazed 'Belfast' type, with a wooden draining board on one side and space for a boiler on the other. Cupboards were to be 'nearby', and a crockery rack was also recommended.

Built-in cupboards were in fact quite usual, but the American idea of a continuous work-surface had not yet arrived: the table was still firmly placed in the middle of the room. However, the ever-diminishing size of some kitchens encouraged the almost universal adoption of the freestanding kitchen cabinet which, unlike the Victorian dresser which was for display, was highly functional. It had high and low cupboards and drawers for housing crockery, pans and other equipment, a baize-lined drawer for cutlery and a zinc-lined drawer for bread. It also had a central compartment with a drop-down flap which created an enamel-topped work surface, and this often contained a metal hopper for dispensing flour. All these features made such devices remarkably useful storage units which could be closed up to produce instant tidiness. The advent of fully fitted kitchens saw their demise, but many have found a second lease of life in the garden shed.

Two of the built-in cupboards were usually of the full height of the room, one for brooms and cleaning equipment and the other a larder. Ideally, the larder was to be north-facing, with a gauze window. It often had a tiled shelf and tiled walls to help to keep food cool.

For the larder, the *Complete Home Book* recommended an electric fan and various other gadgets. Expense often precluded a gas or electric fridge, and ice-boxes and meat safes were still common. Frost boxes were also sold; these were small chests made of a chalky substance that absorbed water like a sponge. The constant evaporation kept the contents cool. Various dishes and bottle covers made of unglazed terracotta worked on the same principle (and are still sold today). It was also suggested that lights be fitted over both sink and stove, although a single central pendant seems to have been the norm in most houses. A linoleum floor was also recommended, in 'battleship brown' with a modest inlaid pattern to camouflage dirt. One can only assume that the writer had never seen a battleship.

In large houses, a small dining recess off the kitchen was provided for use by a maid, who was unlikely to 'live in' any more. If they had no maid, a family might use this space for breakfast, in a precursor of the kitchen/diner of houses built after 1945.

LIGHTING IN THE 1920s AND 1930s

In the 1920s gas and electricity companies competed fiercely, and both systems were commonly used for lighting. Gas systems had remote and even two-way switching devices, and a range of standard, table and bedside lamps was available. Despite the advantage of being dimmable, gas lighting was rarely fitted into newly built housing; the overall superiority of electricity was becoming apparent. Although one or two local authority 'all gas' flats were built, electricity became the standard method of lighting in the 1930s.

▽ The glass or alabaster 'fruit bowl' pendant shade was a firm favourite for many years; these three (top row) are from a 1939 catalogue. The three inverted globes from the same catalogue (bottom row) are intended for gas lights, but similar shades were produced for electricity.

SHADES AND FITTINGS

The Edwardian habit of having bulbs hanging bare or only partially concealed by glass or material shades continued to a certain extent, but improved, brighter lamps meant that more effective shading was necessary to reduce glare. At about the time of the First World War, the first alabaster ceiling pendants appeared. Resembling fruit bowls, these were suspended below the bulb on three chains attached to the ceiling rose, and threw a soft, diffused, greenish or pinkish hue depending on the type of 'alabaster' (actually imitation 'alabastine' or glass). Despite being notorious dust traps and always containing at least one dead fly, these shades remained popular for more than thirty years and are enjoying something of a revival today. Such shades were less suitable for the softer light from incandescent gas mantles; for these a common pendant shade during the 1920s was a shallow upturned dish of opaque white glass with a painted or transfer design around the edge. (Egyptian scenes were especially popular after 1922 when Tutankhamun's tomb was found). These invariably had deep fringes of wooden or, occasionally, coloured glass beads. Many small opaque glass shades with simple painted scenes or flowers were mass-produced at this time, and are often available in second-hand shops. Those with a small hole at the top were for electric pendants, while

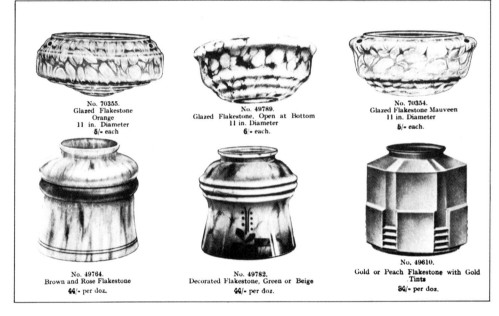

No. 70355.
Glazed Flakestone
Orange
11 in. Diameter
5/- each

No. 49789.
Glazed Flakestone, Open at Bottom
11 in. Diameter
6/- each.

No. 70354.
Glazed Flakestone Mauveen
11 in. Diameter
5/- each.

No. 49764.
Brown and Rose Flakestone
44/- per doz.

No. 49782.
Decorated Flakestone, Green or Beige
44/- per doz.

No. 49610.
Gold or Peach Flakestone with Gold Tints
84/- per doz.

those with the larger holes (about 6 cm) were intended for the brass gallery of a gas fitting.

In the 1930s, lighting took on a much greater importance in the home and more thought was given to it. The *Complete Home Book* of 1937 recommends at least 100 watts of lighting power for the average room 'depending on paintwork', and adds that 'insufficient lighting is not only depressing and a strain on the eyes, but can also cause worse troubles; headaches, indigestion, general lassitude and irritation can often be traced to it'.

The lights chosen to avoid such ail-

ments very much depended on personal taste. Textile shades were out of fashion (except for silk shades on lamp standards), but paper or – even better – parchment was a favourite in cottage-style homes. The 'parchment' was in fact pieces of brownish, opaque plastic, sometimes with a roughened surface, stitched together with twine in numerous different patterns, usually with long silk tassels or fringes. Dull to look at by day, when lit they did produce a homely glow that was well reflected in the polished oak of the lamp-bases and 'Jacobean barley-twist' standards to which they were fitted. Transfer pictures of galleons or flowers were sometimes added to these shades, particularly those made to clip on to bed-headboards as reading lights. Even more elaborately, little panels of parchment inscribed with medieval script might be incorporated into shades to make them look as if they had been made from cut-up legal documents or ancient manuscripts. This curious conceit was particularly popular with small shades on wall brackets, and persisted well into the 1970s. Cottage-style wall brackets and ceiling pendants were either of wood, stained dark and 'rusticated', or of wrought iron, the scrolls of which were painted black or cream. To enhance the effect, tubes resembling candles (complete with drips) were introduced to cover the bulb holders, although this meant that all the bulbs pointed upwards and the emission of light was thus considerably reduced. The desired effect, however, was cosiness rather than brightness, and pools of light from several sources would have achieved this better than a single pendant.

A welcoming glow in the hall was essential, and lamps in the form of a flaming torch to be fixed to the newel-post of the stairs threw a suitably orange hue. Yet even in the most 'olde worlde' of Jacobethan homes functionalism was the order of the day in kitchens and bathrooms, where simple white glass cubes or spheres were used to enclose the bare bulbs pendant from the ceiling in these rooms.

▷ The wall bracket with a choice of rainbow, gold or pink glass mounted on a metal arc shows the influence of Art Deco; likewise the three-light pendant designed to throw the light upwards was considered a most up-to-date design in the 1930s when it was produced. The standard colour finishes of metalwork offered for these light fittings were ivory and gilt or ivory and green.

THE MODERNE HOME

For those with less traditional taste, a variety of up-to-date designs for light fittings influenced by the Art Deco style was introduced. Silver-painted statuettes of girls holding huge illuminated opaque glass orbs in their outstretched arms are something of a cliché for the entire period, and still produced today as such. Pendants made great use of new materials such as clear or yellow perspex, and although many simple, functional designs were produced, others seems to have been inspired by flying saucers. Wall brackets often comprised sheets of glass or metal arranged in an inverted pyramid to conceal the bulb and throw light upwards; a single triangular sheet mounted in a corner fulfilled the same function.

Concealment seems to have been the essential requirement of light fittings in the moderne home of the 1930s. Lights were built into furniture such as wardrobes and cocktail cabinets, to be operated by automatic door switches. In wealthy homes, false walls, ceilings and shelves constructed from occluded glass concealed light sources. The newly invented architectural strip light was recommended by the *Complete Home Book* for behind pillars and the borders of niches to illuminate 'some attractive statuette'. Standard lamps, too, were designed to throw light upwards so that the overall effect was of a room bathed in a soft, diffused, almost mysterious glow rather than the cosy pools of light the traditionalists preferred.

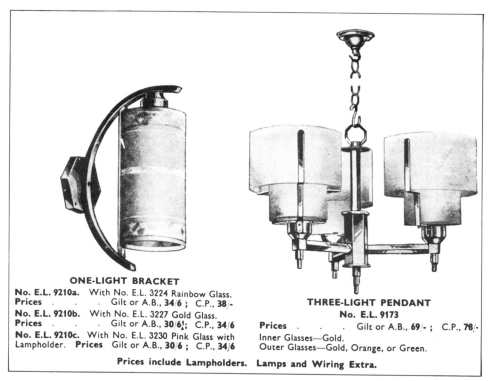

ONE-LIGHT BRACKET
No. E.L. 9210a. With No. E.L. 3224 Rainbow Glass.
Prices   .   .   . Gilt or A.B., **34/6** ; C.P., **38/-**
No. E.L. 9210b. With No. E.L. 3227 Gold Glass.
Prices   .   .   . Gilt or A.B., **30/6** ; C.P., **34/6**
No. E.L. 9210c. With No. E.L. 3230 Pink Glass with Lampholder. **Prices** Gilt or A.B., **30/6** ; C.P., **34/6**

THREE-LIGHT PENDANT
No. E.L. 9173
Prices   .   .   . Gilt or A.B., **69/-** ; C.P., **78/-**
Inner Glasses—Gold.
Outer Glasses—Gold, Orange, or Green.

Prices include Lampholders. Lamps and Wiring Extra.

INFLUENCES ON STYLE: *The Festival of Britain/1*

The Royal Festival Hall on London's South Bank is one of the few reminders of the celebration that was the Festival of Britain in 1951. Significantly, perhaps, it is now unceremoniously lumped together with what popular opinion considers to be the concrete disaster of modern architecture. At the time, however, the architecture and design of the Festival was greeted with considerable enthusiasm.

The idea of the Festival was first mooted by the Royal Society of Arts and was repeated more forcefully by newspaper editor Gerald Barry in 1948; he suggested that it would be appropriate to commemorate the centenary of the Great Exhibition with a 'great trade and cultural exhibition'. The idea was taken up, but for reasons of both time and cost thoughts of an international show were abandoned in favour of a show which would concentrate on Britain or, more precisely, on 'Britain's contribution to civilization – past, present and future'. It was to be the 'autobiography of a nation' as the official programme described it. A co-ordinating team drawn from bodies such as the Council of Industrial Design, the Royal College of Art and young architects and designers, many of whom had been involved in the 'Britain Can Make It' exhibition in 1946, began the task of finding sites, producing designs and 'scripts', and commissioning builders and decorators. A huge variety of problems dogged the planning and building of the Festival, not least the continuing criticism from both establishment and media, which suggested that the whole thing was a monumental waste of time and effort, but it opened as arranged in May 1951, closing five months later.

'A TONIC TO THE NATION'

The principal site for the Festival was London's South Bank, but Belfast and Glasgow also had large exhibitions. Local festivals, particularly of the arts, were also held throughout the country. In addition, there was a funfair at Battersea, a travelling exhibition, a festival boat (the 'Campania') and a fleet of double-decker buses which promoted the show in Europe. The South Bank was undoubtedly the centrepiece, however, and it was here that the underlying theme of the Festival was given full expression. In addition to fun and (it was hoped) optimism-inducing celebration, the Festival was to be educational: there was to be a definite narrative progression to the story of Britain's achievements, which were divided into 'chapters' in different pavilions which charted the development of the Land of Britain

▷ **The Festival of Britain was to have a profound influence on the way people viewed their homes and the environment, and it did this most of all by its own appearance, from the sculpture and furniture to the pavilions themselves. This night-time view of the South Bank site of the Festival highlights the futuristic Skylon tower.**

FESTIVAL OF BRITAIN

1951

MAY 3 – SEPTEMBER 30

MAIN INFORMATION CENTRE · SWAN & EDGAR BUILDING · PICCADILLY CIRCUS · LONDON

and the People of Britain, with the Dome of Discovery in the centre and the Skylon – a futuristic-looking tower – dominating the scene, a symbol of future possibilities.

It is generally agreed that the architecture of the Festival was not revolutionary, reflecting as it did current European trends in the Modern Movement and design ideas that were already common currency before the war. Previously, however, they had been known only to the architectural profession and now they were made accessible to a much wider and apparently enthusiastic public. While contemporary and subsequent critics differ in their opinion and definition of the Festival Style and its influence, there seems to be general agreement that the Festival renewed the public's interest in design in general, if only in some of its more quirky aspects such as the wiry legs with knobs on which quickly appeared on all kinds of furniture.

However, its real significance was as Sir Hugh Casson, quoted in *A Tonic to the Nation* (1976), a retrospective look at the Festival compiled by Mary Banham and Bevis Hillier, explains:

Although there was nothing very revolutionary in the layout or the buildings, there was plenty of serious thinking under the funny hats; many ideas worth passing on were to be adopted by the designers of our environment . . . The nation was alerted to possibilities and opportunities hitherto undreamed of. But the real achievement of the South Bank was that it made people want things to be better and to believe they could be.

◁ **The patriotic symbol of the Festival appeared on posters and later on blocks of 'Festival Flats' built at this time.**

INFLUENCES ON STYLE: *The Festival of Britain/2*

For the visitor from the suburbs the architecture of the Festival was one of the earliest indications of the new ideas emerging in architectural planning, and in particular the renewed interest (born of post-war necessity) in urban renewal, rather than in continuing the suburban thrust into the shrinking countryside. One of the most striking features of this was the attention given to the spaces outside the buildings: murals and sculpture were integrated into buildings and the environment; pedestrian walkways were sensitively landscaped and seating areas were well planned. It was this which heralded the shopping precincts, civic centre plant pots and pseudo-Henry Moore sculptures which were to become the hallmark of urban renewal and development in the next decade.

New ideas in architecture were dealt with in more detail at a 'Live Architecture' exhibition at Lansbury in London's East End. The exhibition was 'live' in that it consisted of part of an actual redevelopment programme which included housing, shops and schools, and which it was hoped would illustrate both town planning themes and actual architectural and building developments. This neighbourhood exhibition was supported by the Town Planning and Building Research pavilions at the South Bank in which were demonstrated (as the guide explains) – with the aid of 'diagrams and models – the principles to be followed in providing for the needs of a new community'. Inevitably the exhibition included a parody of the standard inter-war suburban semi, dubbed 'Gremlin Grange' in which its perceived drawbacks and the architects' solutions were described.

The problems presented by post-war conditions and the emerging ideas about the home also formed the inspiration for the House and Garden pavilion. The pavilion was not devoted to the illustra-

◁Modern urban landscaped squares and shopping precincts, complete with monumental sculpture, are two of the most obvious legacies of the Festival of Britain. Examples of the original inspiration are seen here against a backdrop of the Royal Festival Hall, one of the few remaining Festival buildings.

◁A contemporary and characteristically futuristic drawing of the South Bank site of the Festival by artist James Holland.

tion of luxury homes as might have been expected; on the contrary, they did not even concern themselves with whole rooms, as the Festival guide explains:

Because rooms of today must often serve more than one purpose and because of limits of space, these new proposals for design do not embrace complete rooms. They are, rather, grouped around special features within it – it may be even a corner.

Six schemes in all were displayed, each undertaken by a different group of designers and each dealing with a different situation – the child in the home, hobbies and home entertainment, and with new concepts such as the bedsitting room and the kitchen/diner.

The pavilion was concerned with the economical and practical use of available space in the home, and although the symbolic importance of the home, and in particular the 'parlour', was not forgotten, it was hoped that the need for 'gathering round the fireplace' would be met in a 'twentieth-century style, and

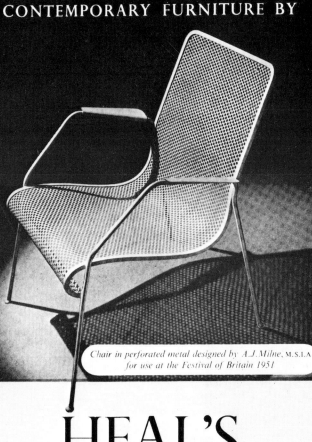

CONTEMPORARY FURNITURE BY

Chair in perforated metal designed by A.J.Milne, M.S.I.A for use at the Festival of Britain 1951

HEAL'S

without a trace of frowstiness'.

As with the architecture, however, the design of the Festival itself was just as influential as the specific exhibitions within it, if not more so. The Council of Industrial Design, which had a large hand in all the arrangements for the Festival, had decided against a separate pavilion devoted to industrial design in favour of having overall control of the selection of all industrially produced and hand-crafted items that would be used in the exhibits. Thus everything from the decor in the restaurants, the chairs and plant pots on the walkways, to the purely functional exhibits in the historical or scientific displays, had been carefully selected to give a particular impression about what was available from British manufacturers and what constituted (in the Council's opinion) 'good' design. Expressed in this way, the message was hard to ignore, and it made a major contribution to the Festival's heightening of public awareness of design possibilities, in terms of both functional furnishings and the use of colour in the home, and of urban spaces.

◁△**Gremlin Grange was the Festival's demonstration of how not to build a house, and an irreverent and dismissive view of the mass of pre-war suburban housing. The Grange was in the 'Live Architecture' exhibition for the Festival in London's East End, which included part of an actual redevelopment programme designed to illustrate new ideas of community planning and architecture.
△Not only the exhibits but all the furniture and fittings for the Festival were carefully selected by the Council of Industrial Design, a point made by Heal's in this advertisement.**

STAINED GLASS

After the First World War, sash windows were almost completely superseded by casement-type windows topped by small horizontally hinged lights. However, the practice of incorporating stained glass into the upper sections of reception-room windows was continued and developed. Similarly, halls, porches, and stairs were popular places for complete glazing in stained glass, since these positions were both seen by visitors and yet needed privacy. Although this practice remained remarkably popular in suburbia for at least another forty years, such overt ornamentation ran directly counter to the decorative philosophies of the architectural elite, and all the designs and patterns then available from builders' suppliers owed their origin and inspiration to the stained-glass craftsmen who were working at the turn of

the century. Pre-eminent among these was Oscar Paterson, who in 1901 described (in an article 'Modern Stained Glass' in *Modern British Architecture and Decoration – The Studio* special number) in rather florid terms the way in which craftsmen of the day had moved away from the medievalism of the Gothic Revival:

Where formerly *tours de force* of colour prevailed, ponderous facts dealt with in a severe didactic manner, overpainted, over-strained, betraying all the grossness of a perverted mechanical dexterity, we now possess simplicity, sweetness and light. The sombre measure of an effete barbarism has given place to the welcome cadence of form and colour . . .

The influence of craftsmen like Paterson was profound, and designs of great restraint, simplicity and delicacy, usually based on slender stylized flowers or 'teardrop' patterns, found their way into many homes. As the country-cottage movement popularized lattice-pattern leaded casements, the lead itself came to be seen as an attractive feature in its own right. Paterson wrote:

An important feature is the prominence given to outline. The lead, formerly looked upon as a necessary evil, has now become the cornerstone of the fabric. Where formerly it was the practice to exhibit a pictorial effect in colour more or less bizarre, the tendency now is to render the theme in freehand drawing throughout; the lead lines marking the outlines . . .

In northern England the practice of decorating single sheets of glass with strips of lead applied in exuberant, almost Art Nouveau, swirls and arabesques, was widespread in the 1920s and 1930s and some of this has succumbed to overzealous window cleaning. In the main, however, stained-glass panels were the genuine article, bought readymade from builders' merchants.

Speculative developers would often

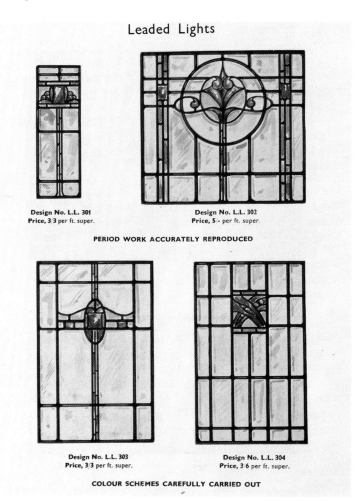

Leaded Lights

Design No. L.L. 301
Price, 3/3 per ft. super.

Design No. L.L. 302
Price, 5/- per ft. super.

PERIOD WORK ACCURATELY REPRODUCED

Design No. L.L. 303
Price, 3/3 per ft. super.

Design No. L.L. 304
Price, 3/6 per ft. super.

COLOUR SCHEMES CAREFULLY CARRIED OUT

◁A vast selection of ready-made leaded lights was available from builders' merchants during the 1920s and 1930s. These are taken from a catalogue of 1939 but owe their inspiration to the Arts and Crafts craftsmen of the turn of the century, who advocated that the lead itself be used to form the pattern, rather than merely to hold patterned glass as in Victorian windows. Many such patterns are still available from architectural salvage companies today, or the original catalogue designs may be copied by a stained-glass artist.

Leaded Lights

Design No. L.L. 367
Price, **7**/- per ft. super.

Design No. L.L. 368
Price, **7**/- per ft. super.
(Bullions extra)

Design No. L.L. 369   Price, **8/6** per ft. super.

Landscape and Seascape Scenes, all worked in Rich Variegated Glass

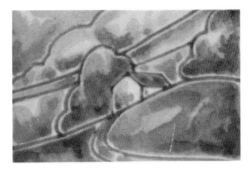

△**Richly coloured land- and seascapes were popular for porches and side windows.**

give first purchasers the opportunity to individualize their homes by choosing from a small selection of designs and, right up to the outbreak of the Second World War, the most popular themes remained those based on Arts and Crafts patterns such as stylized flowers and galleons. Even the rising sun – the most potent symbol of the 1930s – can be seen in a Paterson design of 1900. Also popular later in the 1930s were country cottages and rural scenes. Generally, figures were not as popular in the twentieth century as they had been in the nineteenth, except for baggy-trousered and beclogged Dutch boys in windmill scenes. In the 1930s some lip-service was paid to modernity, and Art Deco chevrons and abstract geometry can be seen in large staircase windows where, in the previous decade, heraldic devices had held sway. Geometrically patterned stained glass can also be found in the opening lights at the top of the bays of many more modest semis built in the 1930s.

◁**In the late 1930s (and, briefly, just after the Second World War) elaborate scenes in leaded glass became popular. The ubiquitous galleon is here sailing on unusually troubled waters. Note the contrived 'repairs' in the small panes beneath the yacht to suggest antiquity.**

▷This wood engraving is from William Robinson's influential book *The English Flower Garden* (1883), in which the author derides the then popular practice of 'bedding out' or 'mosaic culture', where 'the beautiful forms of flowers are degraded to the level of crude colour to make a design, and without reference to the natural form and beauty of plants, clipping being freely done to get the carpets or patterns "true" '. Robinson favoured a more natural style of planting, using hardy perennials in simple borders in the manner of English cottage gardens, as in this illustration with its romantically bordered path leading to a shady bower.

5. GARDENS IN SUBURBIA
Introduction

The nature of British suburbia, with its emphasis on houses with gardens rather than apartment blocks, has done much to make gardening one of the most persistently popular of suburban recreations. Indeed, after an uncertain start, a style of gardening evolved in the late nineteenth century that was particularly suited to middle-class taste and which became a hallmark of suburbia itself. However, as with so many other aspects of suburban style, a large measure of eclecticism has been, if anything, the overriding theme, with gardens laid out using whatever plants or materials the gardener may fancy or inherit. Few gardeners have the chance to start from scratch on virgin soil, and most gardens are the products of many owners' foibles and preferences.

An emphasis on flowering plants rather than vegetables has always epitomized the suburban garden. Until the nineteenth century, gardening was largely restricted either to the poor in rural areas, who needed to supplement their diet by growing vegetables, or to the rich who employed large numbers of gardeners to supply kitchen produce and maintain 'pleasure grounds'. The kitchen garden had always been the most important part of the garden, and food rather than beauty was the main aim. The suburban gardener's plot was usually too small to provide much in the way of produce for a large family, and in any case the new railways which sprang up alongside suburbia in the 1840s ensured a regular supply of fresh fruit and vegetables in urban areas. Most towns and cities were ringed with extensive market gardens, but the new trains brought fresh produce from much further afield – even potatoes from Jersey and Dieppe – and many of the ancient markets were reorganized to cope with the extra traffic (Covent Garden was rebuilt in the 1830s). With such a variety of fruit and vegetables cheaply available, ordinary gardeners could turn their attention to what had previously been regarded as a peripheral activity – the growing of flowers for ornament.

The early popularity of suburban gardening was given a further boost by the universal agreement, still current, that it was a virtuous pursuit and one that even ladies might take an interest in, provided no strenuous effort were involved. There were those who regarded cultivation of the soil as the essential distinction between 'civilized' races and the 'inferior orders' of human beings then being discovered by anthropologists, and who seemed to have no notion that things could be grown. Gardening was also looked upon as a Christian activity – the gardens of Eden and Gethsemane being important Biblical images – and there was a general view that the seasonal growth of plants was God's work on Earth made visible. A piece of popular doggerel carved into Victorian garden stonework, and still cast into sundials and ornaments sold today, sums up this sentiment nicely:

> The kiss of the Sun for a pardon,
> The song of the birds for mirth.
> One is nearer to God in a garden
> Than anywhere else on Earth.

The middle classes also saw gardening among the working classes as a good thing: it was a suitable alternative to the pub and an antidote to political sedition and moral turpitude. Allotment societies were promoted and horticultural clubs flourished; and by the end of the century the notion of gardens for all had become established.

HIGH VICTORIAN FORMALITY/1

A garden, rather an unusual asset to proto-suburban-ites, became a vital feature of the suburban house, and gardening was taken to with the enormous energy and zeal typical of the Victorians, who applied all the scientific, technological, and geographical discoveries of their age to its development. Scientific growing methods and the building of effective glasshouses and conservatories, brought for the first time within reach of the increasingly affluent middle class, made it seem as if Nature were at last controllable. The importation of previously unknown exotic plants from all over the Empire by professional plant hunters and amateur natural-ists – many of them missionaries of the Church – satisfied a taste for the rare and spectacular.

The fashionable style of gardening during this exciting age seems, with hindsight, to have been something of an aberra-tion. The 'English Style' of gardening, as it was called, had always tended towards naturalism and carefully contrived irregularity, but in the Victorian Age, especially in the 1850s and 1860s, the most desirable effect was considered to be a high degree of formality.

◁John Loudon, horticulturalist, writer and founder of *The Gardeners' Magazine* in 1826 and, with his wife Jane, co-author of *The Suburban Gardener and Villa Companion* (1838), was a key figure in the evolution of the suburban garden. He realized that the mainstream of English gardening would in future flow through middle-class suburbia rather than large Gothic estates.

The Influence of Loudon

As with so many other facets of home life, the new middle classes found no shortage of written instruction on the management of their gardens. The pro-lific John Loudon (1783–1843), whose *Encyclopaedia* had done so much to influence the style of houses and furniture, was – in partnership with his wife Jane – even more famous as a gardening journalist. He founded *The Gardeners' Magazine* in 1826 and in 1838 published, among many similar titles, *The Suburban Gardener and Villa Com-panion*. The book's subtitle explains that it is 'intended for those who know little of gardening and rural affairs, and more particularly for the use of ladies', show-ing that it was recognized early on that gardening was a 'rural' activity new to the *emigrés* from the towns and one that might most readily be taken up by the ladies of the house. Indeed, Jane Loudon, who had always worked closely with her husband and after his death revised and

reissued many of his writings as well as producing books and journals of her own on botany and gardening, became, together with Elizabeth Beeton, a par-ticular authority for those who were new to gardening.

John Loudon's book was aimed not only at the owners of 'first-rate suburban gardens' of over fifty acres, but also at 'fourth-rate gardens . . . of houses in a connected row or street; the gardens of double detached houses, that is of houses built in pairs, and forming part of a row, and the gardens of houses which are detached on every side, but which still form part of a row, or line of houses'. The assumption was that the middle classes would emulate the aristocracy in all matters of taste and style, but the scale of the average 'fourth-rate' garden either precluded or made a mockery of much of the grand tradition of English gardening. Loudon impartially sum-marizes the hitherto main trends as the geometric (or architectural) and natural, the latter being 'grounds and plantations formed in flowing lines, in imitation of

nature' the former being 'ground formed into regular slopes and levels, or plan-tations in straight lines, or included in plots, bounded in lines always decidedly artificial . . .'

The Italianate Style

The English Style, which Loudon sub-divided into Picturesque, Gardenesque and Rustic, seemed singularly ill-suited to the severely rectangular plots of most suburban houses, whereas a formal, geometric layout, imported from Italy along with her architecture, seemed par-ticularly appropriate. As with the interior of the house itself, the essence of the mid-Victorian garden was segrega-tion. Gardens were divided into beds, each designed to contain one variety or colour of plant or flower. The beds them-selves were often of complex curved shape (resembling the sets of French curves used by draughtsmen), but the overall plan was symmetrical when viewed from an upstairs window. Gravel paths meandered all over the

The strict formality of mid-nineteenth-century Italianate gardens suited small rectangular suburban plots better than anything from the English tradition of landscape gardening. Segregation and symmetry were important: the garden was seen as an architectural design, and naturalism was spurned.

A shrubbery was *de rigueur* for the fashionable, with evergreens including conifers and other easily clipped or naturally neat shrubs such as laurels and privet.

Gravel paths in the Italian tradition were preferred to lawns, although grass was often used as an edging.

Urns and statuary were placed around the garden at regular intervals or to provide a focal point. A formal pool with classical fountain would be centrally placed.

Bedding plants in ever-changing succession were arranged in blocks of strongly contrasting colours in contrived and geometrical patterns or rigid lines.

A parterre would have been made in larger gardens, with beds in elaborate shapes set into grass.

Ornamental edgings were essential: terracotta or iron was cast into a rope pattern or scalloped shape; concrete was used for low walls.

A terrace with balustrade was favoured, complete with symmetrically placed urns.

garden and separated the flower beds, and the English tradition of wide lawns was discouraged, although small, geometrically shaped areas of grass, neatly contained by gravel paths, were normally part of the overall design, as were areas covered in different-coloured chippings.

Ornate architectural devices were an essential element of the formal Victorian garden, and the more the better. 'Natural' stone and brick were out of the question, but artificial stone and even the newly invented concrete provided the correct smooth appearance. Statuary based on classical figures or a sundial was *de rigueur*, usually in artificial 'Coade-Stone' (named after its manufacturer), and might provide the focal point from which the gravel paths could

radiate. Urns or plant-filled vases would be placed at regular intervals along walls or paths. Large gardens would be landscaped to provide terraces with balustrades and stone steps leading down to *parterres* – flat areas laid out with flower beds, which might be raised a few inches from the paths by low stone retaining walls. In most suburban villas, brown or black ornamental edging tiles delineated the flower beds from path or lawn, and many of these survive today. Water was always a popular adjunct to the plants, and a bigger garden may have had a pool, either circular or rectangular with a stone edge and a fountain, possibly issuing from a statue.

Strict formality was far from universal, however, and 'rustic' designs were also popular. For example, mass-produced

cast-iron garden seats often had designs resembling fern fronds or intertwined branches, and seats made of unbarked timber were also common. Trellis work, made either from cast iron or wood, was used for walls and arches. In the design of the garden, as elsewhere in the home, the suburbanite was more likely to follow personal taste than to stick to an overall style. Rockeries were popular (see page 177), and were given their allotted and carefully marked-out territory. Shrubberies were also common, but they, too, needed grandeur of scale to be impressive. Privet and lilac were frequently planted, along with masses of laurel bushes and aucubas, which withstood a polluted atmosphere well.

The new suburbanites were the first gardeners for whom decorative and not

edible produce was the prime requirement, and kitchen gardens were small, if present at all. Where space allowed, they were also kept separate behind walls or trellises. The cultivation of flowering plants in formal gardens was based upon a system known as 'bedding out'. Seedlings and young plants were raised elsewhere, often under glass, and massed together in the flower beds to produce displays of colour. After flowering the plants were discarded and the beds received another batch of seedlings. The objective was purity of colour, and even plants with mottled or flecked petals were frowned upon (although variegated leaves such as those of the spotted aucuba were admired in the shrubbery). Mixed beds were, however, acceptable, with lines of scarlet geraniums, yellow calceolarias and blue lobelias apparently popular favourites. A variant was 'carpet bedding' in which low plants would be densely packed together to create areas of colour in various patterns, a technique employed by some councils today to make 'floral' clocks and other designs in municipal gardens.

Strict formalists seem to have been offended by the sight of plants past their optimum season, which the 'naturalists' could tolerate. There was, however, some logic in the bedding out method, for many newly discovered plants were half hardy, originating from climates rather milder than Britain's and consequently able to withstand only the summer outdoors. The production of cheap greenhouses enabled great numbers of such plants to be raised in ideal conditions for their brief moment of glory. Bedding out is, however, a labour-intensive system of gardening and a middle-class family wishing to maintain a fashionable garden in the 1850s or 1860s regarded a gardener as an essential member of the domestic staff. 'Fourth-rate' gardens did not, however, justify a full-time hand, and large numbers of jobbing gardeners made a meagre living by looking after several gardens each week, perhaps supplementing a pittance by raising bedding plants in the greenhouse of one client for sale to the others.

Formal gardening in the ornamental Italianate style reached its peak of popularity with the building of the famous gardens around the resurrected Crystal Palace at Sydenham in South London, and many of the huge numbers who visited the site must have been inspired to recreate some sense of the occasion by including an urn or statue on their tiny plot. This public pleasure ground failed financially in the 1880s and went into decline, as did so many of the grand private gardens as labour costs increased. Possibly the best preserved of these is the Terrace Garden at Windsor Castle which may be glimpsed by the public on certain days. The tradition of bedding out is also still practised in municipal parks and gardens to create splashes of colour.

The modern idea of a Victorian garden is often one of dank shrubberies and gloomy statuary, but this is because that is usually all that is left of them; in their heyday they were criticized for their gaudy use of colour. The style, however, demanded a grandeur of scale that was difficult to emulate in small gardens, but some of the more determined attempts to be in fashion must have had a certain charm, at least for the few weeks in the season when the flowers in their formal beds provided a colourful contrast to the groups of evergreens and statuary.

◁ **The Italian Garden at Scarborough has the terraces and balustrades, paths, urns, classical statuary, fountain and formal flower beds of the High Victorian style.**

△ **The cast-iron seat is a reproduction of a mid-Victorian design. It was in reaction to such complex ornamentation that later gardeners favoured simple oak benches.**

HIGH VICTORIAN FORMALITY/3

CONSERVATORIES AND GREENHOUSES

Perhaps the most important innovation for Victorian suburban gardens was glass. It had not only become much cheaper but its novel use as a building material had also caught the public's imagination, largely thanks to the work of that quintessential Victorian Joseph Paxton. Paxton, as head gardener to the Duke of Devonshire at Chatsworth, was responsible for the huge conservatory built there, but it was his design for the Crystal Palace which housed the Great Exhibition (see page 70) that gained him fame, and a knighthood. Henceforth, glass and iron were the building materials which most excited the Victorians, and are the glory of many railway stations and shopping arcades. Many garden greenhouses appeared, described as glazed in the 'Paxtonian system' (although it was actually John Loudon who had invented effective metal glazing bars), but these were perhaps less important than the passion, never fully spent, for building conservatories attached to houses.

The idea of the conservatory was not new. Great houses of the seventeenth century had orangeries, and such 'stoves' or heated rooms remained the principal source of citrus and exotic fruits until Victorian times. In the early nineteenth century Humphrey Repton had advocated attaching the conservatory to the house so that it might become a feature from within, creating a vista which could be doubled in length by the artful placing of a mirror. Victorian suburban villa owners, taking advantage of the cheaper technology, readily adopted the idea, but the small size of such houses precluded any vista, and the layouts of some were singularly unsuitable for the new fashion, often making an already gloomy area even darker, as the conservatory effectively shut out any available light into the dining or morning room adjoining it. But for those lucky enough to have the style and size of house to which a conservatory could successfully be added, they offered the perfect setting for growing examples of the newly discovered exotic plants and flowers or for relaxing on summer evenings. For those wishing to create the same effect today, some of the prettiest Victorian designs for conservatories are available today from many suppliers.

Wardian Cases and Indoor Plants

The Victorians loved indoor plants, which were by no means confined to conservatories. Unfortunately the heat and fumes of gas lighting and the terrible smogs which hung over most British cities for much of the winter were even more harmful to plant life than the central heating of today. To overcome this problem, curious devices called wardian cases became immensely popular throughout Victoria's reign.

Their inventor, Dr Nathanial Ward, had noticed that some seeds, accidentally caught in a sealed jar in which a chrysalis was placed for observation, germinated and thrived for four years, despite the atmosphere in the East End of London where he practised, which apparently precluded all plant life. Ward began to experiment by growing plants in almost airtight glass cases, and found that they thrived in their own microclimate. Such devices were initially used for transporting plants on long sea voyages.

By the 1840s, wardian cases became popular novelties in homes, where glass and iron or mahogany cases housed ferns and other moisture-loving plants.

In the 1850s they fell somewhat out of favour because some commercially made cases were completely airtight, causing the plants to die. But when it was realized that a small circulation of air was necessary (the earlier cases had been inefficient enough to allow this), they found renewed popularity. Later in the century some cases became very elaborate, being built as miniature palaces incorporating fountains or even aquaria.

A further development was to incorporate a wardian case into a window space, resting on the outer sill, so that the window opened directly into the case. This was an effective way of concealing an ugly view, but cut out natural daylight almost completely. Linley Sambourne House in London, run by the Victorian Society, has good examples of these still in position. Most houses would have simply filled the windowsills with pot plants, a practice much more common then than today, and deep sills with iron 'balconettes' were designed for this purpose.

Pot plants were also displayed indoors on quite elaborate cast-iron or wooden stands which were made in a variety of forms. It was of course necessary to conceal the earthenware pots from view, and large ceramic 'art pots', some with matching stands, were mass produced and have become something of a cliché.

◁◁◁**The Victorians had a passion for conservatories, and stocked them with tender and exotic plants which could be viewed from the drawing room.**
◁◁**The Queen Anne window conservatory was designed to fit into an entire window opening and, complete with miniature waterfall and aquarium, could mask an unpleasant view but shut out light.**
◁**The wardian case – the more elaborate the better – was another popular method of growing indoor plants, which thrived in their own microclimate protected from gas fumes which would have killed them.**

HIGH VICTORIAN FORMALITY/4

Read's Patent Garden Watering Engine.

△The greenhouse, a popular feature of many larger Victorian gardens, was built to house the ferns and other moisture-loving or sub-tropical plants intended for indoor decoration. The gardener would have been granted a little more respect than other servants, although rates of pay were generally very low.

△▷Rollers, mowers, garden hoses and other familiar gardening paraphernalia were already available by the mid-nineteenth century. 'Garden engines' were used for spraying water on to plants to rid them of pests (chemicals were not yet available except for infusions of tobacco leaves and limewash which made more effective pest-control sprays).

GARDEN GADGETS

The Victorian middle classes were fascinated by gadgetry, for the garden as much as the house. Many such gadgets were designed to save the backbreaking effort of the traditional spade, fork, rake and hoe, and their desirability increased as labour costs rose. Many, too, were designed to overcome the vicissitudes of the climate or simply as decoration.

'Garden engines' of various types – forerunners of today's spraying machines – were advertised in mid-nineteenth-century magazines for squirting trees and plants with clean water, there being no chemical sprays. A sturdy servant or two was needed to pump the thing but it did double up as a fire engine. Lime wash was used later in the century, and an infusion of tobacco leaves was an effective pest controller.

A mowing machine advertised in *The Gardeners' Magazine* in 1832 was identical in principle to those used to crop millions of suburban lawns for the next hundred years – until motor mowers became widespread. The patentee stated that 'Country gentlemen may find, in using the machine themselves, an amusing, useful and healthy exercise'. By the 1860s mowers which also rolled and collected the grass were being sold, and hose pipes in gutta percha or vulcanized rubber were also available, one type complete with a reel for winding it up and wheeling it away.

ROCKERIES AND GNOMES

Most of the deprecations of suburban gardens have been flung at the ubiquitous garden gnome placed in his rockery. Yet both gnomes and rockeries as garden features have perfectly respectable, even aristocratic, antecedents, being emulations of examples found in stately homes that were, even in Victorian times, avidly visited by the general public. Several rockeries were quite famous and, executed on a grand scale, sought to recreate natural outcrops in the crevices of which mountain plants and trees might be shown to best effect. Waterfalls added to the alpine atmosphere. On a suburban scale the effect is necessarily less dramatic, and 'stoneries' were criticized as early as 1838 for being 'very incongruous, heaps of stones, chiefly irregularly formed things' (C. Mackintosh, *The Flower Garden*). The use of clinker, and shells and pebbles collected from the beach, on suburban rockeries was also condemned as being in the worst taste, although the practice is still thriving.

The garden gnome was introduced in the 1880s, making its first appearance at Sir Charles Isham's famous gardens and rockery at Lamport Hall in Northamptonshire. It seems that Isham was a firm believer in the existence of 'earth spirits' and used gnomes, imported from Germany as matchbox-holders, to represent them and to delight his visitors. Sir Charles thought the great Loudon himself would have approved the gnomes, and in his *Remarks on Rock Gardens, Also Notes on Gnomes* (1890) wrote of them:

It is difficult to see why these useful though occult agencies should be disregarded at the present period of research, especially as it is now acknowledged by many that seeing such things does not indicate mental delusion, but EXTENSION OF FACULTY.

PLANT DISCOVERIES

The passion for flower gardening was fuelled in the mid-nineteenth century by the discovery of a large number of new plants and plant varieties. The western coast of North America yielded many plants which settled happily in Britain, and the opening up of China and Japan to western traders introduced many species that became firm favourites. Many entrepreneurial nurserymen established businesses in the new suburbs to cater for the increased market, and some of these were so successful that they employed their own plant collectors to seek out new plants for them to sell.

◁Clematis Lady Caroline Nevill is one of many hybrid clematis developed during the nineteenth century. They were considered by William Robinson to be 'of the highest value for gardens'.

◁◁Many Victorian plant collectors became minor national heroes for their courage, daring and, sometimes, eccentricity. Joseph Rock, who discovered new varieties of paeony and rhododendron, often dressed as a Mandarin and once had a personal caravan that stretched for half a mile over the mountain roads of China.

One collector, William Lobb (1809–63), employed by the famous nurserymen John and James Veitch (whose firm was founded in 1808 and whose latinized name appears frequently in plant names), introduced the first commercially viable monkey puzzle trees from Chile in 1840, as well as *Berberis darwinii*, escallonia and other shrubs and plants now common in suburban gardens. After Japan's ports were opened in 1858, James Veitch's son James the younger was instrumental in collecting plants

and trees from that country, including the larch (*Larix leptolepis*); the Virginia creeper (*Parthenocissus tricuspidata*) and the golden-rayed lily (*Lilium auratum*), as well as the 'retinosporas' range of conifers that were such favourites in late Victorian and Edwardian gardens. In the 1860s Veitch travelled further in the Far East and Australia, introducing many plants including irises, maples and bamboos.

Another famous collector was Robert Fortune, whose travels in Japan and the

legendary land of Cathay between 1843 and 1862 introduced to Britain many favourites such as mahonia, *Jasminum nudiflorum*, weigela, dicentra, forsythia, *Prunus triloba*, rhododendrons, azaleas, tree paeonies and various chrysanthemums. He also, at great personal risk, obtained by stealth the tea plants from China that established the tea industry in India, and the British habit.

The daredevil adventures and tragic early deaths of many plant collectors made them into minor folk heroes in

1. Sutton's Ruby King.
2. Sutton's Superb White.
3. Sutton's Superb Red.

SUTTON'S SUPERB CINERARIA.

1. Giganteum roseum superbum.
2. Giganteum roseum album.
3. Giganteum roseum.

SUTTON'S 'PERFECTION' CALCEOLARIA.

Victorian times, and the activities of the nursery industry as well as the new learned institutions such as the Royal Horticultural Society and the Royal Botanic Gardens at Kew left no part of the Globe unscoured. Many, if not most, of the new species were, of course, completely unsuited to the British climate, but the character of British gardens today owes much to the work of the plant hunters.

Of equal importance was the relatively unspectacular work of the hybridizers, both amateur and professional, who, without knowledge of genetics, produced by slow and painstaking methods of selection a constant supply of new strains, many of which still delight us today. They developed the delicate imported rhododendrons into the hardy scarlet, pink and white forms loved by the late Victorians, and did the same for the fuchsia which has been a favourite ever since. George Jackman raised the ever-popular hybrid *Clematis jackmanii* in 1863; and in 1867 hybrid tea roses, which, in one form or another, now adorn virtually every suburban garden, were introduced from France – where most of the breeding of this most English of flowers has always been done. The modern gladiolus was also reared in the 1860s, from plants brought from South Africa; and even the native daffodil was not recognized as a garden plant until the 1870s when the introduction of improved forms made it something of a cult object.

◁This page from a Sutton's seed catalogue of 1879 shows some popular hybrid varieties of plants grown in conservatories and greenhouses or as summer bedding. Many varieties of primula (from Asia), cineraria (from the Canary Isles) and calceolaria (from tropical America) were introduced in the nineteenth century, and from them larger and more colourful hybrid strains were developed.

THE VERNACULAR GARDEN/1

The styles of domestic architecture which made their first appearances in the 1880s, and which continued to be popular up to (and indeed after) the First World War, placed a new emphasis on the garden and its relationship with the house. The renewed interest in light, air and the countryside, combined with the influence of the garden suburb and garden city developments, led to a new consideration of the house in relation to its setting. The general lack of basements or back extensions meant that gardens were now readily accessible from the house and more closely related to it. Inspiration for the garden was drawn from the same sources as the architecture, namely Queen Anne and the Vernacular, and there was a reaction against the rigid formality and contrived styles of High Victorian Italianate gardens. Two schools of thought on the most suitable style for gardens arose at this period. There were those who favoured a 'natural' arrangement, in which a garden might be loosely planned but certainly not 'designed', and those who recommended a more formal, old fashioned approach in which the artistry of the design played an important part.

The leading figure of the 'natural' school was William Robinson, a gifted gardener who campaigned fiercely against the highly ornate gardens of his predecessors, describing such figures as Charles Barry and W. A. Nesfield, who had popularized the formal Italianate style, as 'broken brick gardeners' of 'painted gravel gardens'. The reduction of plants to mere elements in an intricate pattern, using the techniques of bedding out and 'carpet bedding', in which the display was gaudy and short-lived, was a particular target for his displeasure. Robinson was also adept at putting his ideas and opinions into print. He started a gardening paper in 1872, called simply *The Garden*, and in addition wrote a number of highly influential books, notably *The Wild Garden* and *The English Flower Garden*. The latter was particularly popular, going into nine editions between 1883, the year of its publication, and 1905. In the preface to the ninth edition, Robinson suggests that those involved in the formal style of gardening are 'meanly trying to rival the tile or wallpaper men', and instead recommends, in an echo of Arts and Crafts principles, that the design of the garden be organically related to its site, that it 'should arise out of its site and conditions as happily as a primrose out of a cool bank'.

For Robinson the most important function of a garden was the display of flowers, plants and shrubs in their natural state, making the most of the play of colour and foliage, rather than trimming and pruning plants into a manicured design. In further contrast to the 'carpet bedding' school, he recommended that planting be done in such a way as to give a changing show the year round, rather than a quickly passing virtuoso display (which he described as 'annual fireworks'), that relied on greenhouses and the energies of a small army of gardeners to make it effective.

The natural garden took its inspiration from the English cottage garden (those who could afford it were in any event buying derelict country cottages of their own) and has a number of distinctive

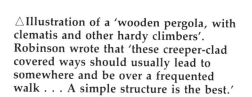

△ **Illustration of a 'wooden pergola, with clematis and other hardy climbers'. Robinson wrote that 'these creeper-clad covered ways should usually lead to somewhere and be over a frequented walk . . . A simple structure is the best.'**

features: wide sweeps of lawn, herbaceous borders, loosely shaped beds containing shrubs and hardy plants, rustic steps and paths and flowering creepers trained over walls. Where possible, flower beds would be 'permanently planted' with shrubs and flowers mixed together, individual species being grouped or mixed to create a complementary effect. Roses, carnations and paeonies might be combined with a range of the newly popular sub-tropical plants such as yucca, dracaena or palms, not to mention 'Indian hemp' (*Cannabis sativa*), which were selected for their striking foliage. Robinson also recommended that ground-cover plants be encouraged in the beds so that no patch of bare earth be seen: dwarf hepaticas, primroses, saxifrage and forget-me-nots were commonly used, as well as alpine

△A charming drawing of Gertrude Jekyll made in about 1896 by the architect Edwin Lutyens, who worked with Jekyll on many houses. Each influenced the other to create a unique and enduring vision of the typically English house and garden.

plants which had the added advantage of creating an evergreen element. Evening primrose, iris and lilies were frequent choices for borders, and garden walls often had wisteria or clematis trained over them.

A significant side-effect of this informal approach to gardens was that they were more practical and less time-consuming to maintain, an important factor to consider when garden help, in common with servants generally, was in short and expensive supply. Those tending the gardens – their owners – wanted time to enjoy them, and not to be trimming and tidying all the time. Robinson emphasized this point, suggesting that garden paths and walks should be reduced to the minimum necessary for enjoyment and practical purposes. Paths, like the gardens themselves, should take as natural a course as possible, and 'follow the line of easiest gradation, and this cannot always be a straight line, and is indeed often a beautiful bent line'. In this Robinson echoed garden city architect Raymond Unwin.

Materials used for paths included gravel, possibly with a layer of crunched shells on top, and stone, like the walks seen in cottage gardens, which were recommended for smaller gardens – thyme, mint or harebells would be encouraged to grow into the cracks. Grass walks, for taking a closer look at a special bed or rockery, were also used.

ART IN THE GARDEN

The style of gardening proposed by William Robinson and those who followed has proved to be an enduring one, but it was also very much of its time. In common with the writers of the period who were concerned with the creation of the 'house beautiful', Robinson was interested in the 'art' of the garden. An artistic effect was also the aim of another school of gardeners, but in a rather more contrived and self-conscious fashion. The 'art' of John Sedding, one of the leading proponents of the Queen Anne or 'old-fashioned' garden style, was based on artifice, incorporating a large degree of formality rather than a purely natural appearance. Sedding maintained that a conscious application of 'art' was necessary if a garden were to complement a home of 'sweetness and light'. In his *Gardencraft Old & New* (1891) he writes:

To bring nature up to the window of your house with a scorn of art sweetness, is not only to betray your own deadness to form, but to cause a sense of unexpected blankness in the visitor's mind on leaving the well-appointed interior of an English home. As the house is Art-production, so is the garden that surrounds it.

Whereas the gardeners of the natural school recommended that the site should to a large extent dictate the plan, those inclined towards the more formal approach – often artists and architects rather than professional gardeners – recommended that a design be the first step, the plants and flowers then being used to fill in. Mark Girouard, in his book about the Queen Anne Movement, *Sweetness and Light* (1977), says that inspiration was drawn from the formal gardens of the late seventeenth and early eighteenth centuries, and featured clipped hedges, topiary and borders of 'old-fashioned' flowers, particularly lilies, standard roses, poppies and the ubiquitous sunflower. The flowers were chosen as much for their 'olde worlde' and symbolic associations as for their shape and colour. Box hedges for edging the beds and borders, trellised walks and bowers, and enclosing walls with flowering climbing plants all assisted in the creation of an 'aesthetic' effect. The self-conscious artistry of the gardens enclosing the 'sweetness and light' homes of the period is described in an article of 1875 for the *Saturday Review* and quoted by Girouard:

. . . They plant passion flowers round the porticoes and train the musk roses, despised but yesterday, to mingle with the ghostly juniper, and to blush on the inhabitants looking at them through the square-paned windows.

The increasing emphasis on the architectural aspect of the garden, as publicized by John Sedding and Reginald Blomfield in *The Formal Garden in England* (1892), further alienated the 'natural'

THE VERNACULAR GARDEN/2

school until Gertrude Jekyll (1843–1932), the most prominent of William Robinson's followers, combined elements of the two approaches in her own gardens. When she first met Robinson she was pursuing a career as an artist, but she soon began to contribute regular articles to *The Garden* (she took over editorship in 1902) and in the 1880s began to design gardens herself, gardens in which woodland and water played an important part. In 1896 she began work on her own house at Munstead Wood in Surrey, near her childhood home. The house was designed by Edwin Lutyens, and this was the first of many collaborations on small houses and gardens between the two. Here was first seen the balancing of architectural and horticultural elements which was to become a trademark of her style. Jekyll, together with Lutyens, created gardens in which 'natural' planting, along the lines of that recommended by Robinson and his school, is combined in a carefully balanced arrangement with architectural elements, such as terracing, fountains and paving. The play of colours and textures, including vistas of dense 'cottage garden' planting leading the eye to a simple seat or sundial, was exploited in a way that could easily be transferred to a suburban garden.

Gertrude Jekyll drew her inspiration from the countryside and from the carefully tended cottage gardens of her native Surrey. She cultivated many wild flowers, giving them a new respectability for the smaller garden (the 'Munstead' strain of primrose is an example of her work), and reintroduced many flowers which had been banished from fashionable gardens and were now often to be found only in old cottage gardens. Among the flowers and shrubs she favoured were wallflowers, double daisies, white bush roses, London Pride, columbines, poppies and honeysuckle. It was perhaps her interest in the smaller

◁The interest in natural gardens was reflected in the choice of garden furniture: elaborate wrought-iron or rusticated furniture was replaced by simple wooden benches in the Arts and Crafts manner.

garden which earned her the enduring affection of many amateur gardeners. Her book *Wood and Garden* (1899), which described many of her ideas and her work at Munstead, went into six editions in the first year of its publication, and she also contributed regularly to *Country Life* and published a further book, *Home and Garden*, in 1900. Her writings are an inspiring mixture of practical information and poetic imagery; for example, gypsophila she says is 'one of the most useful plants . . . its delicate masses of bloom are like clouds of flowering mist settled down upon the flower borders'.

Gertrude Jekyll felt that the most successful gardens were those in which the natural qualities of plants – flowers, shrubs and woodland – were exploited to their full extent, and not simply used as part of a brief, contrived display. Her gardens had different displays for different times of the year, with colour, texture, scent and sound all playing a part, as in her opinion 'the best purpose of a garden is to give delight and to give refreshment of mind, to soothe, to refine and to lift up the heart'.

Garden Furniture

The move to more natural effects in gardening seen in the 1880s was echoed in the choice of garden furniture. The Arts and Crafts Movement, together with the interest in cottage gardens,

combined to create a fashion for simple furniture such as plain oak or elm benches, which soon replaced the uncomfortable ornate ironwork and 'rustic' seats popular in the High Victorian period. These benches might be placed so as to allow the appreciation of a shady walk or vista, or to encircle a large old tree. Other furniture, for example a summerhouse, would also be of a simple, unassuming design.

Further interest might be added by the inclusion of trelliswork or pergolas which would provide shaded walks and, in the words of William Robinson, 'numbers of free growing climbing plants give an abundant and lovely choice of living drapery for them'. Robinson advocated simple constructions: 'on no account let the "rustic" carpenter begin to adorn it with the fantastic branchings he is so fond of'; and he also recommended light arches, possibly made of slender iron, to space a walk at intervals, or to mark the change from flower garden to kitchen garden.

Other items in the garden – terracotta flower pots, water butts, and so on, also took their cue from the cottage garden. For those attempting to create a garden along the lines of those designed by Gertrude Jekyll, a stone sundial was an important accessory, as were low stone troughs or terracotta containers for plants to create an interesting architectural element at the turn of a walkway.

In a Vernacular garden it was essential to have a variety of plants of the kind most suited to the site and climate, with the emphasis on naturalism.

Topiary work was popular with followers of Jekyll who wanted an 'artistic' garden with formal elements, to match their Queen Anne houses and aesthetic furnishings.

Water was a favourite element in Jekyll's gardens, particularly ponds with water lilies.

Pergolas and summerhouses, simply constructed from natural materials, were recommended, and as with old brick walls, climbers such as wisteria, honeysuckle and clematis were trained over them.

Paths of brick or stone were to be kept to a minimum, and if possible lead to a vista or focal point, and be softened by alpines between the stones.

Herbaceous borders were essential, with a backdrop of greenery or plants trained against a wall to give height. Favoured plants included *Kerria japonica*, lilies, pansies, primroses, cranesbill, irises, phlox, columbines and pinks.

The lawn, said by Robinson to be 'the heart of the English garden' was to be a bold, informal sweep.

A terrace was to be a planned element, but not too contrived.

THE SEMI-DETACHED GARDEN/1

In the miles of semi-detached suburbia built between the wars, the garden was at least as important a feature as it had been for its Edwardian predecessor. The garden was an integral part of the Jacobethan cottage image.

As Alan Jackson points out in *Semi-Detached London* (1973), for those moving into a new house on a new estate, it was unlikely that the garden was prepared in any way, except perhaps with a layer of rapidly browning turf at the front. Some lucky owners might have gardens with rich soil if the estate had been built on the site of an old orchard or market garden, but for many merely a thin layer of topsoil covered an unpromising base of hard clay or flint, bricks and stones. Aware of the important selling point of well-presented front gardens on their estates, many builders encouraged front-garden competitions among the first buyers, to reduce the area's bare, newly built look. In any event, gardening quickly became a favourite pastime for the new generation of sub-urbanites, who were assisted by longer summer evenings – 'Daylight Saving' (Summer Time) had been introduced in 1916 – and a reduction in working hours. The many gardening magazines, societies and radio programmes that were established in the inter-war years also ensured that every new homeowner could soon become a knowledgeable gardener. The rapid development of fertilizers and insecticides in this period helped in the creation of what were usually fairly formal, orderly gardens.

Front and back gardens served markedly different purposes. Social pressure on owner-occupiers ensured that front gardens were neatly maintained, and primarily an area of display – to serve as an indication of the diligence and industry of the occupants. By contrast, the back had a more practical and private aspect, being a combination of fruit and vegetable garden, play area for the children and relaxation space for the adults.

The lack of privacy at the front was in marked contrast to Victorian sub-urban front gardens, which were often screened with high hedges and railings. Instead, the new semis had low brick walls, often topped with a symbolic barrier of a chain slung between posts along their length. In this way passers-by had a clear view of the garden in which prize roses and dahlias in rigorously neat beds, a small, neat patch of lawn and a 'crazy' paving (or 'crazy' patterned concrete) path to the front door were typical features. A number of decorative pieces of statuary might also be included in the front garden, for example gnomes, a pair of storks or seated lions, and possibly even a small pond or rockery.

◁▽ **These new houses in Southgate, north London, with their low garden walls and sunray gates, each have a clearly delineated front garden, an essential part of the image of inter-war suburbia.**
▽ **A back garden in another London suburb, Edmonton, in 1936, displays some of the more typical elements: crazy paving, neat lawns, formal beds with hard edging, Victorian-style pots and fruit trees.**

The back garden, which might be 24 to 60 m (80 to 200 feet) long, was often carefully screened by high weatherboarding fences from the neighbours, and invariably divided into two sections: the area furthest from the house was the fruit and vegetable garden, that nearest to the house, and approached from French windows, was for family recreation. A rose-covered trellis might screen

▷ **The back garden of a substantial inter-war house, illustrating the mix of formal and natural elements that exemplifies most suburban gardens of the period. Manicured lawns and flower-beds are combined with more rustic features such as the arches at each end of the path, covered in roses and clematis. The photograph was probably taken from the vegetable garden.**
▽ **In 1953 vegetable growing was encouraged by Food Production Councils, and the vegetable plot was a major feature of Mr Hawes' garden in Norwich, where, beyond his lawn and flower borders just in front of his windows, were vegetables, fruit and runs for pullets and rabbits.**

THE SEMI-DETACHED GARDEN/2

the vegetable area from the house, and further trellises might be added on top of the fence to give further privacy for the six feet or so that a paved terrace extended from the house. A garden shed was an essential item, serving the dual purpose of storeroom for garden implements and tools, and refuge for the gardener from the rough and tumble of domestic life. Summerhouses, some of which revolved, were also fashionable accessories in larger gardens. Other accessories included bird tables (thatched-cottage style) and bird baths, small fountains and the still-popular sundial; and a rustic wooden seat.

The planting of the back garden in most suburban semis owed much to the work of William Robinson and Gertrude Jekyll, but now had a rather more orderly aspect than these two gardeners had advocated. Loosely shaped beds would frame the lawn, and featured many of the plants and flowers they had popularized, but in a somehow less abundant display. Gardens in houses built after 1945 followed much the same pattern, perhaps becoming still plainer; and by the beginning of the 1960s the 'town' garden style, designed for the very small plots of town houses, effectively put an end to the cottage-garden feel in favour of 'contemporary' paved areas with plants in containers.

◁△**An illustration of a small garden terrace from** *Modern Homes Illustrated* **(1947) shows how the garden was now being seen as an extension of the house. The up-to-date furniture co-ordinates with the canopy, which could be rolled up against the house when not required.**

△**These two back gardens demonstrate the post-war emphasis on order, with the rectangular lawns, square paving stones regularly placed, and single tree centrally positioned in the lawn. The dense planting inspired by Jekyll and Robinson has given way to less abundant displays in which the shape of each plant may be seen surrounded by areas of bare earth.**

The garden of many suburban semis was long and narrow, and thus lent itself well to division into two separate areas with quite different functions.

The vegetable garden, sited at the far end and screened from the house and the rest of the garden by a high hedge or covered trellis, was considered essential. A small greenhouse for tomatoes or seedlings might be included in this area, and a garden shed and compost heap.

The decorative area of the garden, designed to be seen from the house, was fairly formally if practically laid out. Crazy paving (or 'crazed concrete') for both the terrace and path which ran straight from house to vegetable patch was usual, as was a wide, carefully maintained lawn containing rectangular or circular beds, and perhaps an apple or cherry tree or two.

Flowers and shrubs were planted in formal beds, either piercing the lawn or in narrow borders along the boundary fences. The most popular plants included standard roses and summer bedding such as alyssum and lobelia, begonias and geraniums, in straight lines and arranged so that their colours alternated.

A terrace, usually reached by French windows from the house, might be bounded by low walls planted with bedding plants, and large enough for seating which often included an upholstered swing-seat.

◁This early twentieth-century house is a fine example of how suburbia adopted traditional vernacular features: the horizontal leaded windows, simple canopy porch, deep eaves and 'catslide' roof are all arranged in a loose asymmetrical design whose balance would be lost by any alteration.

△By the 1930s the vernacular tradition had become the full-blown mock Tudor or 'Jacobethan' of these semis. Although lacking the more subtle charm of the earlier vernacular house on the left, the individual features of these houses have been combined to create a distinctive style.

6. PRESERVATION AND RESTORATION
Introduction

The restoration and preservation of domestic architecture has become a more fashionable option since the late 1960s, but is still often only applied to 'elegant' Georgian terraces or 'charming' Victorian cottages; it has yet to become a serious consideration for the mass of suburban housing built over the last hundred years or so. It is hoped that this book has highlighted the fact that modest suburban homes of other, more recent periods also have a wealth of original features that are equally well worth preserving. The fact that many estate agents are now increasingly emphasizing these original features as opposed to extensive modernizations is a further (financial) incentive to maintain a house as nearly as possible in its original style.

The main reason, however, for preserving the original design and features of a house is that these usually have an appropriateness and aesthetic appeal that no amount of 'modernizing' can improve. The original designs of most suburban housing have a sense of proportion and rightness that is timeless. This is not to say that no aspect of the house must be touched, or that improvements based on a different way of life cannot be made (bathrooms and kitchens, for example, will inevitably incorporate primarily modern design). But changes can be made in such a way as to be sensitive to the style of the house. This is particularly true of the exterior, which is part of the environment, after all, and it is important to take into account its appearance in relation to the

PRESERVATION AND RESTORATION/2

adjacent buildings, whether it is part of a terrace or one half of a semi. Once again, this is not to say that additions or improvements should not be made, but it is possible – for example in the case of adding an extension such as a garage to an Edwardian or Victorian house – to take some care over the use of materials (matching bricks and so on), and the selection of an unobtrusive design complementary to that of the house.

MAINTAINING THE STYLE OF YOUR HOME

Taste has changed in the matter of housing and no doubt will continue to do so. In the 1950s magazines on the home were already giving information on radically modernizing standard 1930s semis by flattening the bay windows and replacing them with a plainer type, and adding a streamlined porch. By the 1970s flower-power-inspired home-owners were painting the outsides of their Georgian terrace houses in bright colours, and adding shutters and murals, all of which now seems very dated and highly unattractive, and an embarrassing reminder today of a passing fashion. In the same way that one would be unlikely to put castors and plastic handles on a finely detailed Victorian cabinet, why impose a modern 'Yorkstone' fireplace on an Edwardian dining room or aluminium-framed picture windows on a 1930s semi? Also to be avoided is the temptation, which has often afflicted suburban houses, to confuse old with 'olde' when undertaking restoration or improvements. This is a fashion which has caused many simple Victorian cottages to be embellished with 'bulls-eye' panes of glass in a vaguely Georgian frame in place of their original sliding sash bays, or Edwardian porches to be enlivened with 'coach lamps'.

It is more interesting and ultimately more rewarding to discover as much as possible about how a house would have looked when originally built, and to improve it by restoring it to this design. A closer look at almost any row of suburban houses, so long dismissed as identical units, will reveal a wealth of individual detail. For example, a row of fairly standard Victorian double-bay houses will feature several styles of window, some with coloured glass, and with carved capitols on the columns of the bays, some depicting flowers and foliage, others with faces or emblems; and there will be a wealth of different types of tiles decorating the porches. In a row of semis built between the wars, there will be a huge range of stained-glass and leaded-light detailing in the

◁Stone cladding and a storm porch are common examples of thoughtless exterior 'improvements' which bear no relation to the original style of a house or its neighbours.

◁Another example of misguided modernization: such inappropriate individualism spoils the visual unity of the neighbourhood.

▷ A basically unassuming house has been turned into an eclectic nightmare by such additions as the Italianate balustrade and the porch which is, if anything, in the Queen Anne idiom.

windows, with Art Deco, Art Nouveau or simple geometric patterns and beautiful jewel-like colours.

Another good reason for recommending maintenance and restoration rather than wholesale modernizing is a practical one. By and large, Victorian and Edwardian houses, and indeed 1930s semis and their post-war counterparts, were solidly and reliably built, often with materials of a quality not easily obtainable today. For this reason it is worth making every attempt to preserve the original fabric in a sound condition; new replacement materials are likely to have a shorter life than the original ones.

The current revival of interest in vernacular styles for modern domestic architecture, with architectural and building awards going to developments with all sorts of eclectic details, is a further indication of the new value being placed on architecture on a comfortable domestic scale and with some style of its own, however idiosyncratic. It is also a reflection of a view that is now becoming more and more accepted, by architects and suburban dwellers alike: that every suburban house, no matter what its period and no matter how modest, is worth preserving in, or restoring to, its original state.

▷A well-restored early Victorian terraced house (below) which retains its original mouldings, four-panelled front door, iron balconette and glazing bars: all the elements which give it a coherence of style with pleasing proportions. Its neighbour (above) has undergone some (now very dated) modernization. The metal windows, lost mouldings and fully glazed door, intended to give an unadorned 'contemporary' appearance, in fact look blank and uninteresting. Painted brickwork soon looks shabby, and here only serves to accentuate the waste pipe.

THE EXTERIOR: *Walls*

With proper maintenance the exterior walls of suburban houses should present few problems, and there therefore seems little point in making major changes, especially as these are bound drastically to alter the character of the property and will possibly reduce its value. Walls are liable to crack and bulge quite harmlessly, especially after prolonged drought or rain, and it is rare to have to undertake drastic and expensive action such as underpinning. It is, however, always essential to seek expert advice if large cracks appear in any walls, especially if it happens over a short period, as this suggests that subsidence is occurring.

It is well worth making a point of carrying out a regular inspection of the exterior walls of your house, including the guttering and downpipes, to check for deterioration of any of the fabric. It is also a good idea to look periodically in bay windows and behind any large pieces of furniture (a piano or sideboard for example) placed against an exterior wall, for signs of damp, which can lead eventually to dry rot or wet rot.

Rising Damp

If rising damp is a problem (i.e. the bricks are soaking up the natural moisture of the ground), then the original damp-proof course (DPC) has probably broken down. To prevent damp, builders in Victorian times often used two layers of slate set into the wall about 15 mm (6 in) above ground level, and later on used layers of felt impregnated with bitumen; natural movement may have cracked them, or age may have reduced their effectiveness. In any event it is not worth trying to replace the original mechanism. The modern solution of injecting a silicone-based fluid into the bricks is cheap, effective, and easily done and hardly noticeable if well done.

Penetrating Damp

Penetrating damp is caused by rain being absorbed by bricks which have lost their waterproof surface and become porous, and can be a problem in the solid brick walls common in houses built before 1930 (after which the double-layer cavity wall became the norm). The fault usually lies in the pointing rather than the brickwork, but if the bricks are to blame a transparent silicone fluid can be sprayed on them to repel water.

Bricks

Brickwork has never had the snob value of stonework, although properly made bricks can last much longer. Brick also gives a warm appearance and mellows beautifully, and is the material of some of Britain's favourite stately homes, including Hampton Court and Compton Wynyates. Bricks in very old houses show regional variations because they tended to be made from local clays fired in a 'clamp' in local brickfields, and many colours from different regions are still available. The growth of the railway system meant that bricks no longer needed to be confined to one area, and builders exploited this by developing polychrome brickwork – walls intricately patterned with different-coloured bricks. Such features are well worth preserving, and if odd bricks are flaking they can usually be cut out, matched and replaced. Professional cleaning can also transform grimy brickwork into an attractively patterned wall, as will a carefully used stiff brush. Never use a wire brush, which will destroy the surface of the bricks and start erosion. Never block air bricks: they are vital to the circulation of air, and to the prevention of rot in timber floors and condensation in rooms.

Pointing

Pointing is the weatherproof finish applied to the mortar between bricks. Unfortunately it tends to break down, let in rain and look shabby after about fifty years, but it is always worth repointing brickwork rather than rendering an entire wall, practically and aesthetically.

Victorian bricklayers regarded pointing as something of an art form, and it is often practically impossible to copy their exact techniques. However, it is worth looking at neighbouring houses to see if special tricks were employed, such as blackening the mortar with lamp-black or colouring it to match the brick and scratching a thin line to create the illusion of a very fine joint. However it is done, ensure that your builder rakes out the old mortar to a depth of at least 13 mm ($\frac{1}{2}$ in) and matches the colour with the original – after a year or two it will mellow and should last for many more years. (If you suspect your repointing, always check it at a comparatively inaccessible place; builders know that shoddy work will be noticed at eye level and near doors, so check the work adjacent to, say, an upstairs window.)

Stonework and Rendering

More common in suburban houses of the north and west of Britain, stonework usually has a regional character it would be criminal to destroy. Repointing is sometimes necessary, but it is probably not worth copying the raised-joint techniques of Victorian builders, whereby the pointing protrudes from the surface by 13 mm ($\frac{1}{2}$ in) or so. The effect often detracts from the natural beauty of the stone, and the more usual flush joint is less obtrusive, easier and cheaper.

Stucco rendering used to imitate stone is an essential feature of much Georgian and early Victorian housing, and should always be preserved. Fortunately the lime-based plasters that were used have a certain amount of flexibility, and have resisted the effects of time very well, but any cracks are soon penetrated by water and should therefore always be repaired quickly. Sadly, modern cement-based plasters are not flexible, so systems employing fibreglass reinforcement should always be used, or cracks will re-open. The same treatment can be applied to the smooth rendered walls popular on many 1930s suburban houses which seem to have survived less well than their Georgian counterparts. Pebble-dash (small stones embedded in plaster) was popular in the early twentieth century; based on 'harling', a traditional technique in north-western Britain, it is always worth preserving. Cracked areas, or sites where pieces have broken away from the wall, can be hacked off and repaired. Provided that the stones are matched for size, the new patches should mellow after a few years and blend in with the surrounding wall.

Stone Cladding

On no account be tempted to buy artificial stone cladding: the adhesive used to bond it to your walls will permanently destroy the facing of the bricks, making its removal impossible. Moreover, penetrating damp is likely to be worsened by water becoming trapped behind the 'stones'. Houses given this treatment not only spoil the harmony of the street and make their owners unpopular with the neighbours, but are also very likely to reduce the house's resale value. If you suffer from stone cladding, some relief may be obtained by training a fast-growing climbing plant such as Virginia creeper up the walls.

△ Brick or terracotta decorative wall panels were often used to add an

Aesthetic touch to houses of the late nineteenth and early twentieth century.

△ Rendered walls and fussy out-of-period glazing on the door and windows

(right) spoil the straightforward style (left) of a mid-Victorian house.

△ Late Victorian decorative wall panels lend a faintly ecclesiastical air.

△ Rendering and brickwork contrived as ancient repairs on these houses of 1938.

THE EXTERIOR: *Doors*

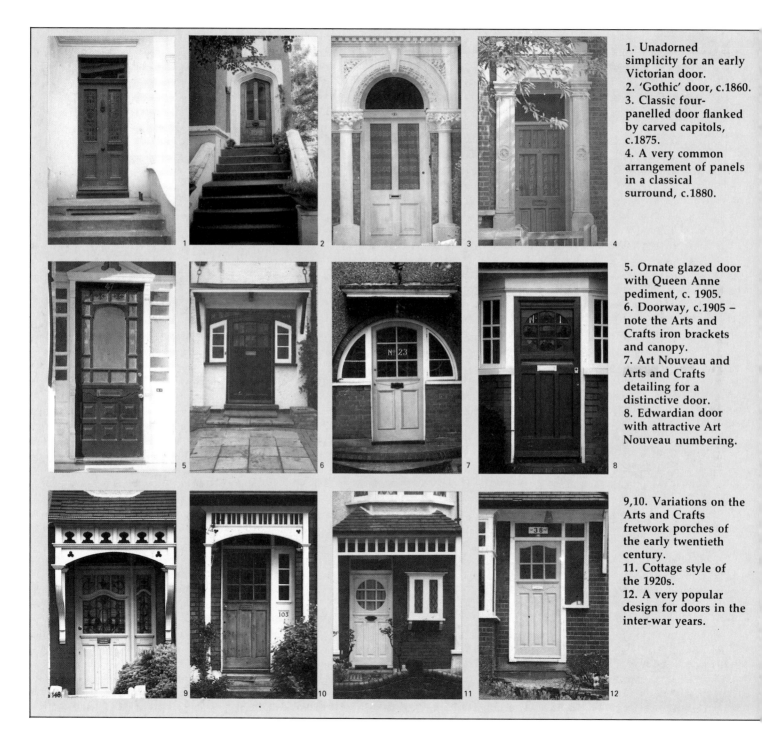

1. Unadorned simplicity for an early Victorian door.
2. 'Gothic' door, c.1860.
3. Classic four-panelled door flanked by carved capitols, c.1875.
4. A very common arrangement of panels in a classical surround, c.1880.

5. Ornate glazed door with Queen Anne pediment, c. 1905.
6. Doorway, c.1905 – note the Arts and Crafts iron brackets and canopy.
7. Art Nouveau and Arts and Crafts detailing for a distinctive door.
8. Edwardian door with attractive Art Nouveau numbering.

9,10. Variations on the Arts and Crafts fretwork porches of the early twentieth century.
11. Cottage style of the 1920s.
12. A very popular design for doors in the inter-war years.

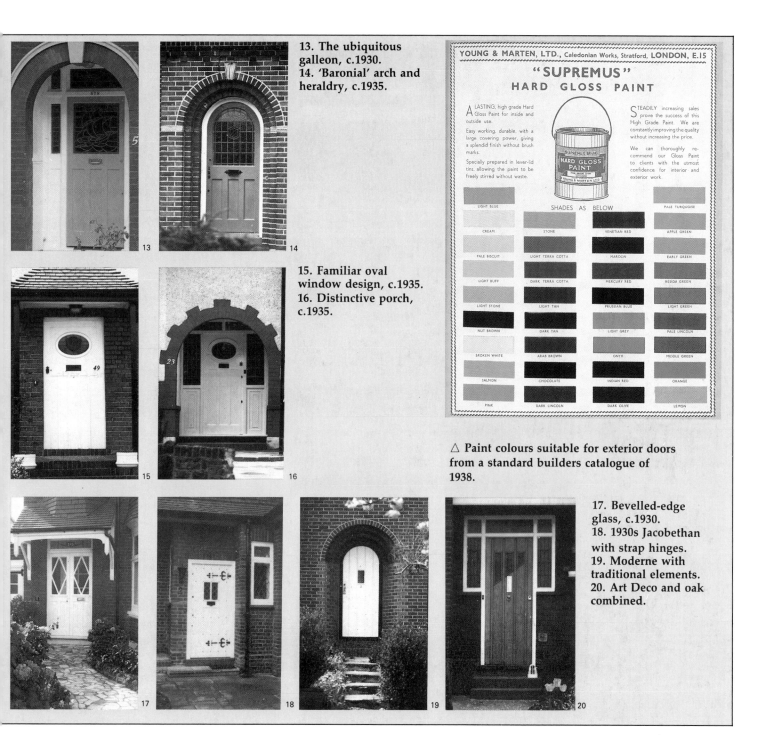

13. The ubiquitous galleon, c.1930.
14. 'Baronial' arch and heraldry, c.1935.

15. Familiar oval window design, c.1935.
16. Distinctive porch, c.1935.

YOUNG & MARTEN, LTD., Caledonian Works, Stratford, **LONDON, E.15**

"SUPREMUS"
HARD GLOSS PAINT

A LASTING, high grade Hard Gloss Paint for inside and outside use.

Easy working, durable, with a large covering power, giving a splendid finish without brush marks.

Specially prepared in lever-lid tins, allowing the paint to be freely stirred without waste.

HARD GLOSS PAINT

S TEADILY increasing sales prove the success of this High Grade Paint. We are constantly improving the quality without increasing the price.

We can thoroughly recommend our Gloss Paint to clients with the utmost confidence for interior and exterior work.

SHADES AS BELOW

LIGHT BLUE			PALE TURQUOISE
CREAM	STONE	VENETIAN RED	APPLE GREEN
PALE BISCUIT	LIGHT TERRA COTTA	MAROON	EARLY GREEN
LIGHT BUFF	DARK TERRA COTTA	MERCURY RED	RESIDA GREEN
LIGHT STONE	LIGHT TAN	PRUSSIAN BLUE	LIGHT GREEN
NUT BROWN	DARK TAN	LIGHT GREY	PALE LINCOLN
BROKEN WHITE	ARAB BROWN	ONYX	MIDDLE GREEN
SALMON	CHOCOLATE	INDIAN RED	ORANGE
PINK	DARK LINCOLN	DARK OLIVE	LEMON

△ Paint colours suitable for exterior doors from a standard builders catalogue of 1938.

17. Bevelled-edge glass, c.1930.
18. 1930s Jacobethan with strap hinges.
19. Moderne with traditional elements.
20. Art Deco and oak combined.

THE EXTERIOR: *Windows/1*

Hardly anything changes the appearance of a house more than alteration to its windows; even the loss of quite small details such as glazing bars can radically alter the overall character of the elevation. Many houses, even ones as recently built as the 1930s, have fallen victim to the persuasions of double-glazing companies and been fitted with quite unsuitable and unnecessary replacement windows. On a practical level, the money saved on heating in no way recoups the huge outlay on new windows; good loft insulation and simple, cheap draught-exclusion strips around doors and windows are a far more cost-effective way of reducing heat loss. Secondly, the replacements are usually completely out of character with the style of the house: large picture windows may seem a good idea but usually necessitate net curtains to ensure privacy, and are hardly suitable on a cottage-style Jacobethan semi or Edwardian villa. In any event, replacement windows are hardly ever necessary, as simple maintenance will ensure the indefinite life of even long-neglected timber windows at a fraction of the cost of new ones. Added security is another reason why many people unnecessarily change their existing windows. Simple, cheap but very effective window catches and locks can now be fitted to all metal and timber windows, and will deter all but the most professional burglar or lunatic vandal.

On practical and aesthetic grounds, therefore, replacement windows are rarely beneficial, except perhaps where it is necessary to provide sound insulation, and even here the most effective answer may be to add secondary glazing to existing windows. To reduce sound transmission satisfactorily, the air gap between the panes of glass should be at least 10 cm (4 in), not the 1 cm ($\frac{3}{8}$ in) or less that is usual in double-glazing units (the minimum to prevent heat loss). Secondary glazing, fitted unobtrusively inside the windows, cuts down noise, prevents draughts and provides a good deal of heat insulation, and does not affect the appearance of your house or reduce its resale value.

Maintenance

Window maintenance usually consists of no more than a couple of coats of paint every four years or so, but frames which catch the midday sun should be inspected more frequently since ultraviolet rays affect paintwork. The trick is to repair before the paint has begun to split and peel off. Once this has happened, the old flaky paint must be stripped off before a new coat can be applied, making the job much more time-consuming and expensive: a weekend of DIY painting can become weeks of labour for a professional decorator in only twelve months, so check every six months. If the paintwork has been neglected, the wood may well have become wet and been attacked by wet rot fungus – a very common but not particularly serious condition. The wood turns soft and spongy and can be dug away with a screwdriver; but a carpenter can cut away these pieces and scarf in new wood with surprising ease. If the new wood is treated with preservative and maintained regularly the repair should be permanent. Other window repairs, such as broken putty and rotten sash cords, are well within the capabilities of a determined do-it-yourselfer; even replacing the sills is not that difficult a task. If, however, you have a timber window that is completely beyond repair, there are many small carpenters' firms which can make a replacement to match your original design. Try your Yellow Pages.

Metal windows can create a bigger problem. Sometimes they become distorted, causing gaps around the frame, or more commonly they rust, resulting in expansion which cracks the glass. One answer is to remove all glass, putty and paint, clean out vigorously with a wire brush, and treat with rust inhibitor, before reglazing and painting. This is not difficult but is obviously a very time-consuming and drastic measure. If total replacement is necessary, Crittalls, the firm which made so many metal windows used in houses built in between the wars, is worth contacting to see if they can supply exact replacements. Nowadays their windows do not rust.

Looking after stained or leaded glass worries many people, but is always worth doing as any such feature is a valuable asset when it comes to resale. The glass itself needs no maintenance, and fortunately there are many small firms which will repair and make stained-glass and leaded windows. A common problem is rain leaking in where the glass fits into the grooved lead strips (called cames). This can be rectified by prising open the came slightly with an old chisel and working in putty mixed with gold-size (available from builders' merchants), and then pressing the came back into place and trimming off any excess putty. It is best to work from the outside to prevent the repair being seen. (Probably the most difficult task is spotting exactly which pane is leaking – examine the windows while it is raining and mark the glass with a crayon.) Broken panes of glass can be replaced using the same putty but, as some soldering of the joints may be required, a glazier should be called in. Improve the appearance of leaded windows by brushing Plumbers' Black or Zebrite grate polish onto the lead.

△Vernacular features such as leaded lights give this 1930s semi its 'cosy cottage' charm.

△The stark picture windows on this identical house render it curiously characterless.

△ A pair of inter-war 'chalet style' semis for which picture windows are singularly ill-suited.

△ A well-restored small Edwardian house contrasts with its sadly transformed neighbour.

THE EXTERIOR: *Windows/2*

△ An early example of an Edwardian oriel window.

△This unusual Arts and Crafts balcony is a distinctive Edwardian feature.

△The standard double bay of an inter-war semi often incorporated stained glass.

△Oriel windows are also often found on inter-war housing.

▷△This window, with its attractive turned wood balcony, is typical of many Arts-and-Crafts inspired details to be found on Edwardian houses.

▷Cast-iron balconies, often based on Classical designs, are sometimes found on Victorian houses, as in this terraced example. Note the later Vernacular door and window.

△Leaded lights and an attractive corner window are distinctive Vernacular features.

△ A combination of leaded and sheet glass was a common late Victorian fashion.

△ Typical suntrap windows of the 1930s moderne house.

△ Art Deco detailing for hall or staircase windows was common in the 1930s.

△ Leaded windows and other Vernacular features often work surprisingly well on large-scale buildings such as flats.

△ Stone mullions are an old English tradition revived by Voysey in the 1900s and used in many Arts and Crafts houses.

△▷ These finely detailed turn-of-the-century windows with lead lights in the cottage tradition set the style for suburban windows for the next forty years. Note the metal gutter brackets in the lower picture; they are in the style of Mackintosh, which successfully unified Art Nouveau curves with crisp angularity.

THE EXTERIOR: Roofs and Chimneys

With one or two exceptions, such as Georgian terraces and moderne houses of the 1920s and 1930s, roofs are a major feature of the overall appearance of a house and should be preserved as closely as possible to their original style.

Standard materials for roofs are clay tiles, which have an almost unlimited life, and slate, a good-quality variety of which should last well over 150 years. Problems may be caused by the metal nails, used to fix the tiles or slates in place, breaking down in time and causing slippage, which results in leaks. More commonly, however, the box gutters and centre valley gutters found on Victorian houses cause the worst problems. These gutters, wooden troughs lined with a malleable metal such as zinc or lead, eventually corrode after a hundred years or so of exposure to the natural acidity in rain, and develop tiny holes. A coating of thick bituminous paint in the gutter may solve the problem for a few years, but once a roof is reaching the last decades of its life it becomes delicate and any repairs are likely to disturb other parts which will then spring leaks. The only permanent answer to problems like these is to strip and recover the roof – an expensive undertaking, and often done badly.

Roof Replacement

Thousands of firms specialize in roof replacement, but choosing one needs care as it is a business notorious for 'cowboys'. If possible, make your choice on the basis of a recommendation, or select an established firm and look at samples of their work. Get several estimates and discuss the work with their surveyors. There are several indicators of good-quality work: the firm should use lead or zinc 'soakers' (where the slates or tiles abut a parapet wall, dormer or chimney) since cheaper felt soakers, or a simple fillet of mortar, are very much less reliable; the same applies to the 'flashings', where the edge of a roof slope abuts a wall. On the other hand, good-quality bituminous felt (provided it is sprinkled with gravel chippings to reflect the sun's damaging ultraviolet rays) is a perfectly satisfactory covering for unseen parts of Victorian roofs, although it will not last nearly as long as the more expensive lead or copper sheeting.

Slates are now very expensive, but there are several imitation alternatives on the market which look quite satisfactory. Second-hand slates are also available, and are a good idea if your builder can save and re-use some of your existing slates, as they can be blended in easily. When purchasing second-hand slates, look out for any that are chipped or have hairline splits along the grain or which are flaking heavily, as these have reached the end of their useful life.

If at all possible, do not be persuaded into having an old roof recovered in red tiles. Modern tiles are made of concrete coated in red sand for decorative effect. They usually have a ribbed finish which looks completely out of place, and being three times heavier than slates they could overstrain the roof timbers severely unless these are reinforced. Beware also the cheap alternative to reroofing now being offered: this entails 'sealing' the roof by coating the tiles or slates with a thick bituminous solution reinforced with fabric or fibreglass. Such coatings not only look bad but tend to last only two or three years, make the inevitable recovering job more difficult, prevent the slates or tiles being re-used, and can cause condensation and rot in the roof timbers.

The ornamental ridge tiles and decorative ironwork finials which are so much a part of Victorian roofs should be retained wherever possible or if these are missing, sought out from architectural salvage firms and refitted. It is important to maintain the roof line of a terrace of Victorian houses, and a small turret over a bay window is well worth retaining, since a flat roof will break the rhythm of the line of roofs. If you wish to have dormers installed when the roof is recovered, care should be taken to keep them in proportion with neighbouring houses, and not to unbalance the whole elevation visually – the best answer is to have them installed at the back.

Chimneys

Chimneystacks on older houses are often now redundant, but should be retained for appearance's sake, as well as for the practical purpose of providing vital ventilation to the rooms below. In any event, attempts to 'deal with them' very often lead to more trouble. Victorian pots in yellow or red clay were often very attractive but are surprisingly large and heavy. The mortar flaunching into which they are set sometimes deteriorates and cracks, however, and should be repaired before an accident occurs. The brickwork to the stack itself may be repointed at the same time. Beware the builder who offers to remove the pots and cap off the stack 'to keep the rain out'. Penetrating rain is rarely a problem, but if it is, clay ridge tiles can be fitted over the pots (special metal caps that you drop into position yourself, using a long pole, are also available); these will do the trick, retain the right appearance and provide the essential ventilation. If air cannot pass through a flue, dampness will be caused by condensation. (For the same reason a blocked fireplace must have a vent.)

△ The roofline of semi-detached or terraced housing has an important unifying effect.

△ The haphazard addition of dormers breaks the line of this arrangement and results in an ugly and messy appearance.

◁ Decorative finials on the ridge tiles, pargetting on the dormers and fish-scale slates: a good example of the kind of decorative roofs that can be seen on many otherwise modest Victorian houses.

◁ The chimneys are often a prominent feature of houses built in the Arts and Crafts style, echoing the massive inglenooks of rural cottages. They are integral to the design of such houses and should always be preserved even if there are no working fireplaces.

◁ The red tiles have been arranged in a decorative pattern on this Edwardian dormer – such distinctive vernacular features are all too often lost with insensitive re-roofing.

◁ Many byelaw houses built towards the end of the nineteenth century featured impressive 'turrets' topping off the bay window, and they were particularly distinctive where the house had a corner site. They are often removed when a roof is being refurbished, but they enliven the roof-line of the terrace and should be preserved.

THE INTERIOR: *Plasterwork*

Until the turn of the century, only the very meanest of rooms were built without a plaster cornice of some sort, and its restoration or replacement is essential to recreate the style of all Victorian and some Edwardian rooms.

Early Victorian cornices were based on the classically inspired late eighteenth-century styles, and were often quite plain. They were usually 'run' on the spot, i.e., formed by running a shaped metal template along the wet plaster. In the 1850s fibrous plaster was introduced in which the plaster was strengthened with hessian or similar material, enabling quite large and complex cornices to be cast in one piece and then fitted into position. Later in the nineteenth century, cornices became very elaborate and might be run on the spot with cast pieces added for extra ornamentation.

Ceiling roses, brackets and other plaster ornaments were mass-produced, and even quite modest Victorian homes could boast elaborate pieces, generally based on acanthus leaf, egg and dart, dentil (a series of tooth-like rectangular blocks) and other designs that drew their inspiration from the work of Robert Adam. After 1880 the Arts and Crafts Movement helped to establish a preference for English rather than foreign styles, and Tudor and Jacobean plasterwork became fashionable in many houses, usually in the form of ribbed ceilings, and persisted in better Jacobethan homes until 1939.

Original plasterwork can be damaged by many things. Dampness, often caused by leaking roofs in bay windows, causes plaster to lose its key and fall off. The partitioning of rooms when large houses are converted to flats is also frequently done with complete disregard for existing cornices and moulded ceilings. Also, when not actually damaged, the fine detailing on the plasterwork may have been obliterated by layers of paint. None of these problems is insurmountable, however.

Removing Paint

Where several layers of paint have hidden the detail of plaster mouldings, there are usually two steps to its removal. If a coat (or coats) of vinyl emulsion or gloss paint has been applied, then a standard chemical stripper should be used. The process of removing the original layers of water-based paint is more time-consuming and delicate, and should be tackled in the following way: using a sprayer, soak a 30 cm (1 foot) length of the cornice with clean water; let this penetrate for thirty minutes and then pick off the paint with a small screwdriver or knife while the next section is soaking. Take care not to oversoak the plaster itself, and for an ornate cornice allow at least one hour per foot for the whole process.

Repairs

Broken or missing pieces of plaster can be easily replaced by a professional plasterer, either by 'running' or by casting new pieces from vinyl moulds taken from the existing pattern (preferably using a section cleaned as described above to ensure a sharp finish). A simpler alternative is to buy ready-made lengths of cornice or plaster details from the numerous firms still producing them, often to the exact designs of a century or more ago. These can be nailed into position, and any small gaps filled with plaster of Paris.

If your ceilings are cracked and look shabby, a competent plasterer should be able to restore them to their original splendour at a reasonable cost, although if the plaster is breaking away from the laths that hold it up, it may have to be replaced entirely before it falls. Whatever the case, take expert advice, and do not have your ceiling 'artexed', a process in which a slightly flexible plaster is spread over the ceiling and manipulated with a sponge to form little stalactites or combed into 'decorative' swirls. It will not hold up a collapsing ceiling, and is difficult to remove. (If you already have one that you hate, it may be possible to remove it with a special textured-paint remover.)

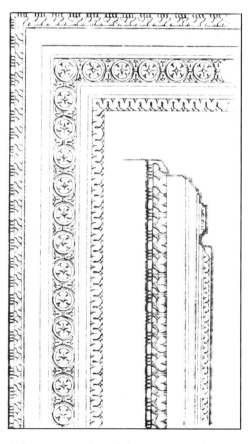

△ **Some examples of the more popular mid-Victorian designs for plasterwork cornices. Cornices, plain and elaborate, were standard features, and replacing them is a comparatively simple and highly effective restorative measure.**

Fig. 6.

Fig. 7.

Fig. 5.

Fig. 2.

Fig. 1.

Fig. 3.

Fig. 4.

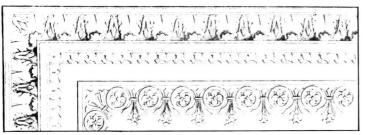

△Ceiling roses (fig. 1) as their name implies, were often very decorative items resplendent with plaster 'foliage'. Towards the end of the nineteenth century, rather more geometric designs based on Tudor or Jacobean plasterwork (figs. 2, 3, 5 and 6) began to be fashionable for both ceilings and walls, a taste which continued into the 1920s. Also popular for walls in the 1880s were the plasterwork panels of the Adam Revival (fig. 4).

◁Many patterns for cornices were based on classical Georgian designs such as acanthus leaves. (All these patterns are still made).

THE INTERIOR: *Woodwork*

The woodwork is one of the most distinctive interior features of period houses, and is all too often found to be damaged or removed. Fortunately, repair and replacement is usually very easy.

Picture Rails

Many Victorian and Edwardian houses have lost their picture rails, which were removed *en masse* in the 1950s and 1960s, when they were regarded as dust traps. Their original function was practical, for lath and plaster walls could not support the numerous heavy picture frames with which the Victorians loved to adorn their walls, and the rail, nailed to the uprights behind the walls, distributed the pictures' weight. They also serve an aesthetic purpose, improving the balance and proportions of a high wall as well as creating an area for interesting decorative treatment. The space between the rail and cornice may be decorated to match the ceiling or the wall, and thus apparently raise or lower the height of the room. A well-preserved cornice also looks quite lost without its picture rail. Most good timber merchants stock moulded picture rails in Victorian and early twentieth-century patterns, which can be easily nailed or pinned directly to the wall. The exact position of the original can usually be seen when wallpaper is stripped down to the plaster. The corners must be mitred and any gaps between the rail and the wall repaired with cellulose filler before decorating. This is one of the cheapest and easiest ways to restore something of a room's original style.

Dado Rails and Dados

Dado rails, sometimes called chair rails, were common in Victorian dining rooms and halls and they and the dado below them served to protect walls from damage from chair backs or the inevitable knocks in a busy passageway. Dado rails are easy to obtain and replace, in much the same way as picture rails. The dado, the space between the rail and the skirting board, was usually filled with a hard-wearing paper such as Anaglypta and gloss-painted a dark colour, a process which is easily repeated today. A common alternative in narrow halls was the older tradition of panelling the lower section of the wall in simple matchboard to form a high wainscot. This protected the wall in much the same way as the dado, but was sometimes added specifically to cover signs of rising damp – not a good practice, as damp timber is affected by both wet and dry rot. Matchboarding to wainscot height (or of entire walls) is a reasonably authentic way of dealing with the walls of kitchens and bathrooms in pre-First World War houses, and helps to insulate the walls. The wood should be gloss-painted, after which it is easily cleaned.

Skirting Boards

Ornate Victorian skirting boards are often removed during 'modernization', and very basic plain and narrow boards substituted for them. These should be replaced if at all possible with moulded boards appropriate to the period of the house. These are still made in mouldings to suit Victorian and early twentieth-century houses, and in any case a good timber yard should be able to copy an original sample very easily. Victorian skirtings were often very high, and this effect can sometimes be copied by combining two or more mouldings.

Shutters

Internal shutters were a common feature of many Victorian middle-class homes, yet their popularity died out almost completely between the wars and many were simply nailed back into their alcoves. Shutters are once again a much-desired feature, and well worth restoring. They look good, keep draughts out and heat in, and deter burglars. A good carpenter can replace or repair shutters, or you may be lucky enough to find shutters in junk shops or architectural salvage shops which will fit your windows if the originals have been removed. In any event, these shops are likely to be a good source of the large strap-latches which are used to keep the shutters closed.

Staircases

The staircase was designed as a major feature of most houses throughout the period, and should be restored with care. Victorian stairs sometimes had cast-iron balusters, but turned wooden ones were much more common. Replacements for broken or damaged ones are still made to the most common Victorian designs and can be readily obtained, and are easily fitted. Balusters were usually painted, but the handrails were invariably polished. Where these have been painted, they can be stripped, stained and oiled or varnished. On particularly fine handrails and newel posts, a professional French polisher may be employed. In Arts and Crafts houses, oak staircases with galleried landings became popular. Between the wars, turned wood disappeared in favour of simple square-section balusters, often arranged in groups of three. The balusters of Victorian and Edwardian houses were commonly boxed in with hardboard (those dust-traps again) after 1950; removing this can sometimes reveal delightful features needing only a coat of paint to restore them to their original splendour.

Doors

The passion for flush doors in the 1950s caused many Victorian and Edwardian and even inter-war homes to have their panelled doors given the hardboard treatment, or to have panels of reeded or decorative glass inserted. The hardboard can usually be removed and the pin-holes filled very easily, although any original mouldings around the panels may have to be replaced.

Replacement doors, both original and reproduction, are easily found, but it is important to get the right type. Victorian doors usually had four panels with the longer ones at the top. The panels were embellished with mouldings of a complexity that varied according to the importance of the room. The doors were invariably painted, often in imitation wood grain, and handles were plain brass or white porcelain knobs. Polished mahogany doors were only seen in very grand houses. The Arts and Crafts houses built in the late nineteenth century favoured oak doors, often based on cottage or vernacular styles with prominent iron hinges and latches, a theme still popular in the 1930s. The late nineteenth-century Adam Revival popularized six-panelled doors.

Inter-war doors and architraves were generally much plainer, with a variety of panel arrangements – often a square panel above three vertical panels. Generally the centre rail (the main horizontal member of the door) was much higher than was the case for Victorian or Edwardian doors, and as this is the strongest section, into which the door handle is fitted, the handles (often made of bakelite in Art Deco designs) were set much higher than in doors before the First World War. Flush doors and lever-type handles also appeared in the 1930s, but did not become generally popular until after 1945.

Some companies are now producing features such as panelling, beams, corbels, friezes and Delft racks in fibreglass and polyurethane material which often bears an uncanny resemblance to dark oak. Such items, once made only for pubs, are now sold for the home, and while it would not match the plain oak panelling of an Arts and Crafts house, their design may suit a Jacobethan hall or dining room.

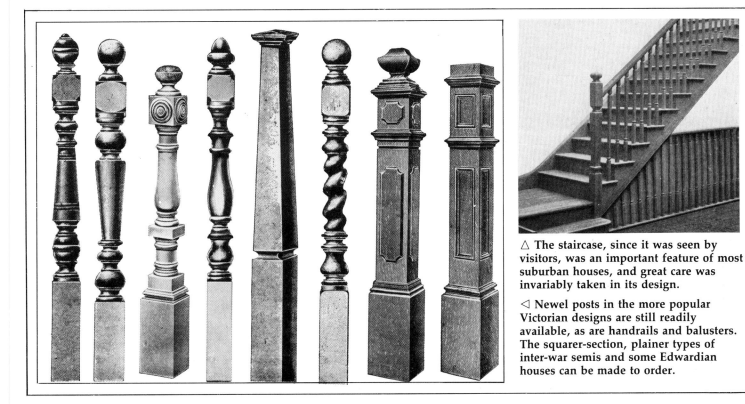

△ The staircase, since it was seen by visitors, was an important feature of most suburban houses, and great care was invariably taken in its design.

◁ Newel posts in the more popular Victorian designs are still readily available, as are handrails and balusters. The squarer-section, plainer types of inter-war semis and some Edwardian houses can be made to order.

THE INTERIOR: *Decorative Finishes/1*

Once interior woodwork and plasterwork have been restored and fireplaces installed or renovated, it is time to consider the decor. It is unlikely that any suburban houseowner would want to reproduce exactly the interior decoration that would have been typical of the house when it was first occupied: the heavily patterned and brightly coloured wallpapers and carpets of the Victorians, for example – not to mention the drapery that would have obscured, among other items, the fireplace – are unsympathetic to the modern eye in undiluted form, as are the bilious colours of a fashionable late Victorian or early Edwardian home, and the porridgey wallpapers of the 1930s. In any case, individual decorative schemes are easily changed by successive occupiers, and an 'antique' environment need not be slavishly reproduced in order to create a decor that is appropriate to a particular style of house.

The foregoing chapters have given an indication of the more usual treatments for walls, floors and window draperies, together with suggestions for suitable colour schemes. Many companies today stock wide ranges of reproduction designs for wallpapers, carpets and fabrics, as well as patterns using the original printing blocks by designers such as William Morris. Careful selection of furniture and fittings that are in proportion and generally in keeping with the size and style of the house is usually cheaper and often just as effective as seeking out only period items.

Some recently revived painting techniques are particularly useful for old houses, especially those of the Victorian and Edwardian periods. They are cheaper than wallpaper and no less effective; they also give a softer appearance than flat paint finishes, help to mask any roughness or unevenness of plaster or woodwork, and are usually sympathetic to other period features of a room. With all the techniques described below, it is important to practise the method on a hidden area or on a piece of scrap paper first, in order to work out how to achieve the effect you want.

Marbling

Marbling is an authentic Victorian technique that can be particularly effective on painted stone, slate or wooden fireplaces. It requires some skill, but the results can be well worth the effort. Examine a piece of real marble before attempting the technique yourself; alternatively, it is possible to have it done professionally. It is best to prepare the surface for marbling with an undercoat followed by an oil-based eggshell or satin-finish paint, then to use oil-based paints in various colours to create the marbling, since their slow drying gives the time needed to create the right effects. The veins are applied to the still-

MARBLING
1. A glaze of white eggshell oil-based paint, thinned with half as much white spirit and a spot of dye, is dabbed over the dry base coat with a paintbrush.

2. The wet glaze is lightly dabbed with a rag or sponge.

3. Lightly brush and dab with a coarse cloth to create the desired effect.

Doers

The passion for flush doors in the 1950s caused many Victorian and Edwardian and even inter-war homes to have their panelled doors given the hardboard treatment, or to have panels of reeded or decorative glass inserted. The hardboard can usually be removed and the pin-holes filled very easily, although any original mouldings around the panels may have to be replaced.

Replacement doors, both original and reproduction, are easily found, but it is important to get the right type. Victorian doors usually had four panels with the longer ones at the top. The panels were embellished with mouldings of a complexity that varied according to the importance of the room. The doors were invariably painted, often in imitation wood grain, and handles were plain brass or white porcelain knobs. Polished mahogany doors were only seen in very grand houses. The Arts and Crafts houses built in the late nineteenth century favoured oak doors, often based on cottage or vernacular styles with prominent iron hinges and latches, a theme still popular in the 1930s. The late nineteenth-century Adam Revival popularized six-panelled doors.

Inter-war doors and architraves were generally much plainer, with a variety of panel arrangements – often a square panel above three vertical panels. Generally the centre rail (the main horizontal member of the door) was much higher than was the case for Victorian or Edwardian doors, and as this is the strongest section, into which the door handle is fitted, the handles (often made of bakelite in Art Deco designs) were set much higher than in doors before the First World War. Flush doors and lever-type handles also appeared in the 1930s, but did not become generally popular until after 1945.

Some companies are now producing features such as panelling, beams, corbels, friezes and Delft racks in fibreglass and polyurethane material which often bears an uncanny resemblance to dark oak. Such items, once made only for pubs, are now sold for the home, and while it would not match the plain oak panelling of an Arts and Crafts house, their design may suit a Jacobethan hall or dining room.

△ The staircase, since it was seen by visitors, was an important feature of most suburban houses, and great care was invariably taken in its design.

◁ Newel posts in the more popular Victorian designs are still readily available, as are handrails and balusters. The squarer-section, plainer types of inter-war semis and some Edwardian houses can be made to order.

THE INTERIOR: *Fireplaces*

Until the 1950s, the hearth with its roaring fire was the focal point of every home, and had been for generations. Things began to change when the Clean Air Act of 1956 forbade the burning of coal in many suburban areas, and the replacement smokeless fuels burnt less attractively and produced less heat. Fairly cheap central-heating systems also became available, so that the fireplace could be removed, boarded up or simply ignored, and the TV moved to centre stage. By the 1970s many new houses were being built without any chimneys at all.

This trend has now very firmly been reversed, and an open fireplace is regarded as a tremendous asset in a home, especially if it is a period piece. Unblocking a fireplace in an old house can be great fun because it may reveal a real gem, perhaps in need of no restoration, though it might also reveal nothing more than a gaping hole. Fortunately there is now a lively market in salvaged fireplaces, and also increasingly in faithful reproductions, so it is usually possible to find a suitable replacement fairly easily. The message is quite clear if you have an original *in situ*: hold on to it.

If you buy a renovated fireplace, the seller will probably be able to arrange for it to be installed by an expert. The proper construction of the throat behind the fireplace is vital to ensure an efficient updraught, and Local Authority regulations also have to be met in order to prevent any fire hazard. None of this is particularly complicated but it is not really a job for an inexperienced enthusiast.

If you have a fireplace that has not been used for many years, it is essential to have the chimney swept before you do so. If you want to tackle this yourself, sets of drain rods can double for this purpose when fitted with a large brush. A specially made, closely woven cloth to cover the fireplace is also a good idea, as large amounts of soot can fall with surprising force. Alternatively, chimney sweeps, once a dying breed, are easily found in the Yellow Pages.

Flues

If your flue is cracked or blocked, smoke and fumes may leak out, usually into an upstairs room. This is a serious matter, requiring the services of a builder, but is not insurmountable: the chimney will have to be relined. The old-fashioned way to do this is to knock holes at intervals all the way up the chimney breast and insert clay cylinders to form a tube the length of the flue, but nowadays flexible metal flue-liners can be installed without damaging walls and ruining decorations. If your flue does not create enough updraught to evacuate all the smoke efficiently (a problem that constantly vexed the Victorians), then a cowl in one of various designs may help to prevent downdraughts. Even more efficient is a cowl that incorporates an electric extractor fan.

Grates

The grate itself may also need attention before the fire can be used. Mid-Victorian grates were often made entirely of cast iron which becomes distorted by intense heat, and they are difficult to repair. Later in the century the backs and eventually the sides of the grate were made of fireclay, which if cracked is much easier to repair or replace, but metal 'baskets' were still used at the front to retain the coals. These were detachable, with lugs that fitted into small slots on each side of the grate, and have often been lost as a result of modernization. Shops selling second-hand fireplaces usually have plenty of these, however, and will generally be able to sell you one to fit your grate at a reasonable price. If you buy a basket with a bow or serpentine front rather than a flat front, you must ensure that it is compatible with the fixed horizontal grate or there will be a gap through which the coals can drop. If the register plate is missing or broken, a dealer may also have a suitable replacement lying around waiting for a home. All these metal parts should be thoroughly wire-brushed to remove any rust, and the visible parts brushed with Zebrite grate polish, the nearest thing to old-fashioned black-lead. This is applied like shoe polish with a small stiff brush and burnished with a softer brush to a sheen which looks good and prevents rust.

The fireclay parts should also be cleaned with a stiff brush and carefully inspected; even small cracks will allow smoke and fumes to penetrate behind the fireplace and possibly damage the structure of the chimney. They can, however, be easily filled with plastic fireclay, obtainable from builders' merchants. The cracks should be well raked out with a sharp point and brushed to remove loose dirt. It is important to splash plenty of water into the cracks before pressing the fireclay in firmly with a trowel or knife and then smoothing off with a wet finger – the initial wetting prevents the very dry firebrick from sucking the moisture out of the clay too quickly and thus causing hairline cracks. The clay should then be allowed to dry for at least twenty-four hours before a fire is lit.

Twentieth-century grates are usually much easier to repair. Freestanding grates replaced the fixed type, and these were set closer to the floor, raised on small legs and hidden behind an ashpit cover. They are still sold today in

ironmongers, usually in 35 and 40 cm (14 and 16 in) widths. The choice of ashpit fronts is uninspiring – they are generally in enamel or lustreware – but this is ideal for an authentic touch in houses built between 1930 and the 1950s. The back and sides of a grate of this period will probably be moulded from one piece of fireclay, which can be repaired if necessary as described above, or replaced with one that comes in two sections, so that it can be fitted without removing the entire fireplace. A replacement of this kind is a job for the experts.

Fireplace Surrounds

Fireplace surrounds are made in a wide variety of materials, all of which may suffer great damage over the years. Mid-Victorian surrounds of polished marble, stone or slate need careful restorative treatment. They can be cleaned with a strong solution of detergent in warm water, but it is best to experiment on a small, unseen area first, as the polish can be damaged. Stiff brushes and powder or creme abrasives must not be used, and nor should acids as these will erode the stone. Stains which have penetrated the surface may be ineradicable, but broken pieces of marble or stone can be glued back into place with an epoxy-resin adhesive. Epoxy resin, mixed with vegetable dye (obtainable from builders' merchants) to match the stone, can also be used as a filler for chipped or deeply gouged marble or stone. When hardened it should be rubbed down with a coarse Carborundum stone and then polished with fine Carborundum (called a slip), which may also be used to smooth out fine scratches.

Later Victorian surrounds were often made of cast iron, and usually incorporated decorative tiles. If either the metal or the tiles have been covered with layers of paint, it can be removed with a chemical paint stripper without damaging the glazed surface. You should not, however, use metal scrapers on tiles: a wooden spatula works well. When the bare metal is reached, the surround should be painted except for the hood or canopy which should be given the Zebrite treatment, as for the grate (this will not clog up the pattern and is heatproof). The tiles will probably need no treatment apart from regrouting; if any are missing you may well be able to replace them in fireplace or architectural salvage shops, which often stock second-hand tiles in sets of twelve (six for each side); and ranges of reproduction tiles are also now available. Fireplace shops will also strip cast-iron fireplaces by sandblasting, which burnishes the metal to a steely blue-grey colour.

Timber fire surrounds (of hardwood such as oak or mahogany) were used increasingly from the 1880s onwards, particularly in Arts and Crafts houses. These often copied Adam styles or incorporated small shelves, mirrors and overmantels. The timber was either painted (in a pale colour, or grained or marbled) or polished, in which case a coat of paint or a good furniture polish is all that is needed to restore it. Grates had canopies or hoods which were often made of brass or even copper; if you are lucky enough to possess one of these a chemical stripper will remove any paint, but on no account use stiff brushes or abrasives. Even metal polishes will eventually wear any pattern away and should be used infrequently. It is often suggested that clear polyurethane varnish be applied to preserve the shine, but it discolours with heat; it is better to let the metal develop its own patina.

▷**Fireplaces typical of their period: from the top, a Victorian marble surround, a more decorative example from later in the century, and Art Deco styling of the 1930s.**

THE INTERIOR: Decorative Finishes/1

Once interior woodwork and plasterwork have been restored and fireplaces installed or renovated, it is time to consider the decor. It is unlikely that any suburban houseowner would want to reproduce exactly the interior decoration that would have been typical of the house when it was first occupied: the heavily patterned and brightly coloured wallpapers and carpets of the Victorians, for example – not to mention the drapery that would have obscured, among other items, the fireplace – are unsympathetic to the modern eye in undiluted form, as are the bilious colours of a fashionable late Victorian or early Edwardian home, and the porridgey wallpapers of the 1930s. In any case, individual decorative schemes are easily changed by successive occupiers, and an 'antique' environment need not be slavishly reproduced in order to create a decor that is appropriate to a particular style of house.

The foregoing chapters have given an indication of the more usual treatments for walls, floors and window draperies, together with suggestions for suitable colour schemes. Many companies today stock wide ranges of reproduction designs for wallpapers, carpets and fabrics, as well as patterns using the original printing blocks by designers such as William Morris. Careful selection of furniture and fittings that are in proportion and generally in keeping with the size and style of the house is usually cheaper and often just as effective as seeking out only period items.

Some recently revived painting techniques are particularly useful for old houses, especially those of the Victorian and Edwardian periods. They are cheaper than wallpaper and no less effective; they also give a softer appearance than flat paint finishes, help to mask any roughness or unevenness of plaster or woodwork, and are usually sympathetic to other period features of a room. With all the techniques described below, it is important to practise the method on a hidden area or on a piece of scrap paper first, in order to work out how to achieve the effect you want.

Marbling

Marbling is an authentic Victorian technique that can be particularly effective on painted stone, slate or wooden fireplaces. It requires some skill, but the results can be well worth the effort. Examine a piece of real marble before attempting the technique yourself; alternatively, it is possible to have it done professionally. It is best to prepare the surface for marbling with an undercoat followed by an oil-based eggshell or satin-finish paint, then to use oil-based paints in various colours to create the marbling, since their slow drying gives the time needed to create the right effects. The veins are applied to the still-

MARBLING

1. A glaze of white eggshell oil-based paint, thinned with half as much white spirit and a spot of dye, is dabbed over the dry base coat with a paintbrush.

2. The wet glaze is lightly dabbed with a rag or sponge.

3. Lightly brush and dab with a coarse cloth to create the desired effect.

damp base coat with a fine artist's brush, and then softened by brushing gently with a soft, dry brush so that they blend into the base. Veins of different colours may be added and softened in the same way. Small patches of another colour may also be added for a stronger effect. The surface should then be sealed with two coats of varnish. (A richer marble-like translucent effect can be created by applying several layers of glaze and veining over each layer.)

APPLYING VEINS
Although the intention of marbling with paint is to give an overall impression of marble rather than an exact copy, it is important to look at some real marble before attempting the technique. Using a fine brush, practise drawing veins on a piece of scrap paper first. They should not peter out but join up to form irregular diamond shapes over the surface.

4. While the glaze is still wet, paint in the veins in irregular wandering diagonal lines.

5. Dab off excess paint from the veins and dry-brush them lightly in one direction, then the other, to blur the edges.

6. When this is dry, add more veins in the same way to add depth to the marbled effect.

THE INTERIOR: *Decorative Finishes/2*

Graining

Graining is another authentic technique that was popular for interior doors and woodwork in houses from Victorian times up to the 1930s, despite the regular remonstrations of the fashionable writers on the home. It was designed to imitate the appearance of a more expensive type of wood than the deal used in most houses. The graining is done by drawing patterns in an oil scumble with a variety of tools specially designed for the job. Suppliers will generally be able to offer an undercoat or ground colour that goes with the scumble selected. When the ground colour has been applied and is completely dry and hard, the scumble is applied in small sections and then dragged to produce a straight grain. Combs, rollers and 'veining horns' are then used to create the different configurations and dapples characteristic of a particular wood.

Stencilling

Stencilling is perhaps one of the easiest decorative effects to try, and certainly one which can produce the most immediately striking effects. It was popular with those later Victorians who aspired to an 'artistic' house, and they enthusiastically stencilled on built-in cupboards in morning rooms and dining rooms, and created friezes in rooms where the wall was divided into 'dado, filling and frieze' in the Aesthetic manner. It can also be a simple way of creating borders and corner details on the walls of an inter-war semi.

Many stencil designs are commercially available, cut out of acetate sheet or stencil paper and ready to use, but it is not difficult to make your own, perhaps drawing on collections of designs and motifs of the period in question. Designs may be enlarged or reduced photographically, or by being scaled up or down on squared paper. Clear acetate sheet is the easiest material to use for making your own stencils, as it can be placed over the design and the outline traced directly on to it. A separate stencil should be prepared for each colour that will be applied.

To stencil a surface, first paint it in the desired basecoat. When this is completely dry and smooth, carefully mark the position of the stencils on it. Stencil paint should be of a creamy consistency and quick-drying – poster or acrylic paints are most suitable – and applied with a stencil brush (one with stiff bristles bluntly cut). Load the brush with a small amount of paint and dab rather than brush it on, to avoid any seepage under the stencil. Alternatively, use cans of acrylic spray paint, which gives a soft effect. Allow each colour in the design to dry completely before applying the next, and when the work is complete give the whole design a protective coat of clear varnish.

WOODGRAINING
This technique was commonly applied to woodwork from the nineteenth century onwards until the 1950s, and was particularly popular in the 1920s and 1930s.

1. The scumble or glaze coat applied over a damp base coat is 'dragged' with a dry brush to create a fine grained effect.

2. Various brushes or combs are then used to draw lines into the wet glaze, to approximate the grain of real wood.

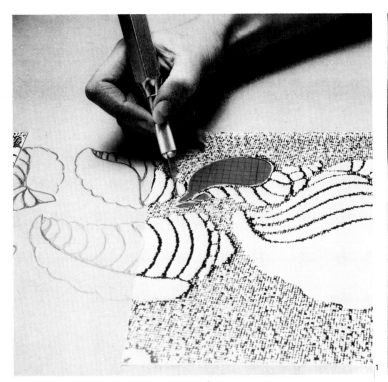

STENCILLING

1. Whether you use clear acetate sheet, thin card or special oiled stencil board, a scalpel or Stanley knife is essential for cutting intricate designs.

2. The paint should be thick and creamy and quick-drying, and is applied using a stipple action with a stubby brush.

3. Designs of more than one colour may be built up using several stencils, each one carefully aligned wth the pattern already on the wall. Clear acetate sheet would be the best material to use for multicoloured designs.

4. Strong colours seem to work better than subtle or sophisticated shades. Stencilling is an ancient tradition that looks particularly good in late nineteenth-century Arts and Crafts houses.

STOCKISTS AND SUPPLIERS/1

△**Gates and railings – whether of cast iron or made of deal – are often obtainable from salvage companies, or can be made to order.**

The following listings give an indication of the range and number of different establishments able to supply period items for your house. As well as the more substantial renovation and restoration requiring building materials and architectural fittings, there are certain small details – door furniture, tiles for porch or fireplace, and carefully chosen bathroom fittings, for example – which are essential finishing touches for an authentically renovated house.

ARCHITECTURAL SALVAGE

There is a growing number of architectural salvage companies throughout the country, and it is always worth making them the first stop in your search for authentic replacements for lost or damaged items in your home: anything from doors and windows, to fireplaces, light fittings, ironmongery, tiles and stained glass can be found there.

Baileys Architectural Antiques, The Engine Shed, Ashburton Industrial Estate, Ross-on-Wye, Herefordshire HR9 7BW.
Brighton Architectural Salvage, 33 Gloucester Road, Brighton.
Glover & Stacey, Malthouse Premises, Main Road, Kingsley, Bordon, Hants.
House of Steel Antiques, 400 Caledonian Road, Islington, London N1 1DN.
London Architectural Salvage and Supply, Mark Street, London EC2A 4ER.
Walcot Reclamation, 108 Walcot Street, Bath.

WALLS AND ROOFS

Sympathetic restoration and renovation of exterior walls and roofs are particularly important, not only because they are an essential part of retaining the character of your home, but also because they affect others as well as yourself. Reclaimed bricks and roof slates, pantiles, ridge tiles and finials can be obtained to match up with the originals. Alternatively, careful selection of modern materials should turn up a reasonably close match.

Brick Advisory Centre, Building Design Centre, Store Street, London WC1.
Up-to-date advice on modern bricks and building and roofing materials, from which you may be able to find suitable replacements.
Cheshire Brick & Slate Company, Brownheath Road, Christleton, Chester.
Suppliers of reclaimed building materials, who also hold stocks of Victorian cast-iron fireplaces.
Cheshire Reclaimed Building Materials, The Old Brick Yard, Junction of Mosley Road and Westinghouse, Trafford Park, Manchester M17 1PY.
Keymer, Nye Road, Burgess Hill, Sussex RH15 0LZ.
Manufacturers, since 1862, of traditional red Wealden clay roof tiles.

GLASS AND WINDOWS

There are several companies which will replace or renew stained glass; the salvage companies stock original pieces, often *in situ* in their original door or window frame (see also under Architectural Salvage).

Philip Bradbury Glass, 83 Blackstock Road, London N4 2JW.
Recreate authentic nineteenth-century patterns on new glass.
The Crafts Council, 12 Waterloo Place, London SW1.
Contact the Council for a list of the designer-craftspeople working in the field of stained glass and leaded lights, and who will work to commission.
Crittall Windows Ltd., Springwood Drive, Braintree, Essex CM7 6DF.

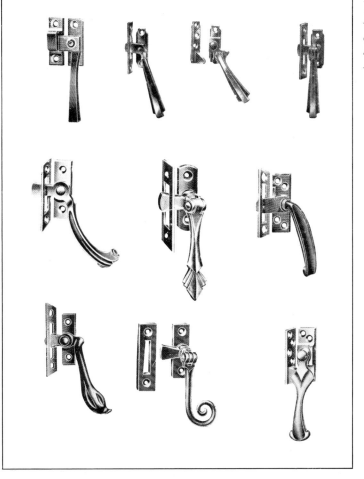

◁ **Casement fasteners for the windows of inter-war houses were often rather ornate and inspired by the Art Deco style.**

The leading manufacturer of metal window frames in the 1930s, Crittall make some of their original designs and replacement parts for the moderne home.
Gifford-Mead, The Furniture Cave, 533 Kings Road, London, SW10 and Unicorn Road, Oswestry, Shropshire SW11 5DD.
Stockists of stained-glass doors and windows, including front doors.
Goddard & Gibbs, 49 Kingsland Road, London E2 8AD.
New stained-glass windows and stained-glass inserts for doors are available here, and the firm also undertakes restoration work.
Matthew Lloyd Stained-glass Studios, 63 Amberley Road, London N13 4BH.
Townsend's Architectural Antiques, 108 Boundary Road, London NW8 0RH.
This branch of the firm specializes in Victorian stained-glass windows and doors.
Whiteway & Waldron, 305 Munster Road, London SW6 6BJ.
Will repair and make stained glass and

STOCKISTS AND SUPPLIERS/2

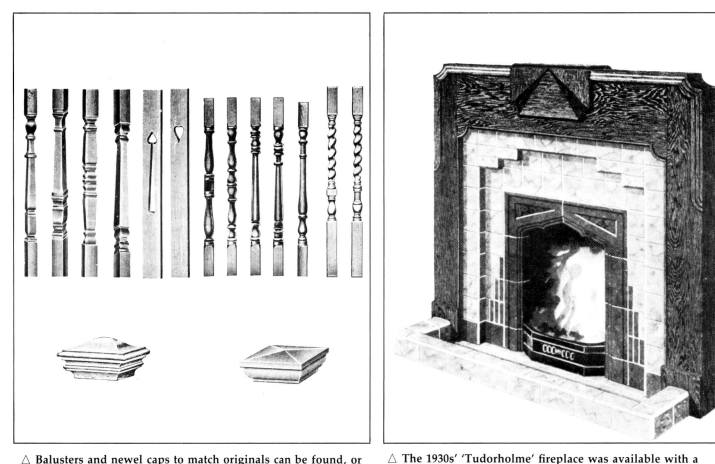

△ Balusters and newel caps to match originals can be found, or made to order.

△ The 1930s' 'Tudorholme' fireplace was available with a mantel of either oak or walnut.

leaded lights to order. (They also stock pine doors and old pine timber, fireplaces, staircases and ironwork.)

WOODWORK AND STAIRCASES

The hall and staircase are important features of a house, and have frequently been the subject of modernizing work. Woodwork in old houses has often been altered, damaged or removed altogether, but it is not difficult to find companies offering copies of original styles of window frame, spindles and newel posts for the staircase, shutters and even Delft racks and panelling for a Jacobethan house. Many firms also make exact replacements to order.

Architectural Woodcraftsmen Ltd., Chivenor, Barnstaple, Devon EX13 4AY.
For purpose-made joinery.
Roy Blackman & Associates, 150 High Road, Chadwell Heath, Romford, Essex.
Specialists in reproduction oak beams and panelling and other wooden features.
Gifford-Mead (see under Glass and Windows) have seven spindle and three newel post patterns in stock, and a number of others available to order. They will also undertake individual work.

Manor Pine Antiques, 1616 Pershore Road, Stirchley, Birmingham B30 3BL.
Oxford Sash Windows, Middleway Workshops, Middleway, Summerton, Oxford.
One of the many firms now supplying traditional sash windows, including double-glazed units; this company can supply to customers in London, the Home Counties and the West Country.

PLASTERWORK

Plasterwork is often another casualty of modernizing work, and in old houses its patterns are often completely obscured by layer upon layer of paint which may be virtually impossible to remove. Fortunately, there are now many plasterers specializing in the restoration and replacement of even elaborate decorative plasterwork.

Architectural Plaster Mouldings, Lower Farmhouse, Lower Blandford Street, Mary, Blandford, Dorset.
Will undertake restoration and match up new pieces with existing cornices and ceiling roses.
Classical Plaster, 109/110 B. M. K. Industrial Units, Wakefield Road, Liversedge, W. Yorks WF15 6BS.
Suppliers of a large range of cornices, ceiling roses and corbels; and will also make to order.
M. Havelock, The Cottage, Dunston Hill Hospital, Gateshead, Tyne and Wear NE11 9QT.
Will match cornices and mouldings.
G. Jackson & Sons, Rathbone Works, Rainville Road, London W6.
An old-established company (in existence since 1780) with their own collection of moulds dating from that time to the present.

FIREPLACES

As well as architectural salvage companies which offer period fireplaces among other items, there are now many specialist stockists of original and fully restored fireplaces, and they will often restore customers' own fireplaces. Fire tools and fenders are often stocked as well, along with ornamental tiles for fire surrounds and hearths.

Acquisitions (Fireplaces), 4 Jamestown Road, London NW1 7BY.
A wide range of refurbished original and reproduction fireplaces.
Amazing Grates, 61 High Road, London N2 8AB.
Stockists of pine fire surrounds as well as those of marble and stone.
British Heritage, Shaftesbury Hall, 3 Holy Bones, Leicester.
Delabole Slate Company, Pengelly Road, Pengelly, Delabole, Cornwall.
Fireplace Designs Ltd., 18 Chepstow Corner, Westbourne Grove, London W2 4XE.
The Fireplace Shop, 108 Glenthorne Road, London W6 0LP.
The Fireside Company, Architectural Metalwork, 92 Carnwath Road, London SW6 3H2.
Grate Fires of London, 223 Royal College Street, London NW1.
Minster Fireplaces, Minsterstone (Wharf Lane), Ilminster, Somerset TA19 9AS.
Neilson Ltd., 76 Coburg Street, Leith, Edinburgh EH6 6HJ.
The Original Choice, 1340 Stratford Road, Hall Green, Birmingham B28 9EH.
A large collection of fireplaces, and also

△ **Jewel Tree, a block-printed linen from 1904, produced by G. P. & J. Baker.**

stained-glass windows and doors and other items of architectural salvage.
Townsend's Architectural Antiques, 81 Abbey Road, London NW8 0AE.
This branch of the firm specializes in fireplaces.

TILES

A collection of late Victorian or Edwardian tiles can make all the difference to a bathroom, kitchen or porch. Careful searches of architectural salvage merchants and antique shops are often rewarding, but there are also a number of reproduction ranges available which have the right quality.

Castelnau Tiles, 175 Church Road, Barnes, London SW13.
Ceramic Tile Specialists, Unit 3, Waterden Road, London E15 2EE.
The Merchant Tiler, Twyford Mill, Oxford Road, Adderbury, Oxford OX17 3HP.
Terrafirma Tiles, 70 Chalk Farm Road, London NW1 8AN.
Townsend's Architectural Antiques, 81 Abbey Road, London NW8.
Stockists of original tiles and also brassware and door fittings, from the early nineteenth to the early twentieth centuries.
World's End Tiles, 9 Langton Street, London SW10 0JL.

WALLPAPER AND FABRICS

Many manufacturers have responded to the demand for the designs and colours of the past, and are reprinting their own original patterns of previous periods or using old designs as the basis for new ones.

G. P. & J. Baker and *Parkertex Fabrics,* 18 Berners Street, London W1.

△ Interior doors: the style on the left dates from Georgian times and became popular again during the Adam Revival ; the other dates from the inter-war period.

△ These door furniture types, popular since the Victorian period and still common until the late 1930s, were of polished brass, 'antique copper bronze' or black iron.

Colefax & Fowler, 39 Brook Street, London W1Y 2JE.

Cole & Son (Wallpapers) Ltd., 18 Mortimer Street, London W1.

Stock a range of traditional hand-blocked wallpapers some of them Owen Jones designs.

Crown Berger Europe Ltd., Crown House, Hollins Road, Darwen, Lancs BB3 0BG.

Makers of two Lincrusta designs, one Edwardian, one in the Art Nouveau style, for dados.

Liberty & Co., Regent Street, London W1R 6AH.

Stockists of a huge range of furnishing fabrics including floral chintzes and William Morris designs.

Osborne & Little Ltd., 49 Temperley Road, London SW12 8QE.

Range includes hand-printed wallpaper based on designs in the Victoria & Albert Museum.

A. Sanderson & Sons, 100 Acres, Uxbridge, Middlesex UB8 1HY.

Among their enormous selection of papers and fabrics are hand-printed Morris papers and fabrics in original colours, made using the original blocks.

DOOR FURNITURE

Having restored original doors, it is important to add the right handles, knobs, locks and finger-plates. Many

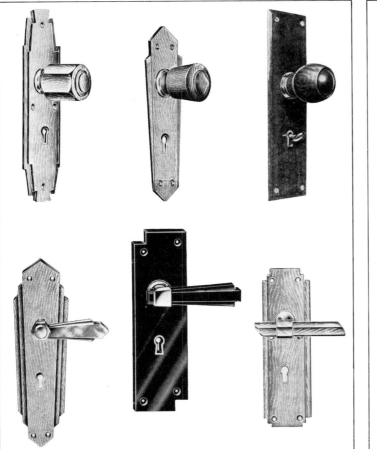

△ **These wood lock sets for interior doors are in designs that became fashionable in the inter-war years, especially for houses furnished in the Art Deco style.**

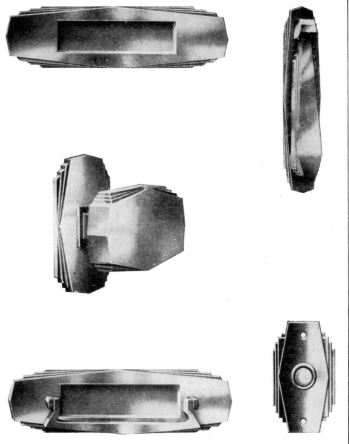

△ **Front-door furniture of the 1930s – in a choice of metals including brass, stainless steel or chromium plate – was available in the geometric Art Deco style for the moderne home.**

companies produce a wide range of reproduction fittings, and salvage companies may be the source of originals, particularly if you are seeking out Victorian letterboxes or the substantial knockers which were fashionable on houses of this period. Broadly speaking, Victorian internal doors would have a matching knob, finger-plate and keyhole cover (escutcheon), either in brass, or, for houses built towards the end of the century, in glass or ceramic. The Arts-

and-Crafts-inspired house might have cottage-style latches, lever handles and possibly even elaborate strap hinges.

For the inter-war semi, bakelite handles were usual (bakelite was also the favoured material for light switches), generally in dark colours, and these are likely to be harder to obtain. When making do with modern fittings, therefore, it is important to remember that whether handles were the lever or the knob type, they were placed high on the

door (as dictated by the door design) and were of plain, Art-Deco-inspired designs.

For the doors themselves, *The Barewood Company*, 196 Broadhurst Gardens, W. Hampstead, London NW6, stocks a range of both interior and front doors, and shutters.

Brass Tacks Hardware, 50–54 Clerkenwell Road, London EC1M 5PS. Supply a huge range of door furniture,

STOCKISTS AND SUPPLIERS/3

including Victorian designs for finger plates, knobs and escutcheons in both brass and ceramic, as well as substantial knockers, knobs and letterboxes for the front door in brass or dull black iron. They are also worth contacting for latches and elaborate strap hinges for a cottage-style house.

Beardmore Architectural Ironmongery, 3–4 Percy Street, London W1P 0EJ.

This firm has a large range of solid brass reproduction fittings, and are worth contacting particularly if you are looking for items for the front door such as centre door knobs, letter-plates or knockers.

Charles Collinge Architectural Ironmongery Ltd., 44 Loman Street, Gt Suffolk Street, London SE1.

Comyn Ching, 110 Golden Lane, London EC1Y 0SS.

In the business for over 250 years, the firm has a huge range of brass fittings, from coat hooks to knockers and elaborate bolts and hinges.

Knobs & Knockers, 385 King's Road, London SW10 0LR.

Stock a large range of both traditional and modern door furniture and have branches throughout the country.

Lionheart Decorative Hardware (Hope Works), Pleck Road, Walsall WS2 9HH.

Victorian designs in matt black or polished wrought iron.

BATHROOM FITTINGS

A large number of companies now pro-duce ranges of sanitary-ware in Victorian and Edwardian styles to meet the demand for their luxurious appearance. The simpler, more functional styles of the 1920s and 1930s are also beginning to reappear. If it is not possible to replace the bathroom suite, traditional fittings such as taps, tiles, lavatory seats and towel-rails will help give an authentic flavour to the room. It is also possible to have an old bath re-enamelled, and is worth considering if your bath is in the right period for your house but looks shabby.

Adamsez NI Ltd., Upper Newtonards Road, Dundonald, Belfast, N. Ireland BT16 0TQ.

Producers of bathrooms since 1870, the firm has a full range of modern and period desings.

Bath Re-enamelling Company, Nantwich, Cheshire CW5 6BR.

Will re-enamel your bath while it is still in position in your bathroom.

Czech & Speake, 39c Jermyn Street, London SW1Y 6DN.

Stock a particularly stylish range of Edwardian taps and towel-rails, as well as a large collection of ceramic jars, soap dishes and so on. They have now introduced a range of sanitary-ware as well.

Hill House Interiors, Rotunda Buildings, Montpelier Circus, Cheltenham, Glos.

Old Fashioned Bathrooms, Village End, Little London Hill, Dedenham, Suffolk IP14 6PW.

Period Bathrooms, Phoenix House, Lingfield Road, East Grinstead, West Sussex RH19 2EV.

Pipe Dreams (Traditional Bathrooms), 70 Gloucester Road, London SW7 4QT.

Both the above are specialists in reproduction Victorian and Edwardian bathrooms.

Sitting Pretty, 131 Dawes Road, London SW6 7EA.

This company started out by specializing in wooden lavatory seats, and now supplies complete suites of both antique and reproduction bathroom furniture as well, including cast-iron rolltop baths, brass and chrome taps and accessories. In addition to their ranges based on Victorian and Edwardian designs, they stock a range called 'Neo-classic', suitable for 1920s and 1930s bathrooms.

ACCESSORIES/LIGHT FITTINGS

For authentic brass light fittings and switches:

Olivers Lighting Company, 6 The Broadway, Crockenhill, Swanley, Kent.

Classicana Ltd., Indiewell Mill, Swimbridge, North Devon EX32 0YP.

For Bakelite phones from the 1920s and 30s:

Ford Halcyon Ltd., 12 Caxton Hill, Hertford SG13 7NF.

Deja Vu Antiques, Hatters Row, Horsemarket Street, Warrington.

GENERAL BIBLIOGRAPHY

Artley, A. (ed.), *Putting Back The Style: A Directory of Authentic Renovation* (Evans Bros., London, 1982)

Banham, M. & Hillier, B., *A Tonic To The Nation* (Thames & Hudson, London, 1976)

Bayley, S., *Taste* (Conran Foundation, London, 1983)

Barnard, J., *The Decorative Tradition* (Architectural Press Ltd., London, 1973)

Bentley, N., *The Victorian Scene* (Weidenfeld & Nicolson, London, 1976)

Betjeman, J., *First And Last Loves* (John Murray, London, 1952)

Betjeman, J., *Ghastly Good Taste* (Chapman & Hall, London, 1933)

Carter, T., *Victorian Gardens* (Bell & Hyman, London, 1984)

Cassell's Household Guide (London 1869–71, and later editions)

Charlish, A. (ed.), *The History of Furniture* (Orbis Publishing, London, 1976)

A Choice of Design 1850–1980: Fabrics by Warner & Son Ltd (Purley Press, Essex, 1981)

Creese, W., *The Search for Environment, the Garden City Before and After* (University Press, New Haven and London, 1966)

Daunton, M. J., *House and Home in the Victorian City* (Edward Arnold, London, 1983)

Dixon, R. & Muthesius, S., *Victorian Architecture* (Thames & Hudson, London, 1978)

Dutton, R., *The Victorian Home* (Batsford Books, London, 1954)

Dyos, H. J. & Wolff, M. (eds.), *The Victorian City* (Routledge & Kegan Paul, London and Boston, 1973)

Dyos, H. J., *Victorian Suburb – A Study of the Growth of Camberwell* (Leicester University Press, Leicester, 1961)

Eveleigh, D. J., *Firegrates and Kitchen Ranges* (Shire Publications, Aylesbury, 1983)

From East to West: Textiles from G. P. & J. Baker (Victoria & Albert Museum Catalogue, London, 1984)

Gledhill, D., *Gas Lighting* (Shire Publications, Aylesbury, 1983)

Gloag, J., *Victorian Comfort* (A. & C. Black, London, 1961)

Gloag, J., *Victorian Taste* (A. & C. Black, London, 1962)

Goodden, S., *A History of Heal's* (Heal & Son Ltd., London 1984)

Hadfield, M., *A History of British Gardening* (Hamlyn Publishing Group, London, 1969)

Hillier, B., *The World of Art Deco* (Rainbird Books, London, 1971)

Homes for Today and Tomorrow, Dept. of Environment (*Parker Morris Report*, 1961)

Jekyll, G., *On Gardening* (Studio Vista, London, 1966)

Massingham, B., *Gertrude Jekyll* (Shire Publications, Aylesbury, 1975)

Muthesius, S., *The English Terraced House* (Yale University Press, New Haven & London, 1982)

Pevsner, N., *Victorian and After* (Thames & Hudson, London, 1962)

Pevsner, N., *High Victorian Design* (Architectural Press, London, 1951)

Pevsner, N., *Pioneers of Modern Design from William Morris to Walter Gropius* (Penguin Books, Harmondsworth, 1960)

Prizeman, J., *Your House: The Outside View* (Quiller Press, London, 1975)

Pyke, B., *The Good-looking House* (Redcliffe Press, Bristol, 1980)

Questions of Building Construction in Connection with the Provision of Dwellings for the Working Classes in England and Wales, and Scotland, Cttee. Rep. (*Tudor Walters Report*, 1918)

Richards, J. M., *Castles on the Ground* (Architectural Press, London, 1946)

Robinson, W., *The English Flower Garden* (John Murray, London, 1883)

Rubinstein, D., *Victorian Homes* (David & Charles, London, 1974)

Service, A. (ed.), *Edwardian Architecture and Its Origins* (Architectural Press, London, 1975)

Service, A., *Edwardian Architecture* (Thames & Hudson, London, 1977)

Simpson, D., *C. F. A. Voysey: An Architect of Individuality* (Lund Humphries, London, 1971)

Thirties – British Art & Design before the War (Arts Council, London, 1979)

Turner, M., *The Silver Studio Collection* (Middlesex Polytechnic, London, 1981)

Unwin, R., *Town Planning in Practice* (T. Fisher Unwin, London, 1909)

Utility Furniture and Fashion, 1941 (Inner London Education Authority, London, 1974)

Weightman, G. & Humphries, J., *The Making of Modern London*, Vols 1 & 2 (Sidgwick & Jackson, London, 1984)

Wentworth Shields, P. & Johnson, K., *Clarisse Cliffe* (L'Odéon, London, 1976)

FURTHER READING/ACKNOWLEDGMENTS

Bentley, I., Davis, I., and Oliver, P., *Dunroamin: The Suburban Semi and Its Enemies* (Barrie & Jenkins, London, 1981)
A collection of papers by the authors – all lecturers in architectural history – exploring the sociology of the inter-war semi, its detractors and its champions.

Burnett, J., *A Social History of Housing, 1815–1970* (Methuen, London, 1980)
A comprehensive and readable study of the social and economic factors which influenced British housing design in the period.

Evans, E. J. & Richards, J., *A Social History of Britain in Postcards 1870–1930* (Longman, London, 1980)
A detailed photographic record of the lives of ordinary British people, showing them at work, at leisure, travelling and shopping.

Girouard, M., *Sweetness & Light: The Queen Anne Movement 1860–1900* (Yale University Press, New Haven and London, 1984)
A scholarly and beautifully illustrated book describing the origins and manifestations of the Queen Anne Movement, including houses, furniture, gardens and furnishings, with a chapter on Bedford Park.

Hackney Houses (A Guide to Renovation) and *From Tower to Tower Block* (Hackney Society, London, 1979)
Two very good examples of the highly informative and useful pamphlets available from local history societies. The hints given on the restoration of Hackney houses are applicable to Victorian houses everywhere.

Jackson, A., *Semi-Detached London: Suburban Development, Life and Transport 1900–39* (Allen & Unwin, London, 1973)
A detailed study of the growth of London's suburbs, and the first to give serious consideration to the inter-war semi. The book nicely captures the lifestyles of the suburbanites of the period.

King, Professor J., *The Bungalow* (Routledge & Kegan Paul, London, 1984)

The definitive study of the bungalow as a worldwide phenomenon.

Marshall, J. & Willox, I., *The Victorian House* (Sidgwick & Jackson, London, 1986)
An illustrated guide to understanding and restoring Victorian houses, from the grand town house to the small terrace.

Muthesius, H. (ed. Dennis Sharp), *The English House* (Crosby, Lockwood Staples, London, 1979)
Originally published in German in 1908 as Das englische Haus, *this is a fascinating contemporary study of the architecture and design of the period that was to be so influential in the development of avant-garde design in Europe.*

Modern Homes Illustrated (1947), *The Complete Home Book* (1937), *Ideal Home Book 1951–2* (London, 1952), and *Yesterday's Shopping* (A reprint of the Army & Navy Stores' mail order catalogue of 1908)
Just a few examples of the many contemporary household annuals and store catalogues which give a fascinating insight into the actual style and taste of furnishing in suburban houses. Similar ones are worth looking out for in second-hand bookshops.

The Reader's Digest Repair Manual (Reader's Digest Association, London, 1972)
One of the best of the standard publications on home DIY. When looking for guidance in this area, beware of books which concentrate on 'improvements'; their suggestions rarely are. Look instead for those which give basic information on repair and maintenance, most of which applies to standard suburban houses. An exception to this rule is: Johnson, A., How to Restore and Improve your Victorian House *(David & Charles, London, 1984). This is a very thorough guide to every aspect of the construction and restoration of Victorian houses.*

The publishers would like to thank the following for their kind permission to reproduce the photographs in this book: Abbey House Museum, Leeds 46–7; Acquisitions Ltd. 207 centre; Armitage Shanks 122; The Architectural Press 137; Associated Newspapers 149 left, 154 below, 154 top; G. P. & J. Baker Ltd. 106 below, 151 top left, 215; BBC Hulton Picture Library 8 left, 25 top, 31 top left, 37 top right, 44, 64, 70 top, 77, 82, 104, 107 below left, 109, 124, 132 below, 144 top, 144 below, 148, 159, 164 top, 165 left, 172, 175, 176 top left, 177, 184 right, 185; Bellings 113; Adam and Charles Black 48; The Bodleian Library, Oxford 110; The British Architectural Library, R.I.B.A., London 11, 34, 38 below, 56, 57, 58, 61, 96, 97, 101, 105 top left, 105 below, 202, 203; The British Library, London 6, 53, 60, 63 centre, 66, 69, 73, 79 below; The Trustees of the British Museum, London 17, 27 top, 79 top, 92 left; Courtesy of Bruce Castle Museum, London 12, 13; Chamberlain and Willows 18 right, 133, 184 left, 207 below; Cheltenham Art Gallery and Museums 76 below; Cheltenham Art Gallery and Museums/Bridgeman Art Library 74; Christies Colour Library 138; City of Bristol Museum and Art Gallery/Bridgeman Art

Library 38; C.O.I. 162, 164 below; Costain Homes 22, 142, 143; The Design Council Picture Library 72 below, 105 top right, 140 top, 146 below, 147, 153, 155 below; E. T. Archive 41; Mary Evans Picture Library 27 below, 49 below, 52, 63 left, 64 below left and right, 65, 120 left, 176 right; First Garden City Heritage Museum, Letchworth 81, 88 below, 112 below, 117 below; John Frost Historical Newspaper Service 21 left and right, 129, 134; The Geffrye Museum, London 78–9; Gladstone, The Working Pottery Museum, Stoke-on-Trent 114; G.L.C. Photographic Library 40, 89 top; Hackney Archives 16; Sonia Halliday 119 top right, 119 below right; Hampstead Garden Suburb Archives 95; Hamptons 145; Robert Harding Picture Library 85 left; Heal's Archive, London 35, 103 top, 121 right, 165 right, 182; Louis Hellman 43; John Henry 207 top; By courtesy of the Company Archives of the House of Fraser plc 25 below; House of Steel Antiques 173; Institute of Agricultural History and Museum of English Rural Life, Reading 76 top; Jesse and Laski Gallery/Design Council Picture Library 146; John Jesse Collection/Philip de Baye 139; Sally Kenny Paint Finishes/Bruce Hemming 208, 209, 210, 211; A. F. Kersting 15,

18, 84, 89 below, 118 below; Linley Sambourne House, London – The Victorian Society/Bridgeman Art Library 78 left, 102 top; London Borough of Haringey 33 top, 85 right; The London Borough of Hounslow Library Services 14 top, 83 top, 93; London Transport/Design Council Picture Library 31; The London Transport Museum 3; The Mansell Collection 29, 39 left, 120 right, 132 top; Enid Marx/Design Council Picture Library 152; Christopher Mendez 141; Merseyside County Council 80; Tania Midgeley 174; The William Morris Gallery, London 103 below; John Murray (Publishers) Ltd./Sir Osbert Lancaster 42; The Museum of London 26–7; National Monuments Record 37 top left; National Museum of Photography, Film and Television, Bradford 112 top; North Thames Gas Museum 24, 116 top, 117 top left, 160; Odhams Press Ltd. 156 top right, 157, 158 top left, 186 left; Popperfoto 136; Port Sunlight Heritage Centre 92 below right; Rainbird/Robert Harding Picture Library 45; © Estate of Eric Ravilious 1987 All rights reserved DACS 38 top; The Jeffrey Richards Collection 155; Ann Ronan Picture Library 8–9; Joseph Rowntree Memorial Housing Trust 92 top right; Royal Academy of Arts, London 45;

Royal Doulton International Collectors Club 123 below; The Salvation Army 10; Arthur Sanderson and Sons Ltd. 67 top and centre right, 111 top and centre left, 111 below right, 150, 151 top right; Silver Studio Collection, Middlesex Polytechnic 108; Sotheby's, New York 59; Suttons Seeds Ltd. 179; Pamla Toler/Orbis Publishing Ltd. 186; Topham Picture Library 33 below, 37 below, 39 right, 128; Twyfords Bathrooms Ltd. 123 top; The Victoria and Albert Museum, London 62, 63 top, 67 below left, 70 below, 71, 88 top, 98, 102 below, 106 top, 107 below right, 111 top centre, 115, 119 left, 155 top, 163; The Victoria and Albert Museum, London/Bridgeman Art Library 107 top; Waring and Gillow (Holdings) plc 116 below, 121 left; Wates Built Homes Ltd. 23, 158 right; The Whitworth Art Gallery, The University of Manchester 67 top left and centre; York Castle Museum 72 top, 75, 127; York Castle Museum/Design Council Picture Library 68; Young and Marten Ltd. 14 below, 140 below, 151 below, 156 left, 161, 166, 167, 195 right, 205, 212, 213, 214, 216, 217. Additional photography by Chris Soczywko.
We apologise to any untraced copyright holders for unintentional omissions.

INDEX

Page numbers in italics refer to illustrations